The definitive report on the most important social revolution of our times: the march of wives into the workplace, which is changing the family, marriage, child-bearing traditions, life at work and everywhere in our society. Women are leaving home for work so fast that on some day in 1979 working wives will outnumber home-makers for the first time in our history.

The Two-Paycheck Marriage documents how this massive shift of power from men to women is amending the marital contract of sex for support, and what it is doing to jobs, politics, markets, schooling, and most of all to the family as we always have known it.

Reluctant homemaker, defiant working wife, vanguard contemporary—all the different kinds of American wives are here, and so are the answers to what the revolution is doing to marriage, sex, children, life-style, and the elusive dream of home.

Caroline Bird, author of The Invisible Scar, Born Female, and The Case Against College has talked with hundreds of women, men, and children and analyzed polls, surveys, biographies, and the findings of behavioral scientists to bring American couples a comprehensive report on how two-career couples cope with the housework, the money they earn, the biological deadline on childbearing—and each other.

They will also find out how two paychecks are liberating husbands from the earning lockstep, how working wives differ from housewives, and what children really think of their working mothers.

This brilliant, three-years-in-the-making report not only documents what sweeping changes this phenomenon is causing in our society, but also shows, through case histories and extensive interviews, how contemporary women and men are coping with this change in their personal lives.

CAROLINE BIRD is the author of five previous books that have established themselves as bellweathers on the scene of social change, among them her most celebrated, Born Female, a landmark report on the conditions that she foresaw were sure to launch the movement for women's independence. The Invisible Scar stands for all time as a definitive report on America's Great Depression. She lives with her husband and teen-age son in Poughkeepsie, New York.

THE TWO-PAYCHECK MARRIAGE

BOOKS BY CAROLINE BIRD

The Invisible Scar

Born Female

The Crowding Syndrome

Everything a Woman Needs to Know to Get Paid What She's Worth

The Case Against College

Enterprising Women

What Women Want

THE TWO-PAYCHECK MARRIAGE

HOW
WOMEN AT WORK
ARE CHANGING
LIFE
IN AMERICA

by Caroline Bird

AN IN-DEPTH REPORT ON THE GREAT REVOLUTION
OF OUR TIMES

Rawson, Wade Publishers, Inc.

NEW YORK

Library of Congress Cataloging in Publication Data
Bird, Caroline.
The two-paycheck marriage.
Includes bibliographical references and index.
1. Wives—Employment—United States.
2. United States—Social life and customs—1971–
I. Title.
HD6055.B45 1979   331.4′3′0973   78–64807
ISBN 0–89256–081–9

Published simultaneously in Canada by McClelland and Stewart, Ltd.
Manufactured in the United States of America
Composition by American–Stratford Graphic Services, Inc.,
Brattleboro, Vermont
Printed and bound by Fairfield Graphics,
Fairfield, Pennsylvania
Designed by Helen Barrow
First Edition

To Andrea, John, and David

ACKNOWLEDGEMENTS

This book would not have been possible without the thousands of husbands and wives who shared their experiences and innermost feelings with us, many of whom did so on the understanding that we respect their anonymity.

Some of the two-paycheck husbands and wives who went out of their way to give me first-hand information included Susan Davis, Will and Pat Dean, Gary Dee, Linda and Bob Dorian, Austin Fitts, Pam Hatch, Mary Hight, Stewart and Linda Hubbard, Marie and Eino Huhtala, Jacqueline Knight, Susan and Terence McCarthy, Amy and Chris Meyer, Bob and Joann Pollard, Linda Puckett, Harriet and Bruce Rabb, Liz Richards, Mrs. Jerry Rainey, Susan Deller Ross, Michael and Jean Salmon, Jane Evans Scheer, Allen and Sandra Shapard, John and Marian Tipton, William and Barbara Trueheart, and Brigitte Weeks.

I am also grateful to the editors of *Family Circle* who helped me frame a Matching Couples questionnaire to accompany "Husbands Talk About Working Wives," the April 1976 article in which Marjorie Godfrey and I reported our initial field research, and who then permitted me to utilize the results of that questionnaire in the preparation of this book. Mark Clements and Estelle Reiter of Mark Clements Research advised and conducted the analysis; Leslie Koempel, Professor of Scociology Emeritus, Vassar Collcgc, and Stanley Morse, doctoral candidate in vocational counseling, consulted; Deborah Nolan, Vassar '77, and Marjorie Godfrey translated thick sheafs of computer printouts into useable statistics and statistics into words.

I want to thank Eleanor Rawson for believing in the book through thick and thin, for suggesting many areas of inquiry, and above all for waiting for three years for it.

I am indebted to Karen Braziller for imaginative and sympathetic suggestions on the structure of the book as well as material used in Chapters 5 and 9.

Kate Olson, researcher for *Psychology Today,* was an insightful interviewer and meticulous checker of facts. Others who interviewed, researched, and checked were Elizabeth Colclough, Grace Graves, Christie K. Leverett, John Mahoney, Jr., Kenneth Norwick, Nancy Peters, and Victoria Strauss.

Specialists who gave of their time and expertise to help us understand difficult facts and social research findings included Carolyn Shaw Bell, Richard Berk, Barbara Bryant, Angus Campbell, Harold Dupuy, John Edwards, Cynthia Epstein, George Farkas, Anita K. Fischer, Eli Ginzberg, William J. Goode, Lois Hart, Marie J. Haug, Marilyn Heins, Lois Wladis Hoffman, Shirley Johnson, Rosabeth Kanter, Betty Kirschner, Helena Lopata, Jacob Mincer, Ruth Moulton, Lucy Rey, Alice Rossi, Isabel Sawhill, Barbara Seaman, Peter Senn, Joanna Sternicke, Leo Srole, Charles Westoff, and Jane Whitbread.

Analysts at the Bureau of the Census and the Bureau of Labor Statistics were generous and patient in retrieving and explaining the wealth of Federal statistics on two-paycheck families, especially Paul C. Glick, Gordon Green, Maurice Moore, and Larry Suter at Census, and Howard Hayghe, Lewis Siegel, and Elizabeth Waldman at BLS.

Information on special points was supplied by Rena Bartos, Mary Bodel, Kathy Bonk, Gazo Cubrera, Catherine East, Lori Gladstein, George Hanford, Helene Mandelbaum, Joshua Miner, Jo Ann Paganetti, and Leonard Sloane.

Elizabeth Bennett, Frances Goudy, Shirley Maul, Jane McGarvey and Joan Murphy were specially helpful librarians.

Esther Vail faithfully typed hundreds of pages of notes talked into the dictating machine over three years. Others who typed drafts of manuscript were Angela Abbate, Margaret Badgley, Susan Bruno, Reine Neumann, and Mildred Tubby.

Finally, this book, like my life, is the better for the unfailing logistical support of my husband, Tom Mahoney.

CONTENTS

INTRODUCTION

THIS BOOK *won't tell you how to juggle family and career, although it has a lot to say about how people do it.*

It won't sell you on adding a second paycheck to the family, but it will give you some facts that may help you decide. Facts about what's bad about two working, as well as what is good.

It will tell you about the options two paychecks offer a couple and the price they are paying for these options.

It will help you understand what a wife's job does to her marriage, her home, her children, and her feelings about herself.

There is a great deal more to understand than meets the eye. Working couples are all around us and they are not new. Most couples have, at some time or another, disposed of two paychecks. But until the decade of the 1970s, most working wives regarded themselves as either temporary or exceptional. The conventions of work, home, and marriage were postponed rather than questioned. "Some day" they'd settle down to the norms of their parents—or the equally mythic anti-norms proposed during the 1960s. This is the way it used to be. Now, in the 1970s, women are breaking new ground.

Traditional wives find themselves working just a little longer for the down payment on the house and soon they no longer feel and act like the traditional women they say they are.

Liberated young women who came out of college spouting feminism find that even if they work, when they marry they can't escape, in daily life, some of the traditional roles they repudiate in theory.

Like childbirth, working for money is a common experience that unites women of widely different backgrounds, incomes, temperaments, and beliefs. The common experience is uncertainty: it is hard to live without rules, and even harder to be one of those creating them, as the pioneer two-paycheck wives of the 1970s were and are doing.

The National Women's Conference of November 18–21, 1977, in Houston, Texas, was the most representative delegated body of women ever assembled in the United States. There were nuns and prostitutes, black, white, brown, yellow, and red, rich and poor. And there was a clear division in their aspirations. This division was not so much on class lines as between the homemakers led by the "Stop ERA," "Right-to-Life" forces and the employed women— often modestly employed at that—who had been out in the world long enough to see the need for some changes in it. High or low, working women were able to see the explicit ways in which they are penalized for earning money in a world that still classes them as economic dependents.

Unlike the feminist protest following the Civil War, and the suffrage movement that won the vote after World War I, the Women's Movement of the 1960s and 1970s clearly is here to stay. Why? Because it is a response to a permanent rather than a temporary increase in the labor force participation of women. This time women are never going back home.

Eli Ginzberg, the Columbia University specialist in human resources who has advised every President of the United States since Franklin Delano Roosevelt, believes that the employment of women outside the home is the most important social change of the twentieth century, more important than the rise of Communism or the

European Common Market. "Its long-term implications are absolutely unchartable," he adds. "It will affect women, men and children, and the cumulative consequences of that will only be revealed in the 21st and 22nd century." We may not have to wait that long.

The thesis of this book is that enough women are now earning enough money to change the terms of both family and work. They are causing the breakup of the lockstep pathway through life historically based on the assumption that all men are or ought to be breadwinning husbands and fathers while all women are "just naturally" homemaking wives and mothers.

Men are beginning to recognize that they no longer need work all their lives at jobs they don't like to support wives and children. Women are beginning to question the ways in which women have adapted their careers to childbearing and some are questioning whether to have children at all. The mere recognition of alternatives to the lockstep is enough to threaten the so-called "stability" of our society.

This book gathers together what is presently known about the impact of a wife's job on the lives of individuals, and the impact of the rise of two-paycheck families on the country as a whole. It draws on the surveys, statistics, opinions of experts, events, biographies, and most of all what hundreds of women and men say.

The first section of the book describes how we became a nation of two-paycheck families and the impact of this dramatic change on our current economic dilemmas. It describes which wives take the new freedom to earn and which remain homemakers.

The second section of the book explores the impact of two paychecks on marriage, home, money management, and children. We find, for instance, that when she works, sex and companionship is clearly better for her, *and slightly less better for* him. *She gains power over how money is spent and he loses a little power, while both lose out on leisure and the housekeeping amenities of a traditional home. The impact on children turns out to be inconclusive with both kinds of mothers making strong pleas for the choice they have made.*

Part Three explores the options two paychecks offer and reports on the experiments some couples are making with choices for which there are no guidelines because they never before were available to any considerable portion of any human population. Especially if she likes her job, a wife doesn't need to have a baby in order to feel fulfilled, so she faces the new decision as to when—and increasingly—even whether to start a family. Especially if he doesn't like his job, the husband of a working wife doesn't have to climb the work ladder in order to support his family. Vanguard young couples are trying to find ways to decide whether to have children and how much of themselves to invest in paid work.

The final section projects how the economic independence of women will alter the terms of family life and the meaning as well as the terms of work.

The most probable future of family life is fewer and better marriages, fewer and more cherished children, and a choice of ways for individuals to get the support—financial and emotional—formerly provided by the traditional family. The most probable future of work is that men and women will have the same career choices and workers will have more influence than at present on the hours and terms on which work is done.

The future, in short, is an exciting world of freedom for individuals.

PART ONE:

THE
TWO-PAYCHECK REVOLUTION

CHAPTER 1

The Exodus to Work

All during the 1970s, wives went out and found themselves jobs. On some unmarked day the inevitable happened. For the first time in American history, the majority of wives had some paid occupation to tell to the Census person.

For quite a while, America had been visualized as a nation of typical families: homemaking mother, breadwinning father, two school-age children, and a dog named Spot. The Bureau of Labor Statistics (BLS) calculated the cost of living on the needs of this family. Politicians weighed the impact of laws on them. Advertisers studied them. Marketers wooed them. Churches extolled them. Everyone regarded them as the backbone of the nation.

The only trouble was that even if you didn't count Spot, only 7 percent of married couples fitted this description by the 1970s. The classic, full-time, lifelong housewife or homemaker was no longer the typical American woman.

Her exodus from the home had come faster than demographers had expected. For more than a decade the Bureau of Labor Statistics had underestimated the number of women they expected would work. In 1973, for instance, BLS projected that it would take twelve years for women to win 42 percent of the jobs. It took only three for women to hold that many by 1975. And if they continue to gain at that rate they may well hold a majority of the nation's jobs before the end of the century.

Social critics sometimes talked as if this exodus from home required an explanation other than that which women gave. They were not quite willing to accept that women were really working "for the money," as they always said when they were asked. Yet it was as simple as that.

The fact is that women have always gone out to work whenever they've been given a chance. In World Wars I and II they eagerly worked at the jobs vacated by servicemen, and some of them had to be all but forcibly ejected when the "boys came home." The biggest creator of permanent jobs for women was the Civil War, which occurred at a time when women *said* they wanted to be clinging vines. Women took the places of men in retail stores, in hospitals, and in schoolrooms, and never gave them back. Clerking and teaching became the first "women's jobs"—jobs women were expected to pass on to younger women when they married.

In the 1970s, women were leaving home to take jobs because after we stopped shipping hardware to Vietnam and the economy wound down, "women's jobs" were just about the only kind opening up. The fastest-growing occupations in the 1970s were the clerical and support work in banks, government, restaurants, hospitals, schools, and other low-paid services that always have relied on cheap female help. These ill-paid, dead-end "women's jobs" grew so much faster than better-paid "men's work" that by 1976 only 40 percent of the jobs in the country paid enough to support a family. With inflation, most husbands needed help with the bills, so most wives went out to work to help them. Even a low salary was better than none, and this influx of low-paid workers widened the gap even more between the average pay of women and the average pay of men.

The housewives flooded into low-paying jobs for the same reasons that attracted previous groups away from unpaid work to a paycheck, no matter how low. European peasants came to the United

States to build railroads in the nineteenth century. Farm boys went to work in the automobile plants in the 1920s. Black sharecroppers came north to work in New York kitchens after World War II. And like these earlier newcomers, the housewives of the 1970s were hired in at the bottom and badmouthed by the workers who were able to move up because there was somebody else below them.

From an economic point of view, the most important thing about all these newcomers was that they were more productive in paid employment than they were when they worked on farms or in homes. "Gains that come to living standards and national income by additional productivity of a new group are not at the expense of the previous groups in society," Paul A. Samuelson, the economist from the Massachusetts Institute of Technology, testified before the Joint Economic Committee of Congress. "No man's masculinity is really going to be threatened, and his paycheck is not going to be threatened. This kind of an effect that I am speaking of has been demonstrated again and again by the history of U.S. immigration, by the long overdue upgrading of black Americans' economic opportunities, and by the increasing education of all classes of American society."

Whether professional or "pink-collar" worker, wives didn't think of themselves in the context of economic history. They had no idea they were creating a revolution and had no intention of doing so. Most of them drifted into jobs "to help out" at home, to save for the down payment on a house, buy clothes for the children, or to meet the rising expenses of college. They eagerly sought part-time jobs, work that wouldn't "interfere" with their families. Instead of keeping women at home, children of the 1970s were the expense that drove women to earn, for wives with children at home were more apt to be earning than women in general.

Mothers took substandard hourly pay for the privilege of being on hand when their children came home from school. Some of them were so successful in maintaining one-paycheck family routines that their school-age children weren't quite sure whether their mothers were working or not.

While many working wives still thought of themselves as exceptions, so did the Conventional Wisdom on which our national policies are based. But as the 1970s progressed, there were enough working wives to confound the rules that had worked for a nation of single-earner families tied to the lockstep of children and career. In the mid-1970s economists, sociologists, and politicians were complaining that they simply couldn't understand what was happening.

ECONOMIC IMPACTS

Economists were the most embarrassed of the wise men. Jobs were being created, but not fast enough to keep up with the new job-seekers, so unemployment was rising. The number of unemployed more than tripled between 1969 and 1975, but there were no riots, no mass marches on Washington, and prices kept rising instead of falling as they were supposed to do when people were unemployed. The economy was growing hardly at all, but somehow most people got by. On polls, individuals said they expected to be better off personally but they expected the country as a whole to be worse off in the future.

Unemployment simply didn't mean what it did when the unemployed were the breadwinning fathers of that standard American family of four—reason enough, said the fiscal conservatives, to stop worrying about it. At the election of 1976, the Republicans claimed that the high unemployment rates really didn't matter because the jobless were "just the women and the kids" who were "just" working for pocket money. If they didn't find jobs, their husbands and fathers would feed and house them.

The unemployment rate of women was higher than that of men, but nothing to worry about. According to Alan Greenspan, economic adviser to President Ford, the whole phenomenon was temporary. More than a million women had "flooded" into the labor market during 1976. This "abnormal growth" was sure to subside. Unemployment would drop when women stopped asking for jobs. And why the flood? Greenspan told reporters that he had no idea why so many women had taken it into their heads to go to work, but he didn't think it had anything to do with the high cost of living.

But during 1977 the flood continued, and the problem of high unemployment and high inflation belonged to Jimmy Carter. The newcomers weren't just the unfortunate single and separated women who were being so blithely ignored. On the contrary, the biggest flood came from married women living with their husbands. "The figures are very puzzling," Commissioner of Labor Statistics Julius Shiskin said of the whole situation, but unlike Greenspan, he predicted that the flood would continue. Asked why, he blamed "social factors" that have led women "to aspire to a life better than that of a full-time housewife."

Working wives were one of the reasons why the traditional trade-off between a decline in inflation following a decline in unemployment was stalled. Stimulate the economy to cut unemployment, and you stimulated women "to aspire to a life better than that of a full-time housewife." And when these newly stimulated women couldn't find jobs, they too began to be counted as unemployed. The economy had to run faster and faster to stay in the same place, because behind the new women were others, less assertive, waiting to look for jobs if enough were created so that they thought they could get them. Women predominated among the hidden unemployed who weren't being counted because they had given up hope of finding a job.

The phenomenon led to an interesting political dialogue. "You can't create jobs enough for all these new people," said the conservatives. "Send them home where they belong and save the value of our money!"

"No," said the liberals, "that's discrimination. We have no right to inquire whether people need jobs or not, so long as they can and will work. It's a whole new world out there, and who's to say that it won't be a better one?"

Yet, in fact, the newly employed wives weren't making things worse. On the contrary, they were the ace-in-the-hole that saved the economy of the 1970s from the ravages unemployment had created during the Depression of the 1930s. About half of the unemployed husbands of the country had wives who were earning. Their earnings kept health insurance policies in force, and prevented the wholesale repossession of goods bought on credit, which had long worried fiscal conservatives.

Working wives helped families maintain their standards of living through inflation. The Bureau of Labor Statistics has calculated that between 1973 and 1974 the real purchasing power of single-earner families dropped 3 percent compared with only 1 percent for families in which the wife was working. The experts and people themselves said it again and again. "With high prices, it takes two to earn." Women especially will put themselves out to defend a standard of living they see threatened.

Women did more than maintain standards. Working wives lifted millions of families into middle-class life. Her pay meant the difference between an apartment and a house, or college for the children. According to a Conference Board analysis, families earning $25,000 or more were an "income elite"—the top 20 percent among families. Two-thirds of these families were working couples, and while wives generally earned less than husbands, their earnings provided the dollars that boosted them to the top. In 1977, the median income was $18,704 when two brought home paychecks.

And working wives were beginning to create a new kind of rich— and, as we shall presently see, a new kind of poor. Couples newly graduated from college and doing well in their chosen professions could easily be earning a total of $50,000 a year before they had babies, mortgages, fuel bills, or debts. Young, childless, and fancy-free, they simply weren't doing what marketers expected them to be doing or buying at their stage of life, and they showed no signs of "settling down."

These new rich couples puzzled marketers accustomed to the predictable pathways of the 1950s. In those days, business planners could figure from the Census how many young families would require new houses, how many would require baby carriages, just as employers could figure, from the size of the high school graduating class, just how many young women would be available to type their letters for the year or two before they married, and how many junior males could be expected to work hard and long and loyally because they had babies at home or on the way. And since these young people had every dollar budgeted, there was much less left over for more than a Saturday night fling. Luxury markets might be small, but they were always reliably stable. The "good life" in the suburbs was a package deal: if you had a $50,000 house (big in those days), the wife was a good prospect for a mink coat and the husband for a Cadillac.

The trouble was the rich, young, childless couples of the 1970s weren't buying the package deal—only the bits and pieces of the good life that happened to appeal to them at the time. If they bought the Cadillac, they might live in a loft and wear denim. One therapist and his counselor wife earn $50,000 between them. They own half a $16,500 airplane, belong to two tennis clubs, take frequent ski vacations, and spend as much as $1,000 a year on art, but they live in a $28,000 house, and he uses his suits until they wear out and she wears primarily jeans.

Older couples with children were only slightly more predictable. A receptionist with two teenage children listed exactly which of "the nicer things of life" her paycheck was adding: "1) a home, 2) a camp in the Adirondacks, 3) a pool." For others it was clothes, or the confidence to buy a $125 tennis racket before consulting the bank balance.

Double-income families were disregarding the axioms of marketing. A flip through market research studies of the mid-1970s spells the message in numbers. Working wives had more money to spend than housewives. They spent it more freely and on more different products. Yet retailers stumbled into serving the working wife almost by accident.

They were slow to adapt to her schedule. Supermarkets that tried the experiment of opening on Sunday, for instance, often discovered an entirely new set of customers had been there waiting for just this schedule—husbands and wives hauling in the week's groceries together. Proud old downtown department stores that did the same were thronged with working couples who had no other time to shop.

Women in advertising tended to be much smarter, but advertising men ignored working wives on the assumption that they would respond like the affluent housewives ad men thought they secretly wanted to be. As recently as 1976, there were only two television campaigns aimed directly at working women: Campbell Soup and Jello. But such is the magic of advertising that the very next year the ignored were discovered. In 1977, the working woman was advertising's woman of the year.

Merchants have always regarded the time of the customer as expendable. Shopping was fun, an outing from home. But to this new kind of customer, time was more important than money. Luxury products that gave her time sold surprisingly well—microwave ovens so that she could have a roast for dinner even if she forgot to take it out of the freezer in the morning, beds "made" with comforters that didn't have to be tucked in to look neat.

It was hard to nail the working wife with the marketing message. The women with the most money to spend weren't watching daytime television and they didn't have time to cut coupons, play games, make extra trips to supermarkets, or paste up blue stamps.

Remember the blue stamps, green stamps, and plaid stamps that cluttered everybody's kitchen drawers in the 1960s? They were aimed at the housewife who had plenty of time but no money except the little her husband gave her to buy groceries. Stamps grew to a billion-dollar business in the late 1960s because they helped housewives squeeze birthday presents out of the only money they controlled. One reason many stores dropped them may well be that working wives hated them. While they had always realized that the so-called "free products" were being paid for in hidden costs, now they began to resent the time they took. One working wife had the cleaning woman paste them up. When her husband complained that the stamps didn't repay the cleaning woman's time, she simply gave them to her for her own use.

There's no way of knowing which purchases are made by two-paycheck couples, but a second income in the family may be the reason why some industries boomed in spite of slow times.

Housing was the sickest patient in the economy of the early 1970s. But late in 1976, housing starts began turning up, and sales of older houses spurted, too. To compound the mystery, a study made by the Urban Institute in Washington found that a higher percentage of *young* families were buying new homes than had been the case in 1970. What happened? Banks began to count the income of wives in giving mortgages. According to a study made by the National Association of Home Builders, more than 47 percent of the families who had bought new houses in 1978 had two wage earners to meet the payments.

Eating away from home became more frequent until Americans were spending as much on food eaten away from home as they were spending on groceries. With the influx of working family patrons, fast-food chains flourished. As a matter of fact, they created more than their share of the jobs that were pulling women out of their homes to work.

Finally, consider the new popularity of preparatory schools among those whose families had not traditionally attended them. During the 1970s, when costs kept rising faster than incomes, boarding schools like Exeter and Andover were able to become more selective and enroll a rising proportion of students whose parents couldn't possibly be described as rich. The appearance of "Mother's Occupation" on application blanks during these years may not be entirely due to a rising consciousness of the women's movement. Some of the first-generation prep school students were there because Mother had a job.

SOCIAL IMPACTS

Feminists denied that jobs for women were breaking up the family as we know it, but the vital statistics were inexorable: Women who worked were marrying later, were more likely never to marry at all, and much more likely to separate or divorce than women wholly dependent on men. Wives who worked had babies later, had fewer of them, and were more likely to have none at all.

Vital statistics dramatized these relationships. During the 1960s and 1970s, marriages were fewer, later, more fragile, and less fertile. More people were spending more of their lives as singles.

Women college students led the rebellion against marriage. No longer did weddings follow graduation. No longer did young women make those "jailbreak marriages" to get away from mother and home. A young editorial assistant two years out of college explained, "I'm alone and I deal with it well, so when I get married, it won't be out of loneliness, as so many people are pressured to do."

The baby-boom babies were flooding the country with young people of marriageable age, but they weren't marrying the way young people used to. In 1970, the marriage rate steadily dropped and in 1976, well over a million Americans had told the Census enumerator that they were living with an unrelated adult of the opposite sex—about 2 percent of the nation's couples (but nowhere near the 12 percent living together without marriage in Sweden where LTAs [Living Together Arrangements] have wider acceptance).

Not only were fewer young people getting into marriage, but more were getting out of it. In 1975, for the first time in our history, there were one million divorces. Social critics advanced all sorts of reasons: higher expectations of marriage, "no fault" divorce laws, and social acceptance of divorce. But divorces have always risen and fallen with the business cycle. A job, or even the hope of a job has made it possible for wives to bury the many dead marriages that were formerly the rule rather than the exception.

Babies were becoming scarce. At the rate women of various childbearing ages were having children in the mid-1970s, they would end up with 1.8 children apiece instead of the 2.1 required to maintain a level population.

Newspapers did not predict the birth rate drop. On the contrary, they reported Census Bureau forecasts of a new baby boomlet as females born during the bumper crop of babies following World War II would start to have babies of their own. In 1968, for instance, the Bureau of the Census predicted that there would be so many more potential young mothers that only a "drastic decline in the age-specific birth rate could forestall another baby boom."

The decline was indeed so "drastic" that by 1978 we had 2 million fewer preschool children in the country than we had in 1970, and 9 million fewer children of grade school age. That year, schools were being closed for lack of children in Newton, Massachusetts; Des Moines, Iowa; Portland, Maine; and even in the suburbs of Santa Barbara, California, and in Fairfield County, Connecticut.

Women postpone having babies and limit the number they have when they find something better to do. During the 1960s and 1970s, that something better was increasingly a job.

Isabel Sawhill, Director of the National Commission for Employment Policy, found that women with little or no earnings were more likely to marry and stay married than women who were able to support themselves. Vassar economist Shirley Johnson has calculated the hazard of divorce in dollar terms: every $1,000 increase in a wife's earnings increases her chances of divorce by 2 percent.

The more money a woman earns, the less likely she is to be married. The relationship cannot be denied, but there are several ways of looking at it.

Professor Gary Becker of the University of Chicago thinks it began with the Pill. He reasons that when women knew they were safe from pregnancy, more of them invested in developing careers, which led to higher salaries which in turn reduced the benefits of marriage and led to higher divorce rates. Becker and his colleague, Robert T. Michael, point out that since 1966 the highest divorce rates have been among women in their twenties. They were the first generation of women young enough to make long-range career plans on the basis of the reliable contraception provided by the Pill.

Another way of looking at it is the impact of a wife's job on her marital dependency. Husbands and wives need each other less when both earn money than when one keeps house and the other wins bread. The more money she earns, the less she has to lose if the marriage falls short of her expectations.

Those expectations are most important. Everyone knows that the more money you earn, the more things you want out of life and the heavier demands you make of your marriage. It's the old story of rising expectations. The higher the expectations, the less the chance of fulfillment and the greater the temptation to split.

But at every income level, wives have problems maintaining their married standard of living as single persons. Those without proven professional skills may find the going unexpectedly rough. Just as jobs for wives have created a new rich, they also have created an excruciatingly painful new kind of poor: single women heads of families.

In 1978, more than eight million families were headed by women. Census demographers projected that more than one out of every three women under thirty would experience the dissolution of a marriage. The experience would thrust them into unexpected poverty.

Few divorced or separated men support their children, and fewer still their former wives. Even though working, divorced women were likely to be worse off economically than when they were married, while divorced men had more money to spend as they pleased. A study made by the National Commission on the Observance of International Women's Year found that only one out of five divorced fathers supported their children. Only 7 percent paid alimony, and most people thought a working wife should not even ask for it. That meant that she was likely to have to live—and very likely support their children, too—on a paycheck that amounted to little more than half of his.

The comedown could be swift and painful. Many of the new poor were women with no training or experience in the art of surviving in poverty. She might come out of a divorce with the family house and what sounded like a fair share of her husband's income, but it often wasn't enough to keep up the taxes and repairs. "Here I was, married 13 years, three children ages 1 to 12, and suddenly I'm divorced," a Florida woman writes. "He was trying to sort out his life, and after all, I had a job, so I didn't take him to court to sue for support until a year and a half later when the $100-a-week I earned selling classified ads just couldn't keep up with living expenses."

Women newly responsible for the full support of their children and who never had worked steadily learned firsthand the many ways in which our society penalizes them by assuming they are dependents of men. Without her husband she lost her credit rating, she lost the health insurance they had through his firm, and she had trouble finding friends, housing, education, insurance, child care, and a really decent job.

The worst discrimination clearly was economic. Very few women were able to earn the $10,481 a year the Labor Department figured a family of four required for a "low standard of living" in 1978. One-third of the escalating number of families headed by women were subsisting on incomes below the poverty level set by the Bureau of the Census. One study made in Jefferson County, Alabama,

showed that court-ordered child support fell far below welfare assistance available to dependent children. Even if fathers could be
made to pay it, court-ordered support averaged $80 a month for a
woman and two children, compared with $300 in cash and services
available from Federal funds for aid to dependent children. Even in
affluent suburbs, middle-class women were going on welfare simply
because they had been divorced and couldn't earn enough at their
jobs to take care of their children unaided.

They tried. They enrolled in the local community college, the
bargain educational institution, hoping to train for better-paying
work. So many went back to school that in 1977, for the first time
in educational history, a majority of the students in these colleges
was women, and the average student was more than 25 years old.
Child care became a burning issue on many of these campuses.

The rising proportion of newly single young adults broke the
stranglehold of couples on community life. They banded together to
rent big old houses in older sections of cities, sharing expenses and
sometimes child care. Those who lived alone gave a boost to the
restaurant business and helped inspire smaller can sizes in the supermarket.

And almost every one of these newly single women, whether with
or without children, saw the point of the women's movement.

POLITICAL IMPACT

The exodus to work has provided a constituency for the women's
movement which earlier feminist protests did not have. Since the
election of 1972, women have been just about as likely to exercise
their right to vote as men, and their consciousness of special grievances has continued to rise. At the 1977 National Women's Conference in Houston, Texas, the resolutions that whistled through
with a minimum of debate were those demanding reform of practices
that specially victimized working wives.

All 2,000 delegates voted for enforcement of equal credit opportunity laws—even the Mormon women from Utah, who voted
as a block against all the feminist issues, and the male delegates, all

of them from Mississippi, some of whom said they were supporting the viewpoint of the Ku Klux Klan.

The National Plan of Action recommended special help for women applicants for loans available from the Small Business Administration, federally funded child care on the basis of ability to pay, and strict enforcement of laws guaranteeing equal access of women to education, including financial aid.

The recommendation on employment demanded not only enforcement of existing laws guaranteeing women equal opportunity and equal pay, but the modification of veterans' preference in hiring and promotion; prohibition of discrimination in employment on the basis of marital status or pregnancy; more part-time and flexi-time jobs; a national policy of full employment; and upgrading of the low wage rates for traditional "women's jobs" by requiring equal pay not only for the same work, but for work of equal value. Under this provision, for instance, the work of an industrial nurse would have to be paid at the same rates paid warehouse workers if a court decided that the nurses—predominantly female—were doing work requiring as much skill, effort, and responsibility as the work that the predominantly male warehousemen were doing.

Other resolutions addressed inequalities in insurance, the collection of statistics, welfare practices, and the legal status of wives. These and many other specific recommendations reflected grievances of working women.

Every working wife has flushed with anger at some law or custom that mistakes her for a dependent. The biggest shock of marriage can be the dent it makes in a bride's paycheck. Income taxes, Social Security, disability and health insurance—every one of the numbers in these little squares on her paycheck stub nibbles away at her paycheck more than it did when she was single.

One woman actually called off her marriage when she discovered, during a budget session with her prospective husband, that she would have to pay $700 more in taxes. She went through with the marriage only when he gallantly promised to transfer $700 from his account to hers every year. This is the "marriage penalty." Its history is amusing. It shows how hard Congress has worked to eliminate discrimination between one rich *man* and another.

The story begins with the community-property law which says that half a man's income really belongs to his wife. That meant that in community-property states men with very high incomes could avoid the high tax rates imposed on those in upper brackets by "splitting" the income with their unearning wives. This enabled these families to drop down to the tax bracket of half their income. The rich in other states became understandably envious, so in 1948, Congress allowed all married couples to split their incomes. Next, single folk complained. So in 1969, Congress "relieved" them by reducing the rate for single individuals. Nobody saw it at the time, but when two worked, the new lower rates for singles meant that a working couple who married found themselves paying more income taxes between them than the sum total of what they had paid as two single persons. At 1978 rates, a husband and wife earning $20,000 apiece would have to pay $1,816 more in federal taxes than they would if they weren't married. This was attacked as an encouragement to immorality, and President Carter wanted to change the law to curb the tax advantage of "living in sin." The tax bill of 1978 reduced, but did not entirely eliminate the tax penalty on marriage for working couples.

Working wives lose out on Social Security, too. The system was devised to transfer income from husbands to wives; it did not anticipate that wives would work. Unless a working wife's earnings are considerable, her contributions entitle her to receive no more in the end than she would have received anyway—without working—as a dependent wife. And if her earnings are so small that they would entitle her to less than the 50 percent of her husband's benefit she gets as a dependent, she and her husband may actually receive a lower pension between them than if their total income had been earned by the husband alone. Disability and health insurance plans are loaded with provisions that limit benefits for women, who seem to be regarded by insurance companies as natural-born malingerers. Discrimination starts with the definition of for what the insurance will be paid out. For men, it means "inability to perform his customary occupation"; for women, "inability to perform any occupation." Men collect if they can't go to the office. Women have to be laid out cold before they are eligible.

All during the 1970s, insurance companies fought efforts to include pregnancy, and the disabilities associated with pregnancy, in health insurance policies. Employer health plans sometimes provided better maternity benefits for the *wives* of employees than for their women employees themselves.

A major blow to all working women was the Supreme Court decision of December 7, 1976, which permitted companies to exclude pregnancy from their sick-pay programs. Insurance companies contended, rather quaintly, that pregnancy was a matter of choice, and did not have to be covered. The decision infuriated women all over the country.

"If you go skiing and get hurt, you're covered," Representative Pat Schroeder of Colorado commented. "If you race cars on weekends and get hurt, you're covered. If you jump horses and get hurt, you're covered. Even if you decide you've had it and attempt suicide—you're covered . . . Now these things are all entered into voluntarily. But the court says pregnancy is the one voluntary act for which you must pay 100 percent."

"The Supreme Court held that it's not sex discrimination to withhold disability benefits," Susan Deller Ross, a professor of law at George Washington University, argued. "But is it then sex discrimination to fire pregnant women? Or force them on long leaves of absence? Or get pregnant women out of the work force entirely?"

Congress finally responded to the outcry. The 1978 pregnancy disability law explicitly prohibited employers from discriminating on the basis of pregnancy, childbirth, or related conditions.

But equal rights to unemployment insurance are a different matter. A wife might be accused of desertion if she did not follow her husband to another city, yet she gets no unemployment benefits if she has to quit a job to do it. And in 1978, court decisions had not yet fully protected pregnant teachers from dismissal which deprived them of unemployment insurance.

Company pension plans sweeten benefits for the *widows* of high-ranking long-term men at the expense of shorter-service women employees. Some women workers leave to have babies before they have worked long enough to qualify. And some women workers are required to pay *more* into the fund and to take *less* monthly benefits in retirement because women live longer than men, although whites are not penalized for living longer than blacks.

Equal treatment of men and women often results in the kind of equality achieved by the law that forbids both rich and poor to sleep under bridges. Take part-time work. It seldom carries fringe benefits, and is often overlooked by banks extending credit. This may sound fair, but it clearly penalizes women, who for family and other reasons are the bulk of the nation's part-time workers.

Or take Social Security. Time gaps in between employment are counted as zero in figuring earnings. Women taking time off for a family are more likely to have these gaps than men.

Medical schools and big law firms pride themselves on sex-blind recruitment of the best and brightest graduates. Private lives are none of their business. If a man or woman wants to have a baby, it is his/her responsibility to arrange it without interfering with work. But by biological necessity childbirth is a scheduling problem only for women.

Under an act creating jobs, called CETA (Comprehensive Education and Training Act), the jobs opened up to relieve unemployment were limited to people who had worked before and had no other means of support. The rule was intended to discourage people from entering the labor force at public expense when they had spouses to support them. The rule sounds even-handed, but most "dependent spouses" who want to enter the labor force are wives.

These are some of the laws and practices women have been lobbying to change. They are bread-and-butter issues a woman is unlikely to feel until she has a paycheck of her own. All of them would be covered by ratification of the Equal Rights Amendment, which forbids discrimination on the basis of sex in laws and government action.

Working women have always led in favoring the Equal Rights Amendment, and support for it grew with the exodus of women to work. In 1977, a majority of women wanted equality for women written into the Constitution and the majority could only grow larger, as the college-educated, younger, gainfully employed women who supported it increased their share of the voting population.

In the mid-1970s, the Amendment was a cliff-hanger issue, which passed or failed ratification in state after state by very few votes. One reason for the closeness of the vote may have been that adult women at this juncture remained equally divided between women who worked and needed its protection and homemakers who could be misled into thinking it would deny them the traditional privileges accorded dependents.

These two groups—homemakers and working women—differed in a number of interesting ways.

CHAPTER 2

Why Some Wives Work
and Others Don't

Newspapers have strict rules for reporting weddings. The story must identify the principals, their parents, and such of their forebears as they currently want to mention. The bride comes first, but schooling, year of debut, and a radiant picture were all the reader used to need to know about her, while the business affiliation of the groom placed him.

Male parents and forebears, identified in terms of their careers, are always mentioned ahead of females, and though the wedding story belongs in many significant ways to the mother of the bride, her maiden name and the exploits of her father used to suffice to identify her. Previous generations of females were nameless and faceless. It used to be that, on the society page, the people getting married sounded very much alike.

Weddings of the 1970s are much more varied. Unless she marries a king, the bride's identity still comes first, but instead of saying ANN OLIVER WEDS, headlines often announce the bride's occupation instead of her name: SECURITY ANALYST MARRIES. And despite less and less space in the paper, the society editor now has to identify the business affiliation not only of the bride, but of the mothers of the bride and groom as well.

"Her father is president of Private Collection Fabrics, a subsidiary of C. Itoh & Company of Osaka, Japan," *The New York Times* wrote of a projected wedding of a member of the graduating class of the University of Pennsylvania Wharton School of Finance and Commerce to a classmate. "Her mother is American marketing director of Ramie Textiles, Inc., a subsidiary of the San Miguel Corporation of Manila; president of Videofashion International and a fashion consultant for Columbia and Universal Pictures."

As for the groom, "His father is marketing consultant with Albert M. Greenfield & Company, the Philadelphia real-estate concern founded in 1905 by his grandfather, the late Albert M. Greenfield, financier and philanthropist. His mother is a real-estate broker. She is a member of the United States Committee for UNICEF and is an officer of the International League for Human Rights."

Like obituaries, wedding stories may be the rare public linking of couples known widely in separate fields. In December 1977, *The New York Times* reported the wedding plans of Jessica Tuchman, section chief for Global Affairs in the National Security Council, and Colin Mathews, a lawyer in the General Counsel's office of the Department of Energy.

"The bride-to-be is a daughter of Dr. and Mrs. Lester R. Tuchman of New York and Cos Cob, Connecticut," the story went on. "Her father is consultant physician to Mount Sinai Hospital and professor emeritus of clinical medicine at the Mount Sinai Medical School. Her mother is Barbara Tuchman, the historian and twice winner of the Pulitzer Prize for general nonfiction."

Of the groom, we learn, "His father is vice president of Craver, Mathews, Smith & Company, management consultants. His mother, Bonnie Mathews, is an editor with the Civil Rights Commission." There follows two more well-packed paragraphs that sound like a *Who's Who* biography.

Such women are becoming less atypical. In the mid-1970s, nearly half of all wives were gainfully employed. *Most of them had more choice about working than their husbands enjoyed.* For the first time in cultural history, there was justification for either option. As many did one as the other.

WHICH WIVES WORK?

Wives are more apt to work if they are young, well educated, and rich. Wives age 20 to 24 are in prime childbearing years, and many are still in school. Yet in 1978 they were the ones most apt to be gainfully employed. Those aged 55 to 64 were the least likely of all working-age wives to be earning.

Schooling was the best predictor of employment. Two-thirds of the wives with college degrees were working, but fewer than a quarter of those who didn't get as far as high school were gainfully employed. As we shall see in greater detail when we talk about working mothers, education was a stronger influence than the presence of very young children on whether or not a wife worked.

Working wives didn't come from the poorest families. Among families with less than $5,000 in income, below the Census-defined poverty level, fewer than a quarter of the wives were working in 1978, compared with two-thirds of those in families with incomes of $20,000 or more. Wives of the *very* highest-paid husbands were less apt to work, it's true, but the sharpest drop-off didn't begin until the husband was earning upward of $25,000 a year, and impressive percentages of the highest-earning husbands had wives who were earners, too. More than a quarter of the wives of men earning $50,000 or more were gainfully employed themselves in 1978.

This is surprising in view of the fact that most wives say they are working for money. Some of the wives of rich men say this, too. No matter how much money you have, you can always use more. According to Tish Baldrige, social secretary for the Kennedy White House, and now head of her own consulting firm in New York, some of the socialites work "to feed their lifestyle."

But most of the wives of affluent husbands work for the reasons that drive some of the independently wealthy to work very hard indeed: they want to feel that they are making a contribution to the world. Some of the most distinguished women achievers have parents who expected as much of their girls as their boys. Sissela Bok, daughter of Gunnar and Alva Myrdal, the Swedish economists, and wife of Derek Bok, President of Harvard, is researching the ethics of medical research at the Harvard School of Medicine. Like Jessica Tuchman Mathews, she comes from a family where achievement and public service are a tradition, regardless of sex.

Before World War I, it was probably safe to assume that most women went out to earn money only when their families were desperately poor or in trouble. But in the 1970s, middle- and even upper-class women earned for the same reasons men in their bracket earned. According to Cornell home economist Ethel Vatter, these reasons are *"need* at the lower level, *want* at the middle income levels, and *self-actualization* at the high income level."

Working for self-actualization has always been a luxury for the rich—and a luxury less available to women than to men. These rich women who work for their own self-actualization are regarded by many as selfish—especially if they take work away from socially mobile women who would dearly like to have their jobs. They are accused of working "just for themselves." And this is a heinous crime for women, rich or poor. The classic opposition to the employment of wives has always been that they "don't need it." That they are working "just" to get out of the house.

The fact is, of course, that the motives of men and women for working are mixed at every level, as we all can testify. But when women make the decision to work they are supposed to put the best interests of their families first. A man may expect his family to sacrifice to help him express himself if he's an artist, or contribute to the world if he's a scientist, but women artists and scientists enjoy no such social support in demanding the same consideration from their families.

What is the best interest of the family? In law and in custom, the husband is the one to determine what it is, and where a wife should work to further it: whether by earning money or doing the housework.

The importance of husbandly support for going to work is implied in what women say. Most concede his right by expressing abject gratitude to husbands who "allow" them to decide for themselves.

"My husband lets me be free to do whatever I want," an Air Force wife declares. "I feel completely liberated in a way I could never be if I were tied to a job every day."

"I am fortunate to have a wonderful husband who has never opposed my desire to work or to be a homemaker (the hardest 'work' of all)."

A teacher with a graduate degree finds her husband "fantastic in that he feels I can do whatever makes me happy." The assumption behind this compliment is that normal, average husbands, husbands who are not "fantastic," presumably do not "let" their wives work where they please. The theory behind a husband's right to tell his wife what to do is based on something abstract, the "family unit" that has interests above and beyond those of its members.

This is called the "family utility" theory. In the 1970s it was seldom stated so baldly. Most couples insisted that husbands and wives made important decisions about the family together. They were supposed to agree on where she would work, at home or outside. Even quite traditional couples didn't like to say what would happen if the couple could not agree on her working. "We've got to agree," they insisted. "It's cause for divorce if we don't." Keep pushing, however, and most husbands and wives said that the wife should have the final say over whether she worked, especially if they were college educated, but they said it as if the husband were unusually idealistic, or advancing a daringly liberal doctrine.

This means that wherever a wife chooses to work, and how comfortable she is in her choice, depends a great deal on the support and approval she gets from her husband. There are really eight different situations in which a wife can find herself if you consider what he wants and what she wants, as well as what she does. The spectrum ranges from Traditional Housewives, who agree with their husbands on staying at home, to Contemporary Wives, who agree with their husbands on earning.

No couple is untouched by the issues two paychecks present. During 1976 and 1977, couples in each of these eight situations were concerned enough to cooperate in an ongoing Study of Matching

Couples. Hundreds of wives and husbands volunteered to talk with us at length or write us long letters. In April 1976, more than 15,000 couples filled out a matching questionnaire on how a wife's job affected housekeeping, child care, budgeting, decision-making, sex, and the feelings of husband and wife about each other. Analysis of the matching couples shows us how their attitudes vary with their situations. (For a description of the study of Matching Couples, see Chapter Notes.)

THE SPECTRUM

1. *Traditional Homemakers* agree with their husbands that a wife should stay at home and they are both quite happy that she's there. They are less likely to have gone to college than the average. They tend to think that working mothers are bad for children, they don't want their daughters to aim for careers, and their husbands would rather go out and get a second job if money were needed than see their wives go out of the house to earn.

Wives who follow a fundamentalist religion have pledged themselves to the traditional role. "My husband and I both are born-again Christians," one wife who opposed the passing of the Equal Rights Amendment explained. "We believe that a wife should work only if (1) it does not interfere with family life; and (2) there's an emergency, such as medical bills, or the husband can't work. Working should not make you financially independent. Your husband should always feel completely responsible for providing for the family."

For Traditional Wives, marriage is a challenging profession that can utilize any skills a wife wishes to bring into it. "If a woman wants to get married," one argued, "then she should stay home and make that her career. What I call being a woman and a homemaker is mowing the lawn, making the garden, laying patio blocks for walkways, painting outside and in, keeping the yard up, washing, ironing, cooking and baking, marketing and bookkeeping, and entertaining. Also being a companion to your husband."

Women who make this investment in their marriages depict their lives as full and rewarding compared with the limited opportunities for self-expression available to the working wives they know: "I feel challenged forming the characters of two children, trying to run a cheerful and warm home efficiently, and providing an atmosphere of stimulation and interest for my husband—while spending some time exploring my own interests."

Traditional husbands frequently turn out to be upper income, or blue-collar workers. Men in both these groups expect to be the sole support of their families, but the emphasis is a little different. The high-income men talk about the personal relationships of a traditional home. "I'm afraid I'm a full-time job for Effie," a dentist told us with a smile. "I'm sure she could find something more worthwhile to do with her time if she really put her mind to it." It is clear that he does not think Effie will put her mind to any activity that could pose a threat to his own domestic tranquillity.

Less secure financially, blue-collar husbands are often defensive of their breadwinning role and they take the housekeeping services of their wives more seriously. "When a wife works, she is always tired," a steel worker who didn't finish high school explains. "You never have normal meals. The house never gets cleaned. She is always getting ready for work, morning and night. Consequently, your marriage, home and sex life change completely for the worse."

Top billing at home seems to agree with husbands who enjoy it. Not surprisingly, husbands in these traditional marriages are slightly more apt than husbands in the other seven marriage categories to say that their marriages are happier than average.

2. *Defiant Homemakers* are our smallest group. They insist on staying at home but their husbands want them to work. The problem isn't usually that the family needs money. Defiant Homemakers had a higher proportion of husbands earning more than $25,000 a year than any other category.

For some of them, children are the basis for the disagreement. Defiant Homemakers think mothers are needed at home for the children's sake longer than her husband thinks that mothers are needed. "It's no fun to come home to an empty house," one Defiant Homemaker writes. "If the mother is working, then she'd be too tired to show an interest and understand the concern that is needed. My husband doesn't agree, but we'll battle that out, if necessary."

But children aren't the whole explanation. More than half of the Defiant Homemakers have no preschool children at home at all; they are most apt to have teenagers. They may be older women who have been left behind by husbands who would like to see them step out and do something on their own. "If only she could find some way to earn money, she'd feel much better about herself," one of these husbands writes. Understandably, his wife bridled at the suggestion. "I don't know what kind of job he expects me to get."

Sometimes homemakers refuse to go to work because they don't trust their husbands to help them at home. "My husband would like me to work but refuses to help me with the kids when I work nights," says a mother of two preschoolers who puts her occupation down as "housewife."

"He'd like the extra money," another explained, "but he wouldn't lift a finger to help me with the work around the house if I did. He wants his cake all the way. He'd resent it if I talked about my exciting day at work and if I made more money or had a better job, he'd go batty."

3. *Submissive Homemakers* want to go to work but their husbands want them to stay home. They often have less schooling than their husbands and they see a job as a way to catch up. "I need something I've achieved myself that I can point to with pride," the wife of a sales manager told her therapist. "I want to go back to school and after I get my college degree I want to get a job. Can part of the reason be to show him just how much I am worth? Or is it to prove to *myself* how much I am worth? My husband doesn't need a full-time homemaker to cater to his whims. I need a full-time life, and we need to continue as partners, independently sharing our life together."

Wives of community leaders and politicians often have to repress an urge to do something on their own. "I'd love to start a little boutique," the wife of a college president confided to a friend, "but I really couldn't do that to Jim. It wouldn't look right. Not in this town." Jim is too preoccupied to realize the depth of her discontent, and she knows better than to bother him with her ambitions.

There are three ways a wife can cope with this attitude. According to John Scanzoni, a sociologist specializing in marriage, she can accept the prohibition as an exercise of legitimate authority: "I don't work because my husband doesn't like the idea."

She can resent it and complain: "According to my husband," one Submissive Homemaker reported sarcastically, "I can't earn enough money to justify the inconvenience of the filthy house and other hassles like dinner at eight and rarely having any clean clothes. So I quit."

Finally, she can resent the prohibition and accept it. "It was great as long as I was working for something we wanted together," a former working wife sighs. "But when he got his degree I had to quit for the sake of peace in the home."

4. *Reluctant Homemakers* are two-time losers. They want to earn, their husbands want them to earn, but something is holding them back. Very frequently they can't find jobs because they aren't trained or merely because the kind of job they would like is hard to find. These women tend to work for self-fulfillment.

"My husband is actively helping me to look for a job in the social work field," one Reluctant Homemaker writes, "not because we need the extra money, but because he knows it is something I need to have and would enjoy very much. He encourages my efforts at every turn and helps me to bolster my confidence when it begins to slip."

Sometimes it's a family problem that keeps her home against her will. "I had always worked until we adopted two children, and then I found I was pregnant," one homemaker explains. "When we found the new baby was deaf, I decided I needed to be at home. The decision was necessary then, and I would do it again. For several months I felt unwanted, unneeded, boring and bored. I was not a person, only an extension of my husband. Finally, I adjusted and actually came to enjoy the joys of free time, of being able to volunteer at my kids' schools, of having a 'gossip' session at a coffee 'klatch,' and of being able to have two and a half hours of 'my' time alone.

"The time, the effort and love I spent in working with my deaf daughter has paid off as she is talking now, understands many concepts and is a happy, well-adjusted child. If I had continued to work, I'm sure she wouldn't have made the same progress. Now I am facing a dilemma about returning to teaching because I need to be known for my talents rather than somebody's mother or somebody's wife."

College-educated wives with career experience tend to feel at loose ends, or vaguely guilty when they stop working to have their families. A high school science teacher who quit her job when her second child was born confesses that she "often feels guilty for not contributing money to the family." She looks back nostalgically on the five years she spent working to put her husband through college, when she was not so "depressed by routine," more "involved with friends outside the home," and less demanding of her husband emotionally. She's looking forward to the time when the children will be in school, and although she believes that mothers should stay at home with little children as she is doing, she would go to work if only she could find decent day care in her community.

These four kinds of homemakers have four working-wife counterparts:

5. *Reluctant Working Wives* are the counterparts of the Reluctant Homemakers. They are doing what neither they nor their husbands prefer. Both wish she didn't have to work. This isn't surprising, because the men tend to be blue-collar workers married to pink-collar workers who rate their jobs lower in status than homemaking. "We would both like a chance for me to be a housewife," an accounting proof clerk with a preschooler confesses, rather wistfully. "Maybe just a dream that keeps us going."

These couples think like the Traditionals, but they don't have the money to live like them, at least at the present. Especially if they are young, the wives look forward to full-time homemaking when the house is bought, or when the baby has arrived. "Being a secretary is a good thing to do if you have to work," one of them admits. "But I'd rather start raising my family. Right now we're saving for the other things we want."

A job can be a protest against the way a woman is treated by her family. Especially sad are the wives who would like to be homemakers if only their husbands appreciated what they want to do

for them. "When first married I did not want a career," a health
care worker in her thirties writes. "Discovered husband did not
appreciate good home and love, so I turned to a professional world
instead of homemaking." She thinks fewer wives would hanker after
jobs if more husbands appreciated women's work at home.

Husbands of wives who are working against their will aren't very
happy about the situation. Almost half of these husbands, a higher
proportion than average, would rather take a second job themselves
than see their wives work, and they look forward to the time when
they can retire her. "Once I can support the family by myself I would
rather she did not work," a young electrician says. Unlike most
fathers, he wants his daughter to be a full-time homemaker when
she grows up.

Layoffs and high prices force women into jobs that they bitterly
resent. "I'd give up my right as a married woman to vote if it meant
that my husband could again earn enough so that I could again
stay at home," the wife of an unemployed worker declared.

6. *Submissive Working Wives* want nothing better than to quit
and keep house but their husbands make them bring in money. It
does not make for a happy home life.

Some husbands can't wait for their wives to get back on a payroll.
Listen to a traffic control engineer married to a registered nurse.
"My wife has not worked since the first child came," he says briskly.
"I expect her to consider a return to her career when our youngest
begins school." This sounds reasonable enough until it develops that
he thinks sex is worse when she works and she thinks that there is
no stage of family life at which a mother should consider working
full time. It is quite likely, however, that she will "return to her
career" when their youngest is in school.

"Working outside the home is killing me by inches," one of these
unhappy women wrote to explain. "I feel like a bug stuck on a pin.

"As I grew up, I dreamed of having a home of my own to fix up,
to cherish, to fill with my handmade things. I dreamed of preparing
good meals and putting out a white, sweet-smelling wash. I dreamed
of a husband to love and care for and children to rear.

"What I have is a dingy mobile home I am too tired to clean.

Husband who sits home watching TV and eating and whose sole contribution to my life is driving me to and from work.

"This happened so slowly that I was trapped before I sensed the danger. When we married, we had nothing. He said it was hard to get going and he would appreciate help for a bit, so I went to work. We were to have a home faster that way. Then he needed a newer car and a boat, and inflation came, and I'm stuck."

Not all Reluctant Working Wives are trapped in dull, pink-collar jobs. A high-powered professional woman who looks as if she had the world by the tail can feel like a bug stuck on a pin, too. "Private law practice is insecure, so two incomes are necessary," an attorney wrote. "But the pressure of 'tough' work is too great for me. Many men find it 'challenging.' The men can *have* it. Of course a woman should be as committed to her job as a man is to his, *if it's a career,* not *just* to earn money!

"I wish there were a way out. Unfortunately, hubby is liberated and says I must support myself. And no judge in the country would require a man to support a woman with a Harvard law degree."

She states her income as over $20,000, and her husband's as higher.

7. *Defiant Working Wives* are classic feminist rebels; they're working because they want to work, and their husbands don't like it. Several studies agree that nearly one working wife out of five thinks her husband resents her job. "My husband makes enough for the three of us," one of these women writes, "but I must have money I can call my own that I don't have to account for."

The husbands of Defiant Working Wives think the children need her longer than she thinks they need her. They disagree about what to do with her money and about what to do if extra money is needed. Income doesn't seem to make much difference in this situation except that husbands in the highest brackets seem to have an easier time keeping their wives at home when the couple disagree.

Sometimes they disagree about whether money really is needed. She wants something he won't buy her, and she marches off to earn it. She's showing him up and he resents it. "I want to go to Greece and see the Acropolis, but my husband says we can't afford that 'culture junk.' I quit work when we married, but I'm back in school doing substitute teaching to make the money for that trip. He's going to be surprised one of these days, because he doesn't think I'll go without him."

Many husbands *are* surprised. "I took a part-time job even though he wasn't very enthusiastic about it," the wife of an affluent automobile dealer told us. "Our daughter is married, a mother, and a full-time homemaker. Funny he thinks that *she* should have a marketable skill but that *I* should be a full-time homemaker."

Although women make less money than men, on the average, until the middle 1970s they have averaged more years of schooling. The inevitable result is that many wives are intrinsically threatening to their husbands because they are better educated and presumably capable of earning for themselves. Teachers do marry truckdrivers, and when they do the stage is set for the smart wife–dumb husband routines that have become a staple of American humor.

8. *Contemporary Working Wives* are working and that's what both they and their husbands want. They tend to be better educated, and of course richer than wives who work only when it is convenient for their families. The most highly publicized are the super career couples who are presented as role models for career-oriented young women.

A surprising number of these supercouples have young children. Proud and supportive college-educated husbands, boundless energy, and two above-average paychecks make it possible for them to live out the college-girl ideal of rearing a family while building a career.

One couple, still in their thirties, earns $50,000 a year between them. She is a marketing executive married to a partner in an advertising agency. They travel frequently to Europe, collect art, own a splendid house and are sending both their children to private schools. "From the very start we both wanted the affluence of dual income," she says. "We're super consumers. And of course our careers are very important to us."

But very few men or women are ambitious professionals. The great majority of Contemporary Working Wives are working because they've always expected to work, and not all of them are

young. Some of them started working in World War II and didn't
go home when the troops returned.

"We were married during World War II and I traveled from post
to post with my husband, each time seeking employment to help
make ends meet," a service wife explains. "We have raised three
children. Our son is a high school teacher, our daughter is in medical
research, and the other daughter is a lieutenant in the United States
Army. They have all made successes of their careers and are highly
respected. We both feel our lives have been happier, fuller, and
with many more benefits as a result of my working and adding to
the finances."

When these women have daughters, the daughters tend to take
work outside the home as a matter of course. A young administrative
secretary in a medical school cheerfully admits she'd "go bananas"
if she didn't work. "I like working as my mother did," she adds.
"She brought us more incentives to become something than my
friends whose mothers didn't work. I like to work and be busy."

It is no accident that wives who work tend to be married to men
who approve, and their approval is more than a rationalization.
Attitudinal studies show that the husbands of working wives take
the feminist side on issues other than working, too. They are more
apt to believe in equal pay, more apt to say sex shouldn't happen
unless both want it, and more willing to share the power of decision-
making and housework.

Husbands of homemakers, on the other hand, are more traditional in their views, and the more money they make, the less
apt their wives are to defy them. In 1976, a study sought out wives
who had given up *good* jobs to stay at home with children. The
report on the findings did not highlight the fact, but every single
one of them happened to be married to a well-heeled man who
thought wives should not work.

But however a woman or her husband feels about her working,
however much or little she adds to the family income, the daily
experience of getting up and going to work makes life better for
her. This may even be true, as we shall see, of the Reluctant and

Submissive working wives who may have dull, ill-paid jobs and think they would much rather be at home.

HOW THEY DIFFER

A lot is known about how working wives differ from homemakers. Physicians compare their physical health, psychiatrists their mental health, sociologists their marriages, child-development psychologists their children. Marketers study how they spend their time and their money. Economists contrive formulas for comparing their contribution to the family's well-being. And over and over, everyone from Gallup to the inquiring photographer tries to find out how many of each kind say they are happy.

The net can be summarized sweepingly: homemakers are more apt to *say* they are happy, but working wives are better off by almost every objective test. Some of the facts are surprising.

Life and health are the most fundamental measures of well-being, and classic studies have shown that working women live longer and feel better all along the way. According to the Public Health Service, working women and men are ill less often than full-time housewives, and this isn't just because housewives tend to be older than working wives. Among young women 17 to 24 years old, ill health restricted the activities of working wives 10.9 days a year compared with 13.3 for housewives of the same age, and the gap widens as they grow older. As one husband put it, "Working gives a woman something more to talk about than her aches and pains."

Housewives used to have so many more psychosomatic symptoms than working wives that Dr. Harold Dupuy of the National Center for Health Statistics lumped them together as "housewife syndrome": nervousness, insomnia, trembling hands, nightmares, perspiring hands, fainting, headaches, dizziness, heart palpitations, "inertia" and fear of nervous breakdown. Employed women actually had more nervous breakdowns—possibly because they could afford to go to psychiatrists who told them that they were breaking down, but the homemakers were more likely to "feel one coming on."

The gap was real enough, but puzzling. Did it mean that there was something about the experience of working that made women healthy, or merely that the ones who went to work were healthier to begin with? If the former, the cure for "housewife syndrome" was obvious: get a job.

There was evidence that it worked both ways. Employment has always attracted the most competent and confident women. A psychologist who tested women college students found that those with high ego strength wanted both husband and career, while those with low ego strength wanted to become homemakers. Those headed for homemaking had "greater dependency and lower personal adequacy and coping ability" and were "other oriented" people who sought their fulfillment through others—nice to be with, perhaps, but not so nice to be.

But there is evidence that a job actually can improve the mental health of a woman. The symptom of psychological distress most common among homemakers, and least common among working women is something Dupuy called "Inertia," or the sinking feeling that you can't get yourself together, can't get going. People with jobs often feel this way when the alarm clock goes off in the morning, but most of the time they drag themselves off to work however they feel, and in the course of the day they feel better for it. Housewives may just crawl back into bed and go on feeling awful all day long.

This common experience has been validated by psychologists Myrna Weissman and Eugene Paykel. They found that a woman who has to get up and go to a job is more apt to carry on through a serious depression than a housewife who has no one around to help pull her out of it. According to them, there is "something protective in the work situation." As a matter of fact, it can be even harder on women who are accustomed to working than it is on men. In 1975, 33 percent of unemployed women sampled in Detroit complained of headaches, depression, tension, and other stress symptoms, compared with 23 percent of housewives and only 18 percent of women who went out to work every day.

Not only can working make a woman healthier, but there is chilling evidence that homemaking can actually stunt her mental and emotional growth. The housewife who complains that her life is making her stupid and "rusting her brains" may be speaking the literal truth. James W. Trent and Leland Medsker tested a high school class at graduation and four years later. They were trying to find out whether four years of college made a graduate smarter than a person of equal intelligence who spent the college years going to work. They weren't particularly interested in housework, but there were girls in the class and a lot of them married when they graduated and spent the next four years keeping house, so they tested them, too.

The results were so dramatic that they could not be ignored. No one expected the homemakers to grow intellectually as much as the women who went to college, but the tests showed that they actually regressed. After four years of homemaking, they scored lower on many intellectual measures than they had at graduation. They became less curious about the world around them, less open-minded, less interested in new experiences, less able to cope with ambiguity and less autonomous.

A woman who quit work to stay with her baby describes how this feels. "I felt that the entire world was happening without me. I felt that my mind was going stale and that I was uninteresting. I had nothing to bring into our conversations at the dinner table except what the kids had done all day and the gossip the neighbors had passed along."

Trent and Medsker discovered that this dry rot was no respecter of social or intellectual privilege. Those who were bright and well off deteriorated proportionately as much as those who were less privileged at the outset. As it happened, the homemakers started a little higher than the working women. In 1960, when they were graduated, marriage was every woman's goal, and the brightest and the best married soonest, but after four years of homemaking they were no brighter than less-favored classmates who had been supporting themselves in paid work.

The picture is brighter for housewives of the 1970s. The poor mental health of women in general and housewives in particular was established by classic surveys of the 1950s and 1960s. But when Dupuy surveyed the psychological well-being of men and women in the early 1970s, he found that homemakers were about as well off as working wives. In 1978 Dupuy and his colleagues were speculating on what had happened to housewives in the late 1960s and early 1970s to cure them of "housewife syndrome."

It could have been the women's movement. In spite of the complaints of homemakers that feminists put them down, the women's movement made all women feel better about themselves, homemakers included. More likely, however, it was the massive application of the obvious cure: in the 1970s, an increasing proportion of housewives had just quit jobs or were expecting to go to work in the immediate future. For younger women, at least, homemaking was no longer a permanent status.

Working wives live longer. Their physical and mental health is better. But their most obvious advantage is that they have more money—one-third more to spend, on the average, than homemakers. The quickest way to see what an extra paycheck in the family means to a wife is to look at what the marketers say a working wife does with it.

The numbers treasured by marketers speak loud and clear: working women have more fun. Compared with homemakers, they are more apt to smoke, drink wine, eat out, travel abroad, join clubs, see films, read magazines, try new recipes, redecorate, cook gourmet meals, keep a dog or cat, follow the news, carry a credit card, insure their lives, keep up with the latest fashions, and go shopping for clothes and the house. They are almost as likely as homemakers to do volunteer work for their communities and make their own clothes (22 percent v. 26 percent according to one study). Just about the only thing they don't do more of is daytime televiewing.

Partly, of course, because they are younger, working wives are more active physically. They are more apt to play tennis, bowl, and tackle major home repairs regarded as "man's work." This just could have something to do with the fact that they also buy fewer laxatives, indigestion remedies, and pain-relieving rubs, although they do buy more aspirin. There's no hard data, but some observers have stated that working women are bigger than homemakers on dieting, jogging, and self-improvement schemes. They buy more diet soda and mentholated cigarettes and they worry more about additives in their foods.

Working wives consume the products that keep the economy growing. They buy more gasoline, securities, traveler's checks, freeze-dried coffee, breath fresheners, frivolous clothes, and fun appliances like electric carving knives. They buy more canned cat food, eye make-up, lip gloss, hair sprays—and more of those "feminine hygiene" sprays that consumer advocates keep saying are unnecessary. As a matter of fact, they buy more of just about everything in the supermarket except baby food, hot cereal, talcum powder, and those laxatives and indigestion remedies.

Longer life, better health, more self-confidence, more money, more fun. By their own report, the working wives have more of everything good. And yet when asked a question about their "happiness" in general, working wives scored lower than housewives. Why?

Happiness is a slippery word. People tend to say they are happy, especially when asked by a stranger, just the way they are inclined to say "fine"' when asked "How are you?" In the early 1970s, when the National Opinion Research Center in Chicago asked a representative sample of Americans what they call a "general happiness question," they were able to compare how homemakers and working wives rated themselves. "Taking all things together, how would you say things are these days? Would you say you are very happy, pretty happy, or not too happy?" The score: 46 percent of the homemakers were "very happy," but only 41 percent of the working wives could say the same.

These results are mysterious. Enough surveys of "general happiness" have been made here and abroad to allow us to know the characteristics of people most likely to say they are happy. Money is the most reliable indicator; all over the world the rich are more apt to confess happiness than the poor. All other things being equal, you're happier if you are young, schooled, skilled, employed, and somewhat surprisingly, if you are free of the care of children. As we have seen, these happiness-making characteristics distinguish working wives from home wives, so they should be happier, but they aren't—or at least they don't say so. It looks as if there might be some experience or feeling of homemaking that makes women happy, but what can it be?

In the early 1960s, Northwestern sociologist Norman Bradburn dug deeper into the feelings and experiences of people who said they were happy, by asking them a long list of questions about what they had done and felt in the course of the week. What made people say they were generally happy, he found, was a preponderance of positive feelings such as "pleased at having accomplished something," "particularly interested or excited about something," "proud because complimented about something." If you had enough of these goodies in the week, you could score yourself "very happy" even if you had a considerable but lesser number of negative experiences, such as feeling bored or angry or so restless you "couldn't sit long in a chair."

But the best predictor of happiness was the number of contacts with people. It didn't seem to matter much how those contacts were made. Happy people had more get-togethers with friends, more outings and meetings, more drives in the car, more meals away from home, more telephone conversations, even more mail.

Now, as everyone knows, the biggest complaint of housewives is the absence of just these happy-making feelings and experiences. They feel "taken for granted." Their work, which has to be redone every day, involves few special achievements, few special excitements. In addition, they feel so deprived of those happiness-making contacts with people that, for many, grocery shopping becomes a welcome diversion.

In his 1965 "Reports on Happiness," Bradburn noted the anomaly but he did not pursue it. He commented, in passing, that employment didn't improve the happiness of women as it did for men. This must have seemed only natural to him, so while he called the discrepancy "startling," from a theoretical point of view, he pigeonholed it for future research.

Early in the 1970s, the alleged happiness of housewives became a fighting issue. On the authority of her credentials as sociologist, wife, and widow, Jessie Bernard flatly charged that traditional marriage made women mentally ill, whatever they said, and whether they knew it or not. Meanwhile, the prestigious Institute for Social Research at the University of Michigan was mounting an ambitious investigation into what they called the Quality of American Life. They asked a national sample of Americans to describe their feelings of well-being or ill-being in order to identify the conditions of life associated with these positive and negative experiences.

The Michigan researchers took a different tack. They tried to find out how people felt about different aspects of their lives—their communities, residences, the nation, their education, their jobs, their amusements, their money, their marriages, and their children as well as their health and their feelings. Instead of talking about "happiness" all the time, they asked people how "satisfied" they were with these aspects of life, and they tried to find out how important satisfaction with work or marriage or housing was in predicting how satisfied people were with their lives in general.

"We have talked about various parts of your life," they said. "Now we want to ask you about your life as a whole these days. How satisfied are you with your life as a whole these days?" The score: 28 percent of housewives were "completely satisfied" with their lives as a whole, but only 23 percent of working wives. The scores were lower than those on the general happiness question. It is apparently a little harder to be "completely satisfied" than "very happy." But housewives outscored the working wives on both questions.

However, the Michigan researchers did not brush this anomaly aside. When they looked at the education of their housewives and working wives they discovered a startling reversal. They found, as Bradburn and others had found, that the more years of schooling, the happier or the more satisfied—*unless you were a housewife*.

Working wives were similar to men. The higher they went in school, the more apt they were to be very satisfied. Same with housewives, too, through high school. But even a little bit of college cut the satisfaction of housewives below that of working wives with less education, and graduation from college could only be interpreted as a disaster. Housewives who were college graduates were no more satisfied with their lives than working women trapped in the dullest pink-collar jobs because they had dropped out of high school. A college education completely wiped out the advantage of high family income. A college-educated housewife whose husband earns enough to retire her to an affluent suburb is apparently no more satisfied with her life than the cleaning woman she employs to do the housework she feels is beneath her! Let her take a job, however, and her chances of being completely satisfied with her life zoom from 56 percent to 79 percent, higher even than the peak score of 72 percent for housewives who quit school with their high school diplomas. In addition, college-educated working wives had better marriages than wives who didn't work. They were not so apt to disagree with their husbands about how much money to spend. They thought that they and their husbands understood each other better. They shared companionship with their husbands more often. And they were less apt to wish, at some time or other, that they had married somebody else instead.

The Michigan team was far too cautious to draw the obvious moral: the way for a woman to be satisfied with life is to get married when she graduates from college and go to work. If she wants to be a housewife, she shouldn't set foot on a college campus, even for one course. "A woman who had learned to relate herself to college people as a reference group finds herself doing the work and being paid the salary of high school education," the Michigan reporters commented. "The failure to complete a college degree apparently has a much more effective 'ceiling' effect on the job achievements of women than it has on those of men."

A study of happiness made by a psychology magazine in 1976 probed every theory about what makes for happiness. Among the more than 50,000 participating were psychologists themselves. But the paradox of the happy housewives held even among those sophisticated respondents: "Although they say they are as happy as employed wives, housewives are much more likely to be anxious and worried (46 percent to 28 percent), lonely (44 percent to 26 percent), and to feel worthless (41 percent to 24 percent). Housewives may have more problems because they are relatively isolated from adult contact. By their own account, they spend more time watching TV, an activity related to worthlessness, and being with their children, which is related to loneliness."

Their conclusion: "The women with the best of all possible worlds are those who are married and employed outside the home. They are happier than the single women and have fewer psychological problems than housewives."

It's worth digging deeper into what makes the happy housewife happy.

Housewives may be telling the truth when they say they are happier than working wives who seem to be better off. Happiness is relative, based on expectations. Housewives have made happiness both their duty and their special work. They may really believe that happiness is nothing more nor less than a happy marriage, and if their marriage is happy, then they must be happy, too.

"Oh, the marriage is happy," one Submissive Homemaker exclaimed. "It's my *life* that's miserable." The distinction is meaningful.

A rather provocative finding of the Michigan Quality of Life study provides one important view. The women most satisfied with their marriages turned out to be those who had never gone beyond grade school. Even happier about marriage were the grade school men. Their explanation for this result is long and wordy. In plain talk, school leads people to expect more out of marriage per se than they are likely to get. Especially women.

We know that housewives have less schooling, on the average, than working wives. Does that make it easier for them to be happy?

Unfortunately, there are bitter truths in the old folk saying that the way to keep a woman happy is to keep her barefoot and pregnant. Before television, a woman without shoes couldn't get far enough from her bedroom to see what she was missing. And without education, most women had little chance of bettering themselves even if they could. These homemakers may adjust to a less than ideal life because they know there is nothing better they can do.

Regularly employed wives have options. They can quit one job for another. Sometimes they can quit and stay home. And they can quit a marriage. Working women are more apt to divorce than housewives, which is not a diabolical social trend, as critics would have us believe, but a benefit of independence and choice. "My job enabled me to get out of a bad marriage," the mother of two children who is working in a paper mill says. "I do not feel, though, that my working has anything to do with our problems."

Jobs for women may indeed be breaking up marriages, but this doesn't mean that marriages are unhappier than they used to be. Just imagine the sheer quantity of marital dreariness that prevailed when wives "adjusted" to intolerable conditions because they could see no exit.

Education raises expectations, and rising expectations lead to discontent from women (and all others) who are barred from realizing them. And unhappiness is allowed to creep into marriages— or the wife's consciousness of her marriage—when other opportunities for work and support are available. By default, then, the "happiest" wives are those not aboard the moving staircase of ambition and opportunity, but those who feel that they have gone as far as they can go by taking their place in the static picture of husband, home, and family.

Housewives tend to say they are happier than working wives with their lives in general and in their marriages, but they are less likely to say they are satisfied with their *work,* by which they mean housework. Many of them profess that what really matters isn't the way they spend their energy but the fact that they are working for their families. And their families are the only thing that matter to them. They are literally working for love—or the hope of love.

"There is no other job as rewarding to me as being a full-time homemaker," one woman said, *"because that is what he wants me to be."*

A nurse who quit her job to become a Traditional Wife found freedom and creativity at home because "My husband likes me exactly the way I am." Traditional Wives talk a great deal about their advantages: "What a wonderful reward it is to me to know that I'm appreciated by the ones who love me."

However they got that way, these women may simply have different psychological needs than working wives who crave the satisfaction of objective achievement. Psychologists Ronald Burke and Tamara Weir found the home-staying wives more passive by nature than the working wives of the 189 Canadian accountants and engineers whose marriages they studied in 1976. The homemakers had a great need to give affection, and their husbands an unusual need to receive it. Husbands of homemakers needed to control other people, and their wives really liked to be told what to do. "Husbands in single-career families appeared to be more dominant and assertive in interactions with others, and appeared to fit the stereotyped notions of the male role better than the husbands of dual-career families."

Homemakers were bossed around, but they liked it. They were bound to their husbands, like electrons to protons, by complementary needs.

But if the relationship of the homemaker couples could be described as interpersonally warm, the two-paycheck couples had to be described as cool.

Both partners of dual-career couples depended less on others for their own self-esteem than the husbands and wives of single-career families. The husbands of dual-career couples were more willing than other husbands to do what other people told them, and the women they married had a higher need than the homemaking wives to take charge of things and tell other people what to do. On all the traits measured, the scores of the dual-career husbands and wives were closer to each other than the scores of the homemakers and their husbands. As a matter of fact, the working wives were more like their husbands than they were like the women who stayed at home. According to Burke and Weir, both husband and wife of the two-paycheck couples were "more self reliant individuals" than the homemakers and their breadwinning husbands.

This psychological matching looks at first like a lucky break. It seems to explain why so many different kinds of couples can claim to be happy. Maybe dominant men need supportive, dependent women and clinging vines need a sturdy oak. But a relationship based on needs can be cruel when the needs don't match. For the homemaker couples, affection was often a one-way street.

Homemakers had the strongest need to receive affection as well as to give it, but, on the average, the men they married were less willing than the "cool" husbands of working wives to give it. These breadwinning husbands were less concerned, too, with "feelings of togetherness and involvement." Homemakers felt it. They complained about it. Homemakers who participated in the happiness study were more likely then working wives to say that they loved their husbands more than their husbands loved them back in return —a devastating confession for women who have staked their whole happiness on love.

Career dedication doesn't make for the happiest marriages, either, even when the career is the husband's, and even when married to Traditional Wives. Whenever they're asked, a majority of men say they get more happiness from their families than their jobs, and, according to an American Management Association study, this was true even for highly paid and motivated top executives. And it is no surprise to find that men who say this have happier marriages than those who get their principal satisfaction out of working. The most companionable marriages in terms of sharing everyday pleasures are those in which the husband derives more satisfaction from his family than from his work and the wife combines marriage with career. The "cool" marriage of likes seems safer and more satisfying, perhaps, than the "hot" marriage of aching needs.

Some wives turn to part-time work as a compromise. But there are a number of reasons why part-time work isn't the ideal solution so many women think it will be. There is evidence that part-time work gives women the worst of both worlds, harried at home and undervalued at jobs which compare even less favorably with those of their husbands than do the jobs of women who work full time. In addition, part-time work can be literally depressing. Labor Department studies tell us that part-time workers are in and out of the labor force, and in their book, *The Depressed Woman,* Myrna M. Weissman and Eugene S. Paykel report that women are especially vulnerable to depressions when starting or quitting a job.

There is, of course, a limit to how far it is useful to generalize. Housewives are all kinds of people. Working wives come in every variety, too. What we can say, however, is that the experience of working changes a woman for the better whatever her reasons for doing it and even if she complains about it at the time. Although they are better off by almost every measure, working wives have a harder time calling themselves "happy" because rising expectation, choice, and a world which in law and custom is not prepared to accommodate their needs combine to create what we are calling "the personal, painful side" of the two-paycheck revolution. As we will see.

PART TWO:

HOME
IS THE NEW FRONTIER

CHAPTER 3

The Personal,
Sometimes Painful Side of It

Meet the Bostwicks. You probably know people like them. They seem to have the best of everything. When the phone rings for Dr. Bostwick, the Dr. Bostwick who answers has to ask, "Which Dr. Bostwick do you want?" Dr. Ethel is a psychiatrist in private practice. Dr. James is a neurosurgeon on the staff of a famous New York hospital. They consider themselves to be an example of really egalitarian marriage.

"It works because we started out being equal," she says. "We went through medical school together and got into the habit of sharing things equally."

Housework?

"I try to help," Dr. James answers. "After all, her time is worth $50 an hour."

"Of course, it helps that we are both M.D.s," she adds. "We understand each other's problems. A lot of doctors would be threatened by another doctor in the family, but I've been lucky enough to find a husband who is too self-confident to worry about his masculinity."

16415

He has another idea about why it works. "Our marriage is *equally important* to both of us. Whatever happens during the day, our evening cocktail together is sacred, medical emergencies excepted, of course."

Their daughter Melissa is proud of having two doctors in the family. "We try to give her special attention so that she won't be jealous of our patients," Dr. Ethel says. "It's easy for the children of doctors to feel neglected."

Money is no problem for the Bostwicks. They just split up the bills. He pays for rent on their New York apartment, and the expense of their weekend house in the mountains. She buys the food and pays the housekeeper and extra help. He pays school tuition, she buys Melissa's clothes. And, of course, they each buy their own cars and clothes.

They sound like the 21st century. Equal at home and at work. But inside, Ethel is doing what physician's wives have always done to build the ego and the prestige of "The Doctor."

First of all, in the 1970s, a professionally successful wife has become a status symbol for a certain kind of professional man who has everything that money can buy. And psychiatry, with its punctual hours, is easily matched to a husband's demands. She schedules sessions so that she is sure to get home in time to get into the long lounge gown he likes, set up the drink tray, build a fire, and plan dinner so that she doesn't have to pop into the kitchen while he's talking. And the talk is always about what's going on at his hospital, and never about what's happening to her patients. He thinks psychiatry is trivial, and it's comfortable for both of them to have him think so.

Ethel hardly remembers the bumps that hurt along the way. They entered medical school together, but a mixup in the dean's office put her a year behind him. James tried to comfort her by saying, over and over, "But what difference does it make?" She cried herself to sleep that night and wouldn't let him hold her.

Another bump was the time a suicidal patient telephoned while she was entertaining some neurosurgeons James had brought home. She didn't think he would like to have her explain to these particular guests that she was called away on a medical emergency, but she couldn't keep her patient talking on the phone. She can't remember anything that evening after he hung up on her. He went through with the suicide.

And then there was the time that James wouldn't take Melissa to the pediatric ward of his hospital for the day, the way the doctor mothers on the hospital staff did when their babysitters didn't turn up. He said he didn't want the nurses talking about his wife the way they talked about the women doctors on the hospital staff.

When he offers to help with the dishes, she declines. He doesn't wipe the counters and that bothers her.

One of the advantages of the separate checking accounts they keep is that he doesn't know how much she has to spend on help to keep up with their lifestyle. If he knew how much money she had to spend to make up for the time she doesn't have to do it herself, he would think her extravagant, creating even more tension.

Sex equality was chic in the 1970s. College presidents sometimes boasted about the careers of their wives, and presidents' wives who had none to display felt a certain pressure to provide a better example for women students. Some of the most persuasive feminists of the 1970s were well-heeled husbands who no more expected to have to do housework than rich Civil Rights advocates of the 1950s expected a black family to move next door. They expected their wives to be doctors or lawyers or clean up in real estate, all without inconveniencing them in any way.

There was snobbery in this view. College students sneered at the sexism of those who expected dinner to be on the table when they got home and didn't mind saying so. Nobody told them that equality is harder at the top than at the bottom.

One reason is economic. The higher a man's income, the more he needs the emotional, social, and housekeeping support of a traditional wife. The higher a woman's income, the less she needs the economic and social support of a husband.

Another reason is psychological. This is more than a hunch. College freshmen who scored high on power motivation on one of those Thematic Apperception Tests that ask you to write a story about a picture, were overwhelmingly less apt to be married to career women ten years after graduation than classmates whose need for power was lower.

Dr. Ruth Moulton, a psychoanalyst of women, reports some of the ploys upper-middle-class husbands use to cool out the ambitions of their wives. "He can threaten to move his work to California or the sun belt; he may try to draw his wife further into his work, depriving her of her autonomy. He may criticize her for neglecting the household, for not taking care of him while he had the flu, etc. There may be sexual withdrawal which often begins with pique and ends in impotence, which he finds a relief because it is also a weapon. He may start an affair with a more available, sexually hungry or dependent and needy woman . . . Another tactic is to belittle the nature of the work the wife chooses to do; it pays too little, lacks prestige, is of no interest to him, will add nothing to family life. He may also complain that she will be less free to entertain his colleagues, clients, friends, although the couple may be at a point where they can now well afford to have more outside help."

One wife who made a pact with her husband that she would quit her new job if after six months he was inconvenienced by it reports that he doubled his demands for home service. In order to delay her from leaving the house, he once tore a button off his coat and demanded that she sew it back on before she went to work.

Beneath the rhetoric of equality lies a dark tangle of fears, guilts, resentments, envies, anxieties, and especially for the women on whom the burden falls, sheer physical fatigue.

These dark emotions sometimes surface in party talk. "Mother reads a lot. She keeps up. But she's still a Southern lady," an engineer reminisced about his Louisiana parents. "Why, she actually told me that she thinks Claire is quote 'coarsening herself' by quote 'getting so deep into men's things' in her job." He makes derisive quotation marks with his fingers in the air, but Claire does not smile. She has not heard this about her mother-in-law before. Is her husband trying to tell her something he doesn't want to discuss in private? Does he agree with his mother?

Husbands don't always realize how patronizing their boasts can be. "She's proving that even after four kids and twenty years of marriage she can step in and do something useful," a businessman said with a straight face.

"Luckily, the company's affirmative-action program came along just when she asked for her promotion," another husband chuckled. Does he write her off as a token?

"Helen's a genius, really. All she needed was a little self-confidence to get going. A push. She doesn't know how good she is. That's why I'm making her aim high." Helen is not flattered. "Oh, he's proud of me all right," she says. "He says to everybody, 'See my wife out there—look what she's doing.' He acts as if I am a puppet dancing on a string."

Pride in possessing a brilliant woman is one reason husbands push wives. Men who are having fun making money often feel sorry for wives who are stuck at home with the kids. But guilt is another reason. "He talks up my commercial greenhouse business," one wife says, "because he's having so much fun making money that he is relieved that I am, too."

Wives feel guilty more often than husbands, and about more things. Sometimes there's no escaping it. A mother who misses the school play to see a long-lost friend in town for the evening is going to be guilty whatever work she does or doesn't do. An executive who lies about taking time off from work to do her part in the PTA fair can be guilty because she hasn't had the courage to give the real reason for her absence. A wife can even feel guilty about feeling guilty.

"He didn't seem to mind and did quite well for the first few times," a minister's wife said of her husband who had undertaken to watch their children while she worked. "But after it went on for awhile he became impatient with it. He didn't say anything, but I knew by the look on his face that he didn't want to be stuck with them, yet I wasn't saying to myself, 'Okay, now you know what I've been going through all these years.' Instead, I was feeling sorry for him, and that bothered me. I was feeling guilty, and I got mad at myself for feeling guilty."

Guilt drives ambitious women to do right by everyone but themselves.

The life of a superwoman is for the hardy. One thirty-nine-year-old lawyer, at the helm of an important firm, is the wife of a physician and the mother of two. She writes briefs on the trains between Manhattan and Westchester and anywhere else she can find a moment's quiet. "Fortunately I don't need a lot of sleep," she says.

A professor married to a fellow anthropologist needs all the mental and physical discipline she learned as a modern dancer. One year she was writing a book, teaching college classes, renovating an old house in the country on weekends, keeping up with New York theater on week nights, without missing the chance to read to her daughter on the bus to school every morning. Sometimes she misses meals. She's thin. "My life doesn't leave me much time to eat," she says.

Wives of these supercouples learn to hide a trail of chores left undone. One woman won't let her guests hang up their own coats for fear they'll open the wrong door and stumble into the black hole of Calcutta into which she pitches low-priority projects. It contains, among other things, two coats that need buttons, a tennis racket to be restrung, a blender to go to the repair shop, an old fur coat good enough to remodel, a Christmas wrapped bottle of perfume she never got around to delivering in person to a shut-in great aunt, mimeographed poetry sent to her by a college chum for review, a dead plant, a rolled-up oil painting of her grandfather to go to the framer's, and a shopping bag full of unanswered letters.

Super-busy women develop stratagems for hiding their workload. One professional woman tucks work from the office into her bag when she packs for a weekend, then during the evening pleads a headache so she can go upstairs and work while the other guests are relaxing. Another wife hates to tell her husband that she can't drop her work to pick up their children on the days he is supposed to, but often finds he's too busy to do it at the last moment. So she has a college boy standing by and pays him out of her own pocket to pick them up.

These are the stratagems used by women now in their forties and fifties. Women undergraduates of the 1970s don't think they'll need them. They think it will be easy to build a rewarding marriage around two really equal careers, but nobody knows how easy this will be because it has seldom been seriously tried.

Sociologists studying the family find very few marriages in which it can honestly be said that her career gets equal billing with his career.

Couples say they regard themselves as equal partners, but most of them don't act that way.

A husband expects a laurel wreath from the National Organization for Women for turning down a promotion that would take his wife away from her job, and lower the family income, or for helping her with "her shopping and her cooking." The laundry, too, is "hers," even though the monthly bills are no longer his alone.

Very few children have had really equal parenting from mother and father. Too often, Father's sacrifice of his Saturday morning to play ball with the male children has been treated as a special favor of Father to Mother. In too many families, the children are "hers" along with the dirty clothes.

Elite young college-educated professional workers don't *think* they feel this way. They associate these attitudes with blue-collar advocates of law and order who don't want their children going to school "with the colored." They and their wives see eye to eye on family policy, *or so they think*.

But there's a little male chauvinism in most husbands' hearts. Husbands are more likely than wives to think that working mothers are bad for children and that women should wait until children are old enough to go to school or even later before working outside the home, that a wife's job hurts sex; and that the husband should make the decision if they disagree on whether or not she should work.

All up and down the lines—whether she thinks of her job as a job or whether she thinks it's a career—two-paycheck couples have similar worries.

They worry that sex won't be as much or as good as it is when the wife stays home.

They worry about what is going to happen to the children.

They worry that her money will make her too independent, so that she won't look up to him and might even leave him.

CHAPTER 4

Sex and Power

Couples don't like to think about it, but what they are promising, on their wedding day, is something more tangible than love eternal. Marriage is a legal contract that obliges a husband to provide money for basic necessities and a wife to give sex, do housework, mind kids, and to go wherever he chooses to take her. Legally, and practically, too, the cards are stacked in his favor. He earns the money, and he has the power.

But marriage is a very special sort of legal contract. You can get into it. You can even get out of it. But you cannot change its terms. What you promised on your wedding day is set by courts and state legislatures, and since courts do not intervene in ongoing marriages, you may not even know what you've undertaken until you apply for a divorce.

During the 1970s, courts and state legislatures were changing the terms of the marital contract to make them more reciprocal. In 1978, for instance, the California Supreme Court established the right of a wife to sex from her husband on an equal basis with his right to sex from her. Before that decision, damages for loss of "consortium," meaning sex and services, had always been awarded to a husband for loss, often through accidental injury, of the services the common law assumed he had coming from his wife.

The support that a wife had coming from her husband was enforceable only through a court award of alimony. But in the 1970s, alimony, too, became a two-way street. Judges began refusing to award alimony to able-bodied wives and even to award it to the husband, if he was not able to support himself in the style to which an affluent wife had accustomed him during the marriage. It is perhaps conceivable—though highly unlikely—that a wife might be obligated to support a husband who stood on his old common-law right to determine where she should live.

As divorces became more common, it was harder for brides and grooms to remain blissfully ignorant of what they were getting into. "I love him," one young professional woman explained, "but I don't want to be a wife." Increasingly, self-supporting women chose to live with men instead of marrying them, or to write their own, individual marriage contracts spelling out what they were willing to do when they were pronounced man and wife.

Attempts to amend the marital contract are as old as feminism itself. The earliest was made by Mary Wollstonecraft, author of "A Vindication of the Rights of Women," the document which in 1792 founded women's rights. She and her husband, William Godwin, agreed to keep separate residences so that "the husband only visits his mistress like a lover when each is dressed, rooms are in order, etc." The pioneer of birth control, Margaret Sanger and her husband, J. Noah H. Slee, had similar arrangements. When Lucy Stone and Henry Blackwell, the political activists of their day, were married in 1855, they wrote a declaration of independence from laws that "refuse to recognize the wife as an independent, rational being, while they confer upon the husband an injurious and unnatural superiority."

Courts have never recognized changes in the personal obligations of marriage, although they have always upheld prenuptial contracts dealing with property. Yet it is control over her own time and domicile that pinches when a wife goes to work. For working couples, the issue is not financial support, but power.

The marriage contracts men and women of the 1970s were writing together showed what they didn't like about the contract. Sometimes the issues were philosophical. "We each offer and accept total openness about feelings toward one another, and about our emotional lives generally. We agree to share one another's lives." Or, "We each offer emotional loyalty and support."

But the issues were also highly practical. They told where the couple anticipated trouble that might threaten the marriage: what to do about relationships with others; what to do about children; who should use birth control and what kind; what to do in the event of an "accidental" pregnancy and who takes care of any children they do have; how to divide money and property; how to spend money; where they will live and on what basis they will decide to move; what to do about careers and career conflicts; who cleans; and how the living space is to be divided between them. Some contracts got so specific that they included who spends which holidays with whose parents, or even how much time each was obliged to spend with the other during the day, or on weekends and vacations.

Contracts usually provided formal business procedures for amending, arbitrating, and terminating the agreement. Some were renewable at intervals such as every five years, but others could be dissolved at a moment's notice. One couple took the "forever" out of their marriage by providing that "this contract can be terminated by mutual consent or at the request of either party at any time."

Various as all these uniquely personal contracts were, they all aimed at recognizing the power that earning brings a wife.

POWER

Open recognition of the power a wife feels her money earns her has inaugurated a time of trouble in American marriages. Like all other powerholders facing challenge, a husband's first reaction is surprise: What am I supposed to do? His next move is to ignore the demand: Too busy to think about it right now. Or to misinterpret it: You don't really want that, honey. Some husbands hold onto their power and fight to the end, until their wives relinquish their demands or the marriage is forced to the point of divorce. Others try for a pyrrhic victory: If it means that much to you, why didn't you say so before? But eventually the conflict becomes real. He has a lot to lose and at some level he knows it.

For the Traditional couple, the transition may be especially hard because it is unexpected. Some husbands may not realize until it has already happened how much they depend on their wives *not* working. Their resentment surfaces in many ways.

"Working was an economic necessity in our house," a wife wrote us about the decision to take a job. "We had five children, over five thousand dollars in uninsured medical bills with the three youngest boys, who seemed to feel oxygen tents and pneumonia were the way every little kid grew up, sporadic periods of unemployment and a house fire. Our youngest was three, and we were not only flat broke but way in debt, so going to work seemed the only solution.

"We discussed it. My husband agreed. All seemed fine. Would you believe that the morning I dressed to go for the first day my husband came completely unglued and spent an hour voicing all the traditional reasons for not having a working wife! His male status was being undermined. I was making him a public embarrassment in front of his friends and family, I was just planning on finding a new, richer husband, the whole grim bit. I went to work anyway, but everything that happened was because I worked. Bad grades, burnt hamburger, empty sock drawer, no sex tonight—all ended up on my doorstep."

Husbands don't always realize how unconsciously they assume that they will be the center of attention. A breadwinner expects the meals to be served when he is ready to eat them. He expects that she will listen when he wants to talk and shush the children when he wants to sleep. When she has a job of her own she may not be able to adjust to his timetable. Even worse, he may discover that she has something else she really would rather do. To her surprise, as well as to his, she may find the company of other women as absorbing as the company of men, and "hen parties" may no longer be restricted to the hours when husbands are working. As wives develop interests and friends of their own, husbands lose the power to keep them at home. They are startled and ashamed to admit a sense of loss when they find that the phone rings for her—and that the conversation is so interesting that she leaves their dinner to cool, or to be served and eaten by others. They are used to being scolded by their wives for leaving the dinner for an important phone call for themselves, but the reverse is inconceivable. And its occurrence can be traumatic.

William J. Goode, a Stanford University sociologist who specializes in family relationships, points out that men have come to expect that women will always assume that whatever a man is doing is more important than whatever it is that a woman is doing herself. He thinks that men resent the loss of this "centrality" in the lives of their women more than they fear the competition of women in the work place. Men like to feel that they are doing something great when they bring home their paychecks, that they are giving the woman they love a gift. Much of their drive to succeed is motivated by an effort to win the admiration of their women. Very few men fail to identify, at some level, with the man surrounded by family, in the life insurance television commercial, who exults, "They need me!"

When women spend more time with each other and with their work, men feel the desertion keenly. It is worse now than in the past, Goode asserts, because they are more dependent on women for solace and intimacy than they were when there were more all-male organizations and clubs than there are now.

In the nineteenth century, the softer, gentler side of a man was channeled to his private, family relationships. The Victorian family ideal put a fence around the family and protected it from the ruthless, Darwinian competition of industrial life outside. This was a great disservice to women, of course, but it also channeled cooperative feelings of husbands to their wives.

In the course of this sex segregation, the tradition of stag parties and male-only bars provided a haven for a man who was having a fight with his wife and an outlet of sorts for one whose wife was overcommitted with the children or unavailable for any other reason.

In the 1960s, the male havens were declining. The women's movement outlawed male bars and relations with women were becoming more difficult because women insisted on being treated as equals. Men were legitimately lonely, and they often complained in inappropriate ways.

To wives, the complaints of their husbands sound trivial, or worse. "I'm not even allowed to read the paper through," one wife reported. "He wants my total attention, like a three-year-old."

Wives who earn part of the family income are not so willing to give their total attention to a man who sounds like a three-year-old. They no longer are content to get their way, as courtiers always have done, by indirection—flattery, flirtatious promises of sex to come, attentions to his comfort, and mostly by close attention to his emotional needs and careful timing of demands to his moments of maximum vulnerability—the "feminine wiles" that worked well when husbands wielded the total power in the family.

Wives who have money of their own no longer are delighted with a husband who "lets them" have their own way. They don't want to be given presents because they are loved or cute. They are not willing to give their husbands the satisfaction of being "generous." They want their own way—or at least their own input as a matter of right.

There is always a struggle when power changes hands. It varies in intensity with the couples, but it goes through similar stages. For Traditional couples, there's a struggle when she goes to work. For Contemporary couples the struggle occurs when her career moves ahead faster than his.

Stage One: Unconscious Hostility

Everyone admired Joyce and Mike. They had a good marriage. They went skiing, golfing, and jogging together. And they had equal and interesting careers. She taught history in the local community college, and he owned the local sporting goods store.

Everything was fine until Joyce was promoted to dean at a salary that topped Mike's take from the store.

Neither of them thought it would make a difference, and at first it didn't. But as the work piled up, Joyce began to feel guilty about the cleaning she couldn't get done and the fancy meals she no longer had time to cook. Mike didn't bother to reassure her. On the contrary, he seemed to enjoy her guilt and even encourage it.

Eventually, he began to grumble about how nice things "used to be" when meals were on time, when the "poor dog" was taken to be groomed on a regular basis, in "the days before there was dust." And he began to find all sorts of little ways to show that he was still the boss.

Sometimes, for instance, he would demand sex when he knew she was tired. "What's the matter?" he would say if she refused. "Don't you love me any more?" It was as if he refused to recognize that anything had changed to give her a right to be tired.

When they went skiing, he spoiled the fun by becoming competitive with her, as if to prove that he was stronger and better. He would insist, for instance, on skiing the only one out of thirty-five slopes that was too hard for her. Not only did that mean that they had to ski separate slopes, but he seemed more interested in proving something about himself than in sharing the pleasure with her.

The strain began to show in social situations. He started cracking jokes at Joyce's expense.

As it often does, the first verbal hostility was in humor. "What can I say?" he once cracked. "She makes more money than I."

"Yes, Madam Dear," he once said mockingly when she asked him to refill her drink while he was refilling his.

At home, Mike lost interest in Joyce's work as she had every reason to become more interested in it. He refused, for instance, even to read a newspaper article about one of her projects which had attracted a great deal of attention among their friends. When they brought it up, he just shrugged and said he hadn't had time yet to read it. The implication, of course, was that his own career was absorbing him totally.

Joyce pretended not to notice these digs. She hoped they would go away. Instead they got worse. Finally she could take it no longer. As she later put it, "Something inside of me snapped."

Stage Two: Open Confrontation

"One night I worked late and when I got home at ten o'clock, there he was sitting complaining 'this house is a mess.' Without a moment's hesitation I looked him in the eye and said, 'I suppose you expect me to stay up until two o'clock to clean up.' And then I flounced off to bed."

This was followed by several days of silence. Silence is a common power ploy: Who will give in first? Who cares more—and is the one most likely to concede? Or, in the pouty words of a child behind the ploy: If you don't care about me, than I just won't bother you anymore.

Joyce was the one who finally insisted they sit down and talk about it. In theory, it was easy to agree. He *wanted* her to enjoy working. He said he was even *proud* of her. And he didn't really care about the house cleaning all that much. He agreed to help around the house and to cut out the jokes that embarrassed Joyce.

"I believe he meant everything he said," Joyce recalls. "But he kept breaking his agreement. And when he broke his side of the bargain, I found ways to retaliate. This kind of volley went on for months."

Joyce and Mike had entered Stage Three.

Stage Three: Conscious Retaliation

Open war had been declared. Life became a duel, a series of retaliations. The first issue was the seemingly innocuous task of washing the car. It was normally his task, but one Saturday he just didn't bother. Pointedly, Joyce didn't bother either.

The next week, Mike went her one better. Not only did he leave the car unwashed, but he went off to play golf with somebody else. This was a two-pronged ploy: it left the car washing to Joyce once again, and proved that he could be quite happy playing golf without her. Formerly, they had always played golf together.

Joyce was equal to the challenge. She just stopped washing the windows. She stopped sewing for him. She stopped picking up his clothes, and when he acted as if this didn't bother him, she pushed them off the chair and onto the floor.

She tried other ways of getting to him. She stopped buying gifts for his family while continuing to buy them for her own. He retaliated by insisting that they plan to have both families to their house for Christmas dinner—an old-fashioned Christmas with cooking and decorations for which he knew Joyce didn't have time.

"No," Joyce said to the proposal. "Absolutely no." But she didn't leave it at that. "We can go to my mother's instead." She knew that he wouldn't want *that*.

The conflagration spread to all areas of their life. They had always done the checks together, but he took to leaving the chore to her. Then he would go out and buy something he knew that they couldn't afford. "If she's going to be earning all that money," he seemed to be saying, "then I'm going to be the one to spend it." It was the classic reaction of dependent wives.

Mike next turned his attention to their daughter. For the first time he began to assert his authority over her comings and goings. He'd tell her that she would have to come in at 11 o'clock on Saturday night when all the other kids were staying out until midnight. This put Joyce in an awkward situation because she had already said that midnight was fine: "He just wanted to prove he had the final say on this as in everything else."

Another fruitful source of conflict was the demands of their careers. As dean, Joyce was invited to faculty parties, but Mike wasn't willing to go with her. The few times he went, he found ways to play dumb. "I wouldn't know a thing about that," he would say in the middle of a casual conversation. "I'm just a shopkeeper. My wife is a college administrator." He managed to embarrass her so much that he got out of ever going with her again.

At home, he found ways to assert the importance of his own work. He demanded absolute quiet when he did the account books for the store on the dining room table after dinner. He wouldn't let her do the dishes. He said he couldn't stand the sound of pots and pans rattling, or the noise of the dishwasher. He couldn't even bear the sound of the can opener when she had to feed the dog. "We had to turn off the television and sit perfectly still," Joyce recalled. "My daughter and I couldn't even whisper to each other, and he'd be upset if I so much as walked through the room."

Stage Four: Crisis

Retaliation at this level cannot, of course, go on forever. Something happens to resolve the crisis or end the marriage. For many couples, the final power ploy is the "other woman"—the "other woman" who he believes is necessary because his wife is neglecting him sexually.

He has been making a case for this for a long time. It begins when he makes sexual demands when he knows that she is too tired to respond. A series of these occurrences convinces him that he really needs another woman. And whether he actually finds her or not, he manages to suggest that perhaps there might be one. He hopes, of course, to bring his wife to her senses, and he does. She may give up the fight to save the marriage or threaten to leave—and mean it.

Joyce and Mike never had to go this far. They went to a marriage counselor who helped them to save their marriage.

A shift of marital power can affect all aspects of life, but it always affects a couple's sex life, even when, as is often the case, neither husband nor wife will admit it.

SEX, HIS AND HERS

Most couples who think that sex is changed when a wife goes to work tend to say that it is changed for the worse. They're too tired, too tense, or their schedules conflict. Many people believe that the tension of professional and business life can cut into sex.

A Defiant Homemaker who has two preschool children thinks that sex was worse when she worked because she was "too tired to enjoy it properly." She's an R.N. who worked long hours and quit because she wanted to be at home with her two children.

Hardworking professional women are too tense themselves to

help their husbands relax enough so that sex is good for them both. "It's hard to be in the mood for sex when both of us are scratching as hard as we can to get some sort of edge over the competition," a Contemporary Wife told us. "I'll bet a lot of couples aren't telling their friends that they aren't sleeping with their husbands."

Ill-matched working hours make it hard for some couples to get together under the right circumstances. In 1977, for instance, a magazine featured a Contemporary couple holding down jobs in different cities. The photographer posed them in night clothes sharing a sofa-bed in the living room of her mother's place where they spent weekends.

Couples who work different shifts to avoid babysitting costs complain that the arrangement cuts into their sex lives. "I'm tired of watching him sleep," one wife complained. A starker report comes from a telephone operator. "My working nights, and husband days. Him babysitting. Me too tired when I got home. He got himself a girl friend, who he had at our house while I was at work! If I had it to do over again, I would not work."

All of these impediments sound plausible, but the fact is, of course, that sex is affected much less by the problems of work than it is by the problems husbands and wives are having with each other.

A machinist who repairs tractors on the night shift has a schedule that seems to leave little time or leisure for sex. "My job is forty miles from my residence and it takes two hours traveling time. Wife works when I'm home. During the week we only see each other about two hours a day." He finds sex worse for her job. She finds it better. "Sometimes there is a strain when my husband feels all his spare time is taken by watching our boy aged three," she adds. It's not so much that they don't have time together as it is that he doesn't think he should have to mind the baby.

A foreman working for a city light department from dawn to early afternoon wrote that working mothers were "bad for husbands" as well as children. "The reason he says that," his working wife explained, "is that he is very tired or sleeping when I get home at 9:30 P.M."

Can this man be acting like a small child who turns his face away from the returning mother who went away when he wanted her to stay? "You weren't here to do what I expected you to do (take care of our boy)," he's saying in body language. "So I'm not here to do what you expected me to do (have sex)."

But, of course, it is wives who are most often "too tired" for sex, and for most, what usually makes *them* "too tired" is the housework. "He doesn't even pick up after himself, much less lend a hand with anything else," a personnel supervisor complained. "Sure his sex life is worse. I'm so exhausted when I go to bed that sex is the last thing in the world I want."

It's not so much that she's tired, it's that secretly she thinks she shouldn't have to do all the housework. No help, no sex.

The connection between sex and housework turns up again and again when you ask husbands and wives separately what they would like to have changed in their marriages. He talks about sex, she about help with the housework:

"More erotic sex," says a high-salaried structural steel engineer.

"Equal cooperation in household duties—for all occupants," says his wife, a warehouse supervisor.

Some wives spell it out. "He was coming home, sitting down reading the paper, while I was in the kitchen, fixing supper with the baby playing under my feet, setting the table, getting supper on, feeding her, getting up, giving her a bath, getting her ready for bed, then doing supper dishes, then doing laundry and then at ten o'clock I could sit down and relax.

"If everything had gone right during the day he'd start in on me at ten o'clock. 'Why didn't you do this? Why didn't you do that?' Then he'd go into another room and come back and say, 'Well, aren't you going to bed with me?'

"Well, I'm not going to take abuse and then give him what he wants—even when I want it, too. It's not that I'm punishing him. If you can't have sexual relations with somebody because you are emotionally upset with them, that's not punishing them. The woman is more punished if she does it when she doesn't feel like it."

"Oh sure, out of my love for him I've done it sometimes when it was too much trouble," the working mother of two small children told us. "You have to get up and get all excited when all you want to do is lie there. I try to tell him that people don't need sex on a day-to-day basis, like vitamin pills. He doesn't see it, so to make my point I waited until he had come home dead beat seven nights in a row, and then I made up to *him*. You wouldn't believe all the excuses he made up for not having sex."

It is no surprise to find that husbands are more apt than wives to think that sex is worse when she works. In our study of Matching Couples, nearly a quarter of husbands complained. Sex, after all, is the main thing husbands are supposed to get out of marriage, and it is worth noting in passing that a great many husbands of homemakers also think they aren't getting their money's worth. A forester from Oregon blames the house, not her job. "Don't know why wife is more of a wife to the house than my lover," he grumbles. "House and yard come first."

It's more surprising, however, to find that more wives than husbands think that the job made sex better (less than a fifth thought working made it worse). In some families, he thinks it's worse, while she thinks it's better. Couples discovered this discrepancy while filling out the questionnaire. Those who talked it out found that they were looking at different aspects of their sex lives.

WORSE FOR HIM

"His reason for stating that sex was worse," one wife wrote, "was only that because I am tired, sex happens less often. But the quality, not the quantity, is more important to me. My reason for stating that it is better is because of the fact that my husband loves and respects me and is concerned for my happiness, and as a result, the sex we have is beautiful and mutually 'love giving.' "

"When I work, I'm sometimes too tired to be interested in sex, so we put off intercourse until we both really want it. . . ." another wife wrote. "Then it's usually quite delightful, so long as we are careful to distinguish between wanting and just being agreeable. So what do we answer? Should we balance lowered frequency against more intense involvement and call sex 'unaffected'? Or should we call it 'better' because it's part of a way of life that *taken as a whole, makes us happiest*?"

Other couples told the same story. Women were interested in the quality of sex, men in the quantity. This difference is mysterious. There is no good physiological reason why less frequent sex makes it better for wives and worse for husbands. Anatomically speaking, it ought to be the other way around. All the sex researchers have found that the more sex a woman has, the better the quality of her orgasms, while the more a man has, the less urgent his desire for more. Something else is involved: control.

The chilling implication is that until they earned money, these wives were having sex when they didn't really want it, or just to be "agreeable." Only when they went to work did they automatically renegotiate the marriage contract that links sex and money. The logic seems to be that if his money gives him control over the timing of sex, then her money ought to give *her* more to say about it, too.

"I don't have to plead a headache, or say something about how it's getting to that time of the month," a wife who had just returned to work exulted. "I can just say no, I don't feel like it now—*and not feel guilty about refusing.*"

It's easy to see why this wife is better off. She doesn't think she has to have sex when she doesn't feel like it. But is sex worse for him when it occurs only when they both feel like it? Surely these husbands cannot be sex machines counting nothing but the number of "outlets" per week.

What couples say about quantity versus quality raises more problems than it solves. "Once your wife goes to work she gets too independent and she's tired all the time," one sex-is-worse husband complains.

His wife has a different explanation. "Before I worked I was clingy and possessive. Now I don't have to relate to the world through my husband."

Why is sex worse for him because she's "not clingy" and "independent"? The only plausible explanation is that he is equating sex with his power over her, that he takes pleasure in making her do what she doesn't want to do. A great many people think this is so.

In the late 1970s, social critics were blaming the rising ambitions of women for what they perceived to be growing sexual problems of males. According to Dr. Edwin Lee, a psychologist chairing the board of Associated Women for A Better Community, psychiatrists' couches were "heaped with young men who are impotent because they are looking for something in a woman they are not getting."

Author Natalie Gittelson charges that men married to successful, competitive women are so angry at losing the dominance they think their due as males that they turn off sex completely.

Scientific sex researchers and psychiatrists deny the charge. They point out that impotence has always been a problem. The only change is that more men are seeking help for it. And all of them specifically deny the ancient principle that male animals—including humans— must dominate to have a satisfying sexual relationship.

The sex-money bargain has enshrined the "macho" view of sex relations as the model, but elegantly designed research has recently demonstrated that male power drive is *sexually* rewarding neither to women nor to men.

In 1960, male students at an elite college took a battery of tests. They were given pictures and asked to write a story about what was happening. They were asked to draw a picture of a man and a woman. Researchers scored them into three classes: high on power drive, average on power drive, low on power drive. Then they scattered to begin careers. Thirteen years later, psychologist David Winter of Wesleyan University and David McClelland of Harvard grilled 136 of the men at a class reunion about what had happened to them since that time.

The high-power men turned out to be classic male chauvinists. They had sex earlier and with more partners, and they were more willing to talk about their exploits with women than men with average power drive. When asked to draw a woman, they exaggerated breasts and drew bizarre, distorted figures. Their fantasies about women showed that they thought women were powerful and dangerous, but necessary for sex. When asked to describe the ideal wife, they emphasized her dependence and powerlessness. In narrating their lives since college they were less likely to mention wives at all, but those who did said things like "settled down in a lovely town with wife and dogs."

These macho males are bad news for women in a variety of ways. Of the men Winter and McClelland studied, the high-power men were less apt to be married to women with careers and less apt to be married at all than the men whose power drive was average or low. The "sex-is-worse" husbands of our own Matching Couples disagreed with their wives not only on what her job was doing to their sex life *but on many other issues as well.*

BETTER FOR HER

How could sex be better for a wife when it was worse for her husband? We have seen that wives benefit by getting out of sessions of sex-as-duty, but there is a great deal of evidence that a job also has a positive effect on the sexual response of women who work.

Women who go back to work or to college after their children are in school often experience a rush of sexual interest that surprises them. "I feel much freer and more uninhibited," one returnee reported. "I have a different view of myself.

"Since I've been working I've felt confident enough to make an appointment for sex, if it was necessary. I used to feel I had to be so subtle about it!"

Anything that improves a woman's self-worth makes her sexually more responsive and nothing improves self-worth more than success at earning money. A twenty-fifth anniversary study of the Harvard Class of 1952 collected some provocative statistics on wives of these generally upscale men. Of the wives earning less than $15,000 in their own right, 42 percent said they were less interested in sex than they had been when they were younger, but 74 percent of those earning more said they were more interested.

Many other studies confirm this phenomenon. Dr. Virginia Abernethy, of Vanderbilt University, has found that women active in the feminist movement earned more of the family income and were sexier than a matching series of traditional women. She found no difference between the two groups in the frequency of coitus, generalized hostility to men, or in the dissatisfaction with marriage in general, but the feminists were much more apt to take the sexual initiative and report satisfaction in the sexual relationship.

Another measure is historical. When women were confined to

subordinate work, sexual hangups were often the problems that brought them to psychiatrists. Of 25 women patients Dr. Ruth Moulton analyzed between 1953 and 1956, 10 had an acute dread of sex, 14 were unable to achieve orgasm by any method, and "a desperate need to find a man to marry was the prominent symptom of ten."

Dr. Moulton rarely sees these conditions today. In contrast with her earlier patients, 20 of a group of 25 patients she treated in the 1970s were established professionals whose main presenting symptom was their conflict between professional and domestic roles. Sexually they were much more active. "Most of the women looking for marriage whom I now see already have been divorced," she says. "Several want better sex with men but no marriage. One woman from the 1950s developed an extramarital affair, whereas eight patients from the 1970s had extramarital affairs, often a whole series of affairs."

Early psychological research established that highly paid women doctors, lawyers, and executives had more active and responsive sex lives than women who looked and acted more traditionally feminine. A study made by Marilyn Whitley and Susan Poulsen while at the University of Washington School of Nursing showed successful women to be sexually more venturesome as well. They queried 45 professional women on 31 sexual practices ranging from "kissing" to "orgasm by other means, please state the means." Those who scored more "competitive," "self-assertive," "independent," and "dominant" on standard psychological tests for these qualities were also the most apt to go in for oral stimulation of both male and female, complex undressing techniques, scents, fantasy, and other exotic sexual stimulants in a way people say is "like men."

Economic success makes women sexy. Perhaps because they have relatively so little of it, even a modest increase in earning power can sexually transfigure a woman. "They ask *me*—at my age—for identification now, when I go to a bar!" a 29-year-old new mother exulted of the changes brought about by her return to work. "My husband wanted me to go to work, I think, because he really wanted back the working girl he married—you know, hair done and clothes and all."

"I'm obviously not young and thin, but I find wives are jealous of me now, and they didn't used to be," a 40-year-old returnee said. "They resent the fact that their husbands want to talk to me in mixed company." She may be projecting her own growing sexual awareness onto the men and women she encounters.

In the study of Matching Couples, three out of four working wives thought their jobs made them more "interesting," but only half of the husbands thought so. This may be because a "more interesting" woman can threaten the dominance of men who think of sex as conquest. Others may fear the sexual appetites of self-confident women.

Promotion to executive status revolutionized a secretary's sexual self-awareness. "I was unattractive before I started making money," she recalls. "I didn't like myself in those days. I didn't like my looks, I didn't like my body, and I wasn't happy sexually. Now I like my looks and body." And that new awareness has changed her life and stimulated her sexual activity.

Husbands who need to dominate may be threatened by a sexual awakening of this kind. "These liberated women want intercourse all night," a male patient told his doctor. "They are insatiable, a bottomless pit. They seem to want to eat a man alive." His fear of being "eaten alive" recalls the bizarre and threatening figures of women drawn by the power-motivated men whom Winter and McClelland interviewed.

Husbands have another fear. A wife newly aglow with success at her work may be attracted to the men she meets through it. This is a marital hazard built into the work of airline stewardesses who are chosen and groomed to be sexually attractive and given maximum exposure and opportunity for extramarital adventure. "Husbands start out thinking it's great to be married to a stewardess," one of them told us. "But as time goes on they have a great big overgrown idea of what their wives are doing all those nights away from home. On my last trip, my husband wanted to know why I was packing a short nightgown instead of the long one I usually took. He was sure I had something special in mind."

Most working couples say that working wives are as faithful as home wives, but the lurking fears persist. Blue-collar couples are most suspicious, but husbands are more suspicious than wives at every educational and occupational level.

Jealous husbands are one of the reasons why Submissive Homemakers stay at home. Much more than husbands in general, these husbands vote to take a second job themselves rather than let their wives go out to earn. Their wives are not flattered.

"A woman home all day, coming in contact with just her children, or perhaps a local merchant, would tend to have an affair easier with the postman, gas man, delivery boy, etc., from sheer boredom," a Reluctant Homemaker remarked.

"I don't trust what she does when she's out of my sight," one man wrote of his Defiant Working Wife. She works on the assembly line of a packing plant when she isn't at home taking care of two small children.

Another Defiant Working Wife is a receptionist married to a carpenter. "He acts as if he would like to lock me up in a glass jar," she complains. "The men who come into our office could look, but they couldn't touch. He wasn't afraid of what I would do. He was afraid of what they would do because it was something he felt he might like to try himself." Kinsey and others have found that blue-collar husbands have more outside sex than white-collar counterparts, so it is not surprising that they were more worried about the fidelity of working wives than the white-collar husbands who answered.

The fears come out when husbands talk about how they feel about their wives going to work. "It would depend on what she did," a barber thought. "I wouldn't want her to be a topless go-go dancer for instance." He was visibly nettled when asked whether his wife wanted to be a topless dancer.

"No, no, of course not!" he shouted.

Another man liked to have his wife at home because "less things can happen." His own case, he went on, was unique because his wife was working with him in his business. If she worked anywhere else, there'd be trouble. Why? "Her being with other people, probably," he replied after a long pause. "There are some jobs I wouldn't want my wife working at, I know that."

Pressed for details, he admitted that maybe he was jealous, but he wasn't sure of what. Of other men? Or of her growing intellectually? "I suppose that way—intellectually—too," he replied, obviously miserable. "I just don't know."

For a surprising number of husbands, "intellectual growth," "broader interests," or even "time away from home" mean just one thing: another man. One husband said he did not want his wife "running around and meeting a lot of people."

Some people laugh at these fears. "Fidelity has nothing to do with where a woman works," one wife insisted. "It depends on how well you are pleased with what you are doing in both your job and your marriage." She's right. Psychologists who have studied infidelity say that it does not occur out of the blue for women, but follows some breakdown in the marriage. Professor Robert Bell, of Temple University, estimates, on the basis of a study in the early 1970s, that more than 40 percent of young wives will have an extramarital affair at some time in their lives. He did not find working wives especially unfaithful, but where, if not at work, is a working wife apt to meet a lover if she is in the mood to take one?

As everyone knows, a great many do. Some of them are eager to confess to a disinterested outsider. "I've just had an affair with a fellow teacher," a mother of two school-age children wrote. "Now I want out of my marriage."

Secretaries are still attracted to their bosses. "Working outside of home has created a desire for physical relationship with co-worker (executive status)," a plant manager's secretary writes. "Husband holds comparable position in another company."

And women turned on by success in their work sometimes do have office affairs. One secretary who was unattractive until she became an executive and started making money has had quite a few, and she talked very frankly about them.

"During the last four years my world has centered around men who are extremely powerful," she explained. "Very powerful people are very exciting to me. The only men I've really been attracted to recently have been significantly older than I and more successful." She believes that there is a traveling salesman cult, "only now there are women in it." Her first affair was with a man who was traveling away from home, too. "I didn't tell my husband then, but I was so naive in those days I thought it was written all over my face. He picked me up at the airport and I felt like Hester Prynne. But nothing happened. I had an affair with that man, and it made my life better. It made my marriage better. Sex was better with my husband. It gave me self-confidence, helped me move ahead."

She is not an isolated example. In a study of sexual behavior in and out of marriage, John N. Edwards, of Virginia Polytechnic Institute and State University, and Alan Booth, of the University of Nebraska, found that wives who scored high on tests of dominance in the family were more apt to have extramarital affairs than wives who were subservient.

BETTER FOR HIM, TOO

Some husbands thought sex was better when she worked. They were, to be sure, a minority. They were apt to be professionals or executives married to college-educated wives and to have children in school. They agree with the "sex-is-worse" husbands that working makes a wife more aggressive, but that's exactly what they say makes sex *better*.

"I sense more aggression from her and I'm more aggressive myself," a banker said of his wife, a health educator. "We have more meaningful things to talk about when we both have been out competing all day long. We're more keyed up, and it spills over into sex. Not more sex, but better, because we have a more complete sharing of what we have done during the day."

His wife was more explicit. "When I'm working we both have parts of our lives that are independent to a degree where we can do things that aren't threatening each other and so we are more comfortable with each other." She recalls the periods when she quit work to have children as times of deprivation and dependence that made her "unavailable emotionally" because she was "concerned with her own sense of deprivation."

A college professor recalls that *he* felt better when his wife went to work because he didn't feel so guilty. "I could come home without feeling that I had been out seeing people all day while she was stuck home with the kids. I'm not saying she felt that way, but I did—and it made our lives better when I knew she was having fun, too."

Wives who are in and out of the labor force identify periods of staying home with dependence. "During the summer when I'm at home, my whole world revolves around Terry," a school teacher explained. "I wait for him to come home, and I'm impatient while he's coming down from his work 'high,' having a drink, unwinding. During the winter, our lives are more on the same wave length. We're both tired when we get home, we both want to relax—and we're both ready for sex at about the same point in the day. Most important for sex, I think, is that we both function better when we both are working."

These "sex-is-better" husbands and wives didn't have housework hangups: they typically shared more household tasks than husbands and wives in general. A banker was unusually relaxed about it. "We don't feel as if it's 'my' job to do the dishes, or take the garbage out. Those are tasks to be done and they get done by whoever is nearest. The house gets picked up when and if someone gets tired of seeing the stuff lying around." No hassle there.

Husbands of working wives deserve more study than they've received, but what we know about them makes them good news for women. According to an early study made by Leland Axelson, of Virginia Polytechnic Institute and State University, they are less apt to stand on their marital "rights" than men married to homemakers and more apt to say that sex should happen only when both want it. And there's reason to believe that husbands married to working wives have more frequent sex and fewer long dry spells of no sex than husbands of homemakers. That, at least, is what Edwards and Booth found when they queried a series of couples about their sex habits.

The marriages of working couples are simply more intense than traditional marriages as we have known them. If the marriage is failing, it is usually failing more dramatically than traditional marriages: more fights, more tension. And more divorce. But if it is good, then the marriage of a working couple tends to be "exceptionally good": better sex, more sex, more companionship, more talk.

Talk is, of course, the most important aphrodisiac, and wives who go back to work report that they have more to say to their husbands —talk that leads to sexual communication, too. "Our marriage is much more exciting," one told a group of women friends. "We've always enjoyed going out to dinner alone together, but now it's a whole new dimension, because it's a two-sided conversation. It's not me listening while he does the talking all the time. We have so much to say to each other that we can hardly stop talking."

"I used to try to help him in his work by entertaining his customers," the wife of a successful real estate developer says. "But now that I have my own thing we have much more to give each other. We used to drive seventy miles without speaking a word, but now we talk all the way."

The most important thing that working couples have more of, however, is equality. When sex stopped completely for a while, as it did for a third of the couples Edwards and Booth studied, something almost always had gone wrong with the marriage. One of the things that the wives said went wrong was "perception that her husband was dominant in family decision-making."

THE DOLLAR VALUE OF POWER

Husbands have always used the veto power of the purse. Like the parents of dependent children, they can threaten to leave the rebel penniless. For the first time in history this power balance between the sexes is shifting. Working wives can challenge this threat.

"I work now, so I'm the boss, too," one Defiant Working Wife told her husband. "I know," her husband retaliated, "but I still make more than you."

The Matching Couples study proves what this couple intuitively knows to be true: the bigger her contribution, the bigger her say. She is more likely to get her own way if she earns $5,000 to his $6,000, than if she earns only $30,000 to his $100,000. On the other hand, the more of the family income he earns the more likely he is to reserve the final decision for himself, and this likelihood rises *directly* with his input. As the gap between her earnings and his increases,

so does the power he wields over how they shall live. Only 49 percent of husbands of homemakers would give her the final decision
on whether she should work if the two disagree, compared with 72
percent of husbands earning the same as their wives and 77 percent
of husbands whose wives outearned them.

It was the same with other issues of marriage equality. The more
of the family income she earned, the more likely he was to approve
of her going back to work before her youngest was in school, to
feel that a woman should be as committed to her work as a man, to
feel he should help with the housework, and to want a career for
his daughter. Whenever couples were analyzed in terms of income
gap, from homemakers who put in zero dollars to wives who outearned their husbands, the percentage of husbands answering in
favor of marriage equality increased as her income neared his—a
nice straight steadily ascending line on the graph.

The ultimate threat to the marriage contract comes when she
earns more money than he does. Neither husband nor wife likes to
contemplate this change in the balance of power. Would he resent
it? More wives than husbands thought so, especially wives who
couldn't imagine doing it. Wives tended to head off his future resentment and husbands preferred to deny the very idea. No one
wanted to speculate.

"Fat chance!" one husband quipped. "No such luck," another
sighed in mock lament. "Frankly, for the field she's going into, and
the field I'm in, that's an impossibility," one more rational husband
explained. "She couldn't earn more than I do unless something very
drastic happened to me. I don't like to think about it."

A Foreign Service Officer couldn't imagine being promoted beyond her husband who was a Foreign Service Officer, too. "Rank
goes with the *person,* not the job," she explained. "If they assign me
to an important mission, they don't have to raise my rank, and they
probably wouldn't." After a few minutes thought she confessed
that a really important mission would be a real marital problem.
"It wouldn't go down too well. I don't know whether I would take
it . . . I think I probably would . . ." Her voice trailed off and
stopped before the unthinkable.

The unthinkable isn't rare. In the late 1970s, nearly 22 percent of wives who worked full time earned as much or more than their husbands. And attitudes were beginning to change. Only three out of ten magazine readers queried in 1978 thought they would turn down a job that paid more than their husbands earned, but those who have the choice don't make it lightly.

"My income for the last year I worked exceeded $50,000, a fact that my husband became very resentful about," wrote a Submissive Homemaker in her forties, who had worked all her life—until recently. "I loved the job. The sense of worthiness, self-confidence, and fulfillment was bliss. Not to mention the financial independence. He could not be happy in my success, although he enjoyed the benefits. It became a choice of marriage or job. I chose marriage. It was a second marriage for each of us, and neither of us wanted it to break up."

A woman from rural Pennsylvania was worried about her marriage because the nursery school she had started in her home was becoming a financial success. "How do you handle the feelings of a traditionally oriented husband who has been cut off from a very successful career because of enforced retirement when you are just beginning to feel the sprouting of your wings?"

"A wife should not make more than her husband or marry a man not equal to her in education," a teacher earning more than $15,000 writes. "Man feels threatened when wife is in job that provides for advancement and salary increases," her husband concurs. He is a city sewerage foreman earning less than $8,000.

Of course some couples adjust to the situation without resentment. "This year I got a promotion that keeps me at the office late many days," a newspaper editor says. "He's not concerned that my salary this year will be close to $20,000 while his remains at $14,-000. There's no jealousy and that makes our relationship even stronger."

Under the marital contract, a husband is entitled to sex and services on demand. We have seen that when a wife earns money, she gains the power to say no. But does it go further? If she outearns him, does her money give her the right to reverse the convention and demand sex and services from him?

No. Her legal obligations remain the same, but the evidence of the Matching Couples shows that her money brings real gains. It often gives her confidence to ask for what she wants, and that's the first step to getting it.

Outearned husbands we talked with were more apt to help with housework, more apt to say sex should occur when both want it, and more apt to follow a wife if a better job opened up somewhere else. Even the *prospect* of bringing in the lion's share of the family income can give a wife power. One wife who gave up a promotion thinks she has benefited because her husband tries to make it up to her. "He cleans the house and does the laundry now," she reports. "He even brings me flowers. If I say I want something, I have it. We eat out a lot."

But which marriages are happiest? Marital happiness is a slippery concept, but a few things seem well established. Imbalance of achievement is a threat to a marriage whether husband or wife is ahead. The happiest marriages are those in which husband and wife are equal—in other words, the one where power is *not* the issue. Happily married couples have renegotiated the marriage contract either deliberately or empirically to make it more equal than the traditional bargain of sex plus services plus obedience for money.

This renegotiation is most apt to happen when her earnings buy her the right to demand more power—a demand that always poses a threat to a marriage. If it can't be restructured to share the power, the marriage may fail, and as we have seen, the rate of divorce rises 2 percent for every additional thousand dollars she earns. Like buildings in an earthquake, only the solid marriages survive. But the solid marriages that survive are more exciting because they allow both partners the room for growth that is denied in marriages based on static social roles.

CHAPTER 5

Coping With the Dream
of a Perfect Home

W ell, why *did* you get married?" the young woman challenged her grandmother.

"To get supported," the grandmother answered.

The young woman glanced at her grandfather, but he was undismayed. "And why did *you* get married?"

"To get my laundry done," he answered matter-of-factly.

The young woman turned to her grandmother. "Did you know that when you married him?"

"Of course," the grandmother answered. "That's always why men get married."

Housework, as noted, is the part of the marriage contract women most want to change. An anthropologist who studied dreams reports that in Africa, Malawi women dream of grinding corn, but in America women do not dream of housework.

What American women dream about is home. The dream is familiar and it has been advertised so widely that it has become the same for all: A house, a yard and a car in the driveway. A fire in the living room fireplace with easy chairs pulled up to it. Polished furniture, spotless carpeting, spotless bathrooms with towels in place.

In the dining room, the table is set. There are flowers on the buffet, a roast beef in the oven and a pie, still warm, is on the kitchen counter. Cupboards, freezer, and refrigerator are packed with food. Upstairs in the bedrooms the beds are made, closets and bureau drawers are neat and full of paired socks and ironed sheets.

But of course the dream of home is more than products advertised on television. It is people. Holidays festive and full of cheer no matter how many aunts, uncles, cousins, and grandmothers crowd into the family room. Answers to the unending daily questions. Where is my watch? What time is the PTA meeting? How am I going to get to baseball practice? And talk. Talk with the children over cookies after school. Talk with a husband over cocktails before dinner. Nothing gets lost. No one is late.

The trouble with this dream of home is that it takes a woman more hours a week to run it than her husband puts in on the average job. This is not an empty boast. Syracuse housewives were averaging 57 hours a week on "purposeful activity performed for providing the goods and services used by the family" when Kathryn Walker of Cornell University clocked them in 1968. The average was 55 hours for a national sample of full-time homemakers who kept time diaries of what they did every 15 minutes in 1966 for the Survey Research Center of the University of Michigan. Updates on these basic studies don't change the surprising conclusion that full-time homemakers spend just as many hours on their homes and families as they did in the 1920s, when the Federal government began to sponsor studies of housework time.

Parkinson based his famous law on offices, but work fills up the available time of homemakers, too. There is, for instance, no denying the convenience of no-iron shirts and washing machines, but time studies show that women spend more time doing laundry than their grandmothers did. Some of the time spent rubbing clothes up and down on a washboard goes into phoning for a repairman and cleaning up the mess when the washing machine floods the floor. And since running it is easy, or even fun—when it works—clothes go through the machinery more often. According to Joann Vanek, a

Queens College sociologist who has analyzed the changes in house-work, improvements have encouraged a rise in the standards of housekeeping which mean that the same time is spent, but in differ-ent ways.

Instead of long hours preparing meals and cleaning up after them in the kitchen, women spend hours choosing from the bewildering array of prepared foods displayed on supermarket shelves, waiting at the check-out counter, and hauling the sacks of groceries home. If you own a food processor or electric mixer, then you are tempted to use it on guacamole, crabmeat soufflé, and milkshakes on demand for the kids. And if the kids are going to take advantage of all those activities the community has to offer—Little League, Girl Scouts, the swimming pool, the library, the crafts center, music lessons—then somebody has to drive them there. Vanek reports that contemporary women spend about one full working day a week on the road and in the store, compared with less than two hours a week for women of the 1920s.

But the dream of home takes more than time. It takes money, more money than most husbands earn. Money for the dream pulls wives out to work. Once they start earning, they suddenly have to weigh time against money. A freelance artist framed the dilemma: "When I'm not working, I never have enough money to make it worthwhile to go into a store. When I work, I never have the time for shopping."

The endless, relentless calculation of time for money goes on every day a wife works. Is the time she spends earning worth the money she brings home? Is the higher price in the delicatessen worth the time saved waiting at the supermarket?

Studies of housework agree that working wives actually spend only about half as many hours doing housework as full-time home-makers. Some manage to do almost as much as they did before they went to work, but 60 percent of working wives queried about their housework in a 1976 magazine survey concluded that the housework suffered. There just isn't time in the day—or night—to do all the things that they feel they should do.

If you think you can't find time for a task, you have three alterna-tives. You can get someone else to do it. You can skip it. Or you can find a way to do it so much faster and better than you thought you could that you *do* have time for it after all. Working wives try all three methods.

Get Someone Else. But who? The classic advice is to hire a reliable live-in housekeeper and let her run the ranch. This solution is obsolete. The Michigan housework time study found that working wives made no greater use of paid household help than wives who were full-time homemakers and the situation cannot have improved any since. In a 1976 survey, for instance, only 3 percent of couples with $25,000 or more had live-in help, and only a third in this high bracket had part-time help of any kind.

Wives can't get out of doing "their" housework even if they become doctors, the highest paid of all professional workers. In 1977, three-fourths of women physicians surveyed in Detroit were doing all the cooking, shopping, child care, and money management for their families, and a third did all the laundry and heavy cleaning with no outside help of any kind. These women physicians didn't earn as much as men physicians, it's true, but they weren't exactly poor. And nearly half of them had husbands who were doctors, too.

So scratch paid help. If she can't get help for money, perhaps she can get it for love. Many, but by no means all working wives feel they deserve a little help with the housework from husbands in exchange for the help they are giving him on his obligation to provide the money.

This sounds fair to husbands. A majority of the husbands of the Matching Couples checked some task they did to help around the house, but they thought they were more help than their wives thought they were. The discrepancy was small but consistent: 59 percent of husbands said they helped with the cleaning, but only 53 percent of their wives corroborated the claim; 58 percent of the husbands but only 52 percent of the wives said he helped with the shopping. On cooking, it was 49 percent and 47 percent. On child care, 47 percent and 45 percent.

"He'll take things to the dishwasher," one wife explained, "but he won't put them in." To her, that meant he didn't help with the cleanup.

Definitions of child care varied, too. "His idea of child care is watching the baby sleep," one wife complained, while another said that his idea of child care was sleeping himself "while the kids tore up the house." Playing with a child was not child care, wives felt, but recreation.

Some of the differences arose because husbands did some things so badly that wives couldn't *let* them help. Shopping is one of the tasks that husbands love to do, but they so often come back with the wrong groceries that wives hate to let them do it. And they are impulse shoppers—particularly with "her" grocery money. A husband who did the marketing while his wife was having a baby put such a big dent into the food budget that his wife wouldn't allow him to go into a supermarket alone ever again.

Standards were a sore point with husbands, too. "When she comes in she gives me hell for putting the knives in the wrong drawer," a husband complained. "She's a neatnik. I'm not. And it's *her* kitchen." The rejoinder of wives is that he doesn't take the responsibility. He's always "helping." That means that she, not he, does the worrying about dinner, even when he does the shopping as well as the cooking. She, not he, does the worrying about the dwindling supply of clean socks, even if he always does "her" laundry.

Wives also felt that husbands sometimes bungled their "help" in order to get out of it. "I asked him to vacuum the bedroom, and he did—all around the edges of the furniture, but not under the dresser or the bed!" Other men seemed to be suffering from inhibitions against doing what they secretly thought they should not be doing, the way a woman can't find her way around another woman's kitchen. "I don't bathe the baby because my hands aren't trained for it," one husband explained. "I might drop the child."

Husbands are more comfortable with husbandly duties—the garbage, the yard, and the snow. They observe a careful division of labor on tasks like "cleaning" and "cooking" which sound like "her" work. He cooked for company, she for everyday. He did the annual taxes, she the monthly bills. He washed floors, shopped for groceries, took clothes to the cleaners. She did the daily things that families undo, like the beds and the laundry. He took the children to outings, she to the doctor or music lessons.

Careful time studies show that while husbands may help a little with a long list of tasks, they are not serious, committed, homemakers. The husbands studied by Kathryn Walker of Cornell averaged no more than 1.6 hours of household work a day, and the Michigan husbands helped only a few hours a week. According to a study of time use sponsored by the United Nations, husbands are much the same all over the world.

What really infuriates wives is that most husbands do the tasks they like when they feel like doing them. This means that the wife gets the most help from her husband in the honeymoon years when it's fun to do the simplest things together. "It's nice to cut up an onion or two so we can go on talking while she cooks," a young husband says. "My idea of heaven is to be making soup with the woman I love." When the children arrive, or when she goes out to work, she gets little or no more help than before, according to all the studies.

Some husbands do help more than others. Some make a conscious effort to divide the work on some basis other than sex. "We share everything," a 26-year-old Contemporary Wife explains. "There are certain things I like to do and I do those, and things he likes he does. I enjoy cooking so I do most of the cooking and he does most of the housework. I hate housework. And he happens to like a clean house, so he does that. The things that we both dislike we do together and take turns. I do my ironing and he does his. Now that we have to go to the laundromat we go together because we both dislike it."

This kind of roommate division of labor is harder to make when there are children, but some families do it. "Our house is looked after by all three of us, my husband, our 12-year-old daughter and me. My husband won't let me mop the floor: he does it. We all have our chores, usually divided up according to who hates what the least, or enjoys doing it the most."

Sharing doesn't always come easily. A college administrator didn't get help from her family until she threatened to quit her job. Her husband and children had promised to help, but they kept forgetting. "Why not let it go?" her teenage daughter suggested. "Nobody really cares if the house is picked up!"

"But *I* care," her mother explained. A heated family confrontation ensued. Out of it emerged a rigid schedule. Her husband cooks three nights a week, she cooks three nights a week, and they all go out on the seventh night. Everyone picks up his or her own room and laundry, and on Saturday all pitch in to clean the rest of the house together.

Which husbands share the housework? The Matching Couples who agreed that the husband did most or all of the household tasks differed from those in which husbands did few in two rather interesting ways. They were more apt to share breadwinning equally. And, as we have seen, couples who shared the housework were more apt to agree that their marriages were happier than the marriages of most people they knew. In part, of course, the sharing may be an expression of partnership. People who love and care about each other naturally like to help each other, whatever the task, and a great many of the sharing couples are newlyweds who were used to companionable sharing of student housekeeping chores.

Husband help, then, is the best, but wives don't get very much of it and they don't get it when they need it. A third possibility is children. There is evidence that when a mother of teenagers goes to work, she may get more help from the kids than she does from her husband. In Cornell families where children were in their teens or older, they contributed 2.7 hours of household work a day.

Families vary in how much the children do to relieve a mother of routine maintenance tasks. Setting the table was the job most often done by the children of 100 working women queried in 1977, followed by making their beds, emptying the garbage, doing the dishes, making breakfast, and laundry. Kids *can* be enlisted to do the occasional muscle jobs such as cleaning the garage and washing the floor —tasks that might otherwise go to their fathers, but kids don't always do more just because their mothers work.

With luck, children can be induced to pack their own lunches, polish their own shoes, wash their own socks, sew on their own buttons, and take care of the personal maintenance chores that men learn to do for themselves before they are married. Working mothers were more apt to let up on their kids to pick up their rooms and require only that they close the door and keep the mess out of sight.

Some couples who share household management find it works best when they itemize the services they regard as essential, split those, and discard what they feel they can do without.

A services account begins with a careful list of nonjob, nonleisure activities each spouse actually has performed in the course of a week. Anyone who ever has kept a time diary of this kind is chagrined to discover how much of a day is spent brushing teeth, phoning dentists, balancing checkbooks, emptying vacuum cleaners and otherwise keeping body and soul together.

These limbo tasks are sorted into two lists. One is *personal* maintenance tasks that no one else could or should do for another, such as going to the doctor, buying gifts, fixing a meal when eating alone. The other is *household* maintenance tasks such as general cleaning, shopping for food, fixing the car, and caring for children too young to care for themselves.

Personal tasks are the responsibility of the person involved. He buys, cleans, repairs, and picks up his clothes, even as she cares for hers.

Household tasks are the problem. They must be defined and assigned. The thing to remember in setting household standards is that they are not a moral but a political issue. They have to be negotiated like a contract or a treaty. She may want the windows washed every month, while he doesn't care if he can't see through them. He may want a big Christmas party she doesn't want even if she does none of the work for it. The trick is to agree on everything that has to be done—and *how well*—and then write it down in black and white.

Skip It. Housework is variable. You can do a little, you can do a lot. You can invent paroxysms of activity much as an old-fashioned spring cleaning, or you can sweep the accumulated crud of the winter into a closet and lock the door. There are no productivity standards, nor even an agreement on what counts as work and what merely play. It is all very well to say that "household work" is any activity that produces goods and services consumed by the family, but that means you'd have to include time spent arranging flowers, making a petit point seat cover, or taking a child to the doctor.

Time-use studies include child care, although they probably should distinguish between the physical maintenance of a child— washing clothes, making lunches, supervising baths—and parenting proper, such as time spent talking a teenager out of smoking or telling him or her how to get over a broken heart.

When a wife goes to work she discovers that some of what she has done for her family will never be missed. Easiest to skip are the tasks that don't show, like washing the top of the refrigerator, cleaning out closets, or ironing sheets. All but two of 100 working women queried on their housekeeping never picked up their children's rooms, and 69 never gave their homes a spring cleaning. An astonishing 34 saw no reason to make the bed for a house that stood empty all day, so they made them up only when they changed the sheets. An equal number never did ironing. One boasted that she didn't even own an iron.

Cooking is the task most women like best, but even those who do cooking as a hobby will serve TV dinners or do-it-yourself peanut butter sandwiches when they are pressed for time. Many eat out one night a week. More and more are using speedy microwave ovens. One working wife has a simple kitchen rule: "If it takes more than half an hour, we don't eat it."

Formal entertaining is the household activity working women miss most keenly. "It's not just the physical work of cleaning the house and making the food," one woman explained. "It's the head time. Figuring out who to have with whom. Writing all those notes. Hanging on the phone. Planning. Come to think of it, a party takes the kind of effort I make all day long at my office." What used to be play has now become work.

Working women aren't less sociable than homemakers and nothing about gainful employment makes them into hermits. In big cities, the more affluent take their friends out to dinner. Younger couples still close to the drop-in practices of college living often get together on the spur of the moment without expecting any special plans for food. If the gang gets hungry, somebody sends out for pizza or scrambles up some eggs.

Older women are defensive about skipping the household niceties even when they resent the idea that they are expected to do them. "I hate myself for ironing my husband's shorts," one newly liberated professional woman confided, "but I can't seem to make myself stop. I was brought up wrong." A woman who doesn't wash the walls admits they would bother her if she were at home all day to look at them. One whose husband doesn't do any housework at all feels she has to give a family reason for cutting out housework. "In the early years we felt that a spotless house and neat closets were important," she says. "However, we have come to realize that these things are not as important as happiness and neat closets and sparkling toilet bowls do not contribute to our happiness." Another ruefully confesses that she no longer subscribes to the idea that anything worth doing is worth doing well. "It's got to the point that when I clean house the kids ask if we're having company, and they are usually right."

Working wives should be skipping many more of the niceties than they do. One reason they don't is that housework is inextricably bound up with the standard of living they often are working to uphold. A Bureau of Labor Statistics study shows that the second biggest expenditure a working woman makes from her earnings is for shelter and household goods.

Be More Efficient. Far too many working women secretly think they ought to be doing everything their mothers did, and a great many of them try—at least some of the time—to juggle it. And since housework *is* variable, the near superwomen almost always achieve it. "It's easier to keep house when I work," one woman says. "I always finish in about three or four hours spent partly on Friday night and partly Saturday morning"—hours of the day homemakers reserve for relaxing with their husbands and children. Richard Berk, a California time-use researcher, reports that working wives simply do housework faster. They get as much done between 6:30 and 8:30 in the morning as the homemakers accomplish between 6:30 and 10:30.

Housework is so inefficient an operation that wonders can be achieved by rudimentary planning. Marketing researchers have found that working wives are more apt to shop with a list and buy more on fewer trips, but some of them feed their families as if it were a military operation. Adelina Diamond, a public relations specialist, installed industrial shelving in her basement and found a store that would accept phone orders and deliver on Saturday. She stocks staples by the case, enough to last three months.

A Massachusetts personnel specialist lays on a traditional New Year's Day reception with home-made pastries, cookies, cakes, salads, gelatin molds, meats, relishes, vegetables, fruit dishes, and eggnog. How does she do it? "In my spare time," she shrugs. "After dinner and before I put the kids to bed. After the kids are in bed and before I do the laundry." She starts using these little squidgets of time a good six months in advance. When the strawberries ripen along the north wall of her house, she makes jam and pie for the freezer. When the rhubarb ripens in the garden, it's more pie and preserves. By the time New Year's Day arrives, she has the feast made.

The most carefully organized women live by lists and plot a day's or a week's work as carefully as an industrial engineer designing a complicated process. They find ways to save time by doing two things at once. They'll be making coffee while washing the dishes, reading the paper while making oatmeal cookies, wolfing down breakfast while packing school lunches, cleaning the bathroom while the washing machine works, emptying the cat box while the clothes are in the dryer, folding the laundry while waiting for the dessert pudding to thicken, shopping for a lamp when a friend they want to see has to go shopping, too.

Women have always doubled up on time. Harriet Beecher Stowe's grandmother is said to have educated herself by finding a way to read while she did her spinning—a feat almost as awesome, though considerably less dangerous, than dictating into a recording machine while driving to work. As a matter of fact, the capacity to split attention may be one of the true biological advantages of women, evolved over the hundreds of generations when survival depended on mothers doing useful work while minding their children. But it's harder to do two things at once than it was before the wonder machines that cut the time but increase the attention required. It's more nerve-wracking to watch a toddler while phoning for a plumber than it is to watch him while hoeing a garden.

MOONLIGHTING AT HOME

In her Cornell study, Kathryn Walker found that the amount of time a woman put in on her house depended more on the size of her family than it did on whether she worked at a job in addition: mothers of three, for instance, were doing eight whole hours of housework a day whether or not they worked outside of the home.

Recent, less elaborate time studies here and abroad confirm the message of the Cornell and Michigan data. Every working wife is a moonlighter. Between her two jobs she spends more hours on productive work than any employer expects of paid workers. Most husbands earn more than their wives, but if you add the value of the housework she does to the money she earns, the gap between them narrows. If their earnings are close, or children are involved, her input easily can be greater. Husbands and wives are remarkably good judges of these relative inputs, but to do it properly you have to estimate the value of her services in dollars.

There are two ways to do it. The simplest method is to add up the hours she spends doing various kinds of household work and value each kind of work at the going wages for comparable services in the labor market. In 1972, Kathryn Walker and William H. Gauger made these calculations in the Cornell study. They assigned all tasks reported in time studies to categories of work: marketing, management, and record keeping for the home; food preparation, after-meal cleanup; home care and maintenance; yard and car care; washing, ironing, and special care of clothing; physical and other care of family members.

Walker and Gauger were conservative in their estimates. They figured costs for child care at the going rate for babysitting, not the pay of the child-care specialists trained at Cornell, even if the mother happened to have such a degree.

When priced out at going wages in upstate New York in 1971, for instance, they found that an employed wife with one school-age child contributed $85 worth of housework services a week, while her husband contributed only $17. That meant that he had to earn $3,500 more a year than she to equal what *she* was doing for the family in services and money.

Calculations of this type are not mere games. Riane Eisler, a California lawyer who has studied the economics of marriage, believes that divorce decrees would be much fairer if the cash value of household work were considered along with money. Courts already face the problem of valuing a homemaker's service when they award damages in accident cases and in the increasing number of states where compensation is awarded to the families of murder victims.

When Delores B. Holmes, of Maryland, was murdered, she was earning $520 a month as well as caring for her family. Testimony figured her household services at $634 a month, for a total of $1,154, more than the Maryland Criminal Injuries Compensation Board had allowed the family. The Court ordered the Compensation Board to consider the monetary loss suffered by the Holmes family due to loss of "maternal services" even though the housework was being assumed by her two adult daughters.

WHAT ARE A FULL-TIME HOMEMAKER'S SERVICES WORTH?

The value of a full-time homemaker's services has been rising along with the things she buys. In 1972, Sylvia Porter figured she was worth $200 a week on the basis of wage rates for 12 skills, but in 1976 she raised the value to $300, or $15,600 a year.

Even higher values were obtained by Dr. Peter Senn, an economist at Wilbur Wright College in Chicago, who worked out a computer program for calculating a woman's value on the basis of the hours she personally put in for her family on each of 23 skills: cook, dishwasher, dietician, baker, waitress, nurse, chambermaid, buyer-shopper, veterinarian, laundress, home economist, seamstress, handyman, hostess, housekeeper, secretary, gardener, chauffeur, interior decorator, bookkeeper, ticket agent, companion, and something else (reserved for an individual's *special* skill). In 1977, Senn valued the services of a mother of three preschoolers at $21,841 a year. His bill included five hours a week chauffeuring, $750 a year; seven hours a week serving family meals, $6,000 a year at waitressing wages. Her husband, a city fireman, would have had little if anything left over if he had been required to pay her at these going rates.

The first reaction to calculations of this kind is to laugh, but they do give pause for thought. Claire Booth Luce points out that very few men could afford the comforts of home if they had to pay even half the value of a wife. Carolyn Shaw Bell, the Wellesley economist, observes that all American husbands are rich because even the poorest is able to command without pay the personal services that have become the rarest commodity in the labor market.

The other way to count the dollar value of a homemaker's services is to figure them at what she could have earned doing something else. This has nothing to do with how much she does for her family, but it is the way women decide whether it's worth their while to take a job. Most top women executives probably could keep a better house, if that's all they did, than anyone they could hire to keep house for them, but it is hard to imagine that their domestic services would be worth more than the money they earn.

THE DIFFERENCE

A majority of working wives think that their housework suffers, but that may simply be what they *think*. Messy closets worry no one but the woman who feels responsible for them. Standards of housekeeping are even harder to measure than hours of housekeeping time. What we can find out, by indirection, does not support the neglect of which working wives accuse themselves.

Marketing studies tell us that working wives buy good food. They spend more grocery money per minute in the supermarket, buy top quality, patronize specialty butchers, try out gourmet recipes, read can labels, figure costs per ounce, and resist bogus advertising claims.

They themselves tell us how hard they work to make up to their families for their absence by going to school events, cooking special foods, taking the kids on trips, going out with husbands to events of his choice, baking birthday cakes, and giving parties.

What gets lost is the *schedule* of the dream of home. The cooking is good, on weekends or special occasions, but it's not meat, potatoes, vegetable, and dessert on the dot every night. Breakfast is catch as catch can, with both husband and wife waiting until they get to work to breakfast from the office coffee wagon.

The real loss is leisure—her leisure. With rare exceptions, working wives from every kind of family put in more hours of paid and unpaid work than their husbands. On one survey, the working wife had ten less hours to herself a week than her husband. The UNESCO study shows that working mothers around the world have less than two-thirds the free time enjoyed by their husbands. They have less leisure than either full-time housewives or working men.

"My life is a complete mess," a working mother wailed. "I can't find time to pay the bills or buy a decent dress! I'd give a month of my life right now for a week of peace and quiet." She is not the only one. More than half the wives responding to a magazine survey said that working deprived them of personal time and more than a third confessed that their dispositions suffered. Time for reading and sewing and letter writing and sports are what working women miss. Or just a day off to loaf or sleep. One dreams of "an idyllic picnic with my lover, if only I had *time* to have a lover."

Working wives complain that the hardest thing is to find time to be alone and think. "There is a doll house downstairs that I wanted to make and I have got the frame cut out," one working wife said, "but it takes a certain amount of preparation, a certain amount of time just to relax, to get into it, and that takes coming home from work, sitting down and having a cup of coffee, and then going down but I never get there. There is always something David, Beth or Cary want you to do with them so that you continue to put off projects that you are thinking of doing."

The moonlighters never get the chance to unwind. Preliminary results from a Use-of-Time Project funded by the National Science Foundation discovered the thought-provoking fact that the average woman worker wastes 35 minutes a day on coffee and nonwork activities on the job, compared with 52 minutes a day of company time frittered away by males. Television watching has become synonymous with leisure, and working women do less of it than either housewives or working men. Holidays and weekends provide extra hours to do housework for her but often more leisure for him. Camping and summer cottage stays, the most popular American vacation, are a change of activity for him, but housekeeping under adverse conditions for her.

Homemakers can plan their work so that they are available to spend leisure time with their husbands and children in the evening and on weekends. The Michigan time-use studies show that working women use this "leisure" time to do the chores that homemakers get done while they are at home alone. "I see too many people working so hard that they can't enjoy life," a Traditional Wife explained as her reason for staying at home. "I feel we are happier than most."

Working or nonworking, a wife is responsible for the family life-style, and as we have seen, it is her day that changes when she goes to work, not his. In order to see just what happens to home when she leaves it to earn, we asked a dozen working and nonworking wives to keep diaries of what they did every day. This isn't scientific, but the slices of their lives that they shared with us reveal important differences in the quality and pacing of life.

The working wives never got a chance to relax. All of them began their day before seven in the morning and most were still going after midnight, while the nonworking wives usually started at eight and stopped at eleven. We found working wives getting up before dawn to write letters and read. A woman who was studying nursing while holding down a part-time job went to bed with her children so that she could study after midnight, when everyone else in the house was sleeping.

What happens to the dream of home when a wife goes to work? Other dreams jostle it for time, but it doesn't go away. Most working wives honor the services clause of the marriage contract. They keep it going by mirrors. The majority of their tasks are performed, hired done, or done without. But what they discover in the attempt is that the priceless center of the dream is the unfailing, 24-hour presence of a woman to respond to immediate needs and make everyone comfortable. When she earns the right to make plans of her own, the dream fades—but it continues to haunt both husband and wife.

CHAPTER 6

The Child-Care Crisis

So this is the baby! The new mother touches the little fingers and toes with her fingertips. She touches the little belly with the palm of her hand. Then she puts her arm around the baby and crooks her neck so that she will be looking directly into his eyes. Why doesn't he open them? When he does, it is the happiest moment of her life. She keeps looking at him as the nurse takes him away.

She can tell his cry from the others because it purses her nipples and hardens her breast with a rush of milk. As he relieves her, she holds him in the crook of her left arm, where he can hear the beat of her heart almost the way he heard it when he was safe inside her. Sucking teaches him that hunger makes food, that wishes come true, a first lesson he will painfully but never wholly unlearn later on. After he's full, he flirts, avoiding her gaze only to return it.

What will he say when he can talk? Her eagerness to know triggers strategies for getting him to respond that do not come naturally to fathers. From the very beginning, she talks to him, eyes wide open, eyebrows raised, facial expressions held fixed, vowels elongated —all ways of exaggerating and prolonging the signal. Mothers talk constantly to their infants, but according to one actual count, a group of fathers averaged only 37.7 seconds a day talking to their babies during the first three months.

Fathers are not mothers. They can be trained to nurture, just as women can be trained to be sharpshooters, but they have less aptitude for the work. During the late 1970s, some thoughtful feminists were beginning to wonder whether equal parenting was the best solution to the care of children when both parents earn. In 1977, sociologist Alice Rossi warned that radical feminists were adopting a "male pattern of relating to children, in which men turn their fathering on and off to suit themselves or their appointments for business or sexual pleasure." She had not expected this outcome when she wrote her famous "Immodest Proposal" for sex equality in 1964, perhaps because her lyrical descriptions of the pleasures of nursing suggest that she is a passionate mother as well as a hard-headed social scientist.

In 1977, she was reminding us that women have always worked, but until the twentieth century, they have specialized in tasks that could be done while caring for little children.

"Reproductive success went to those females capable of two conjoint activities: the bearing and rearing of their young and the hunting of small game and gathering of food within a restricted geographic range compatible with infant and child care," she wrote. "Both these activities involved manual dexterity, physical and emotional endurance, and persistence."

The economics of what Alice Rossi calls "conjoint activities" is the reason why housework and the professions arising out of it become women's work: you can do the washing or make the dinner while you are watching the kids, but you can't spear a bison or pilot an airplane or decide just when to sell short on the stock market. These activities require undivided attention.

Women have always had to work, but in the twentieth century they have had to leave their homes even to do "women's work" in offices, schools, hospitals, and factories. In the 1970s, they began to enter law, medicine, truck driving, policing, and other occupations that require them not only to leave home, but to concentrate on one task at a time, a habit of mind that is not particularly helpful in responding to a three-year-old.

During the lifetime of today's young adults there has been a dramatic shift of mothers to paid employment outside of the home, away from their children. In 1950, when many Contemporary Wives of the 1970s were born, fewer than one mother in five worked outside the home. In 1978, more than half did. The older the child, the more likely the mother to work, but the mothers of the very youngest children have been following the others out to work so fast that in 1978, 38 percent of the mothers of children under three years old were in the labor force.

In the late 1970s women wanted jobs and they wanted children but they weren't at all sure that the two went together. Generally speaking, the idea of a mother working was best accepted and least criticized or questioned by those closest to them, by women more than men, mothers more than fathers, working women more than homemakers, and working mothers most of all.

Men may be more uptight about the absence of mothers from home in part because the mother tie is mysterious to them, just as they sometimes read more into menstrual difficulties than the women who experience them. If only unconsciously, they may be aware of the stake they have in a family system that nurtures *them* along with their children.

Women may be a bit more likely to say that a mother's job does not hurt her children, but a majority of parents think children are worse off when the mother works. Working mothers split evenly on the question. This confidence may be newfound. According to a careful comparison of surveys made at different times, sociologist Karen Mason found that the proportion of working mothers who felt that preschool children "do not necessarily suffer" when their mothers work grew from less than a third in 1970 to almost a half in 1974.

"EXPERTS" MALE AND FEMALE

Experts are almost as equally divided as working mothers themselves about the potential damage separation from mother may do the children. Oddly enough, experts seem to divide along sex lines.

Possibly because they themselves have been working mothers, female behavioral scientists like the late anthropologist Margaret Mead, sociologist Jessie Bernard, and psychologist Lois Hoffman, do not worry about daily separation of mother and child for a few hours.

"You can't expect a mother to be with a small child all the time," Margaret Mead once remarked, with her usual good sense, but in 1978 she shocked feminists by snapping that women don't really have children to put them in day care twelve hours a day, either.

Working women have long contended that the quality of the time they spend with their children makes up for the lesser quantity of time, and the experts continue the argument. Jessie Bernard cites anthropological evidence that mothers in cultures which require them to spend a high proportion of their time caring for children are "somewhat more unstable" in their emotional reactions to their children than are mothers who do not have such exclusive responsibility. This is, of course, a backhanded slap at the feminine mystique of our suburban culture.

No dice, argues child psychologist Lee Salk. "There's no way you can give quality in ten minutes a day," he asserts. "When someone asks me about quality versus quantity, they're asking for permission to do less."

There's the same male-female cleavage over the importance of dispensing cookies and sympathy when a child returns from school.

Eda J. LeShan, a family counselor on parent-child relationships, thinks that adults have romanticized the importance of mother being at home when the children return from school. "Lots of children love to visit other children after school and some like to be left alone to daydream with nobody telling them what to do, and some want to pursue their own special adventures—climbing trees, playing baseball or even taking a piano lesson," she writes. And like most of the women experts, she's practical. "The real issue is whether or not a child knows he or she is safe; is there someone in the house to let him or her in? Has the child memorized both parents' telephone numbers in case of emergency?"

Urie Bronfenbrenner, Professor of Human Development and Family Studies at Cornell, is not so relaxed about the after-school problems. "If there's any reliable predictor of trouble," he declares, "it probably begins with children coming home to an empty house." He agreed with feminist Joan Huber, Professor of Sociology at the University of Illinois, that fathers should help care for children, but he didn't have much faith that they would. He goes on to say, in exasperation, "I don't care whether it's the father who works and the mother who stays home, or the mother who works, and the father who stays home. But please God, let there be somebody!" Like many male developmental psychologists, he believes that nobody, but nobody, takes care of children as well as their mothers.

Huber refused to be railroaded. "The fact is—and people ought to confront it—we don't really know how to rear the kind of children we want. One reason is that no one has ever defined the kind of adult we want."

The difference in viewpoint seems to be that a woman usually thinks in terms of the welfare of an individual child, while a man thinks in terms of society in general. The classic example is the way Austrian-born child psychologist Bruno Bettelheim has favored the kibbutz rearing of the children of Israel. After an intensive on-site investigation he reported that they fared "considerably better than many children raised by their mothers in poverty-stricken homes, and better than quite a few raised at home by their middle-class mothers," but that this was because they grew up in a relatively small society, "where an unusually high degree of consensus exists, where there is very little differentiation in style of life or in property rights, and where the entire society functions like an extended family."

Bettelheim is not the only male to imply or overtly indicate that mothers are responsible for the ills of society in general. In addition to Bettelheim and Urie Bronfenbrenner, Kenneth Keniston, chairman of the Carnegie Commission on Children, and New York Senator and sociologist Daniel Patrick Moynihan, have, on various occasions, blamed working mothers for drug abuse, crime, declining school performance, and rising teenage pregnancy.

Women social scientists, on the other hand, are explicit about the damage they see *contemporary society* is doing to children *and* their mothers. Alice Rossi, Secretary of Commerce, Juanita Kreps, and

Yale sociologist Rosabeth Kanter, author of *Men and Women of the Corporation,* are among the many women social scientists who want work organized so that fathers *and* mothers can spend more time with their children.

THE DEBATE

The views of the experts tell us a lot about the values of the experts, but they don't resolve the worries of working parents. Their fears are hard to pin down, but all of them revolve about what might happen to children separated from their mothers. Sometimes the fears are for the physical safety of the child, but more often the damage is conceived to be psychological. The child will develop slowly, like the pathetic kids in orphan asylums. He will feel unloved or deserted, confused by a succession of caregivers, resentful because his mother isn't on hand when he comes home from school. Worst of all, he might grow up like his babysitter instead of his parents.

"My children are not sure whether we go to a church or a synagogue," a Middle European Jewish father complained—anonymously—of the care his two preschoolers were getting at the hands of a "fine upstanding" Irish Catholic woman with less education than his wife. "They think a calf is called a baby cow and that the commercials they see on TV are the last word in wit and wisdom."

Nursery school teachers and home-care professionals work hard to allay the fears of mothers that they may be supplanted in the affections of the child. One of them says that she makes a point of "reminding a frazzled working mother, leaving her sleeping two-year-old with me, that her child will be happier with her after she gets done what she will do away from the child."

Luckily, these fears are groundless. In 1977 Harvard child-development researcher Jerome Kagan reported an experiment that should reassure every working mother. He found that children turned to their biological mothers for comfort when they were tired or bored rather than to a nurse or care-giver who spent more time with them. This was equally true of children reared by their mothers at home, and children raised from infancy eight hours a day by the same care-giver in a special laboratory setting. He calls this biological tie between child and parent "mysterious."

Mysterious or not, this tie means that children in all kinds of settings grow up like their parents instead of their care-givers. Rich kids learn to talk and act like their mothers and fathers instead of the nannies who do most of the work of bringing them up. And poor kids, alas, seldom profit for very long from compensatory programs which aim to improve the care their biological parents are giving them.

Mothers who think their children are better off because they are working say that their children are more self-reliant, learn to help around the house, and have a better relationship with their parents. They believe that quality of time is more important than quantity, and some of them frankly add that they are better mothers because working makes them happier people.

Lillian Carter is the most august example. "A child is better off not to have the mother every minute of the time," she told a reporter. "Children who cling to their mothers—they grow up being babies, and I think it is good for mother and child to be separated most of the day." President Carter could easily be classified as a neglected child, because during his formative years, his mother worked 12- or 20-hour days as a private-duty nurse either at the nearby hospital or in patients' homes.

President Carter hardly can be described as a failure in life, lacking in self-confidence, ambition, and family feeling, yet that is exactly what one school of self-styled "psychobiographers" is suggesting. They have argued that his indecision on weighty issues confronting the presidency is based on his uncertainty about the attention he could expect from his mother. No doubt Ms. Lillian would argue the reverse. Jimmy might never have run for the presidency if she had kept him tied to her apron strings.

The claim that children become more self-reliant when their mothers work has become a debating point. Those who favor working mothers on other grounds say that they don't. But there is no hard evidence to support either side. Children of working mothers cannot be proven to help more around the house than those whose mothers are there to supervise them, for example.

Most persuasive of all are the mothers who feel their children are better off because staying at home with small children "drives them bananas." There actually is a child-care referral center in Berkeley, California, that *calls* itself "Bananas." "I've really hated staying home all this time," a woman who quit her job to take care of her baby told a reporter. "I've had to resist handing him to my husband at night and saying, 'Here, I've had him all day, now *you* take care of him.'" Dr. Nathan Stockhamer, a physician with the William Alanson White Institute of Psychiatry, in New York City, thinks that mothers who go to work to get away from their children actually may improve their relationship with them.

WHAT CHILDREN NEED

Neither experts nor mothers, then, are objective. In order to find out what a mother's job does to her children we have to look at it from the point of view of the child. What, to begin with, do children really need? Next, what real difference does a mother's employment make to a child? Finally, what do we really know about the difference between the children of working and nonworking mothers that can be attributed to the mother's employment? What do the children themselves say about it, both while their mothers are working, and later as grownups looking back on their childhood?

The needs of children differ at different ages, but all child development specialists agree on a few. A baby needs physical care and physical fondling, preferably from a single nurturing figure who has the absorbing interest which most mothers develop when they care for their babies and nurse them.

When a baby begins to walk and talk, he or she needs, in addition, space in which to crawl, climb, scream, bang, and mess with a minimum of damage to himself.

When he or she is old enough to go to school, the child needs playmates and enough people to see how humans relate to one another and an opportunity to explore the world mentally as well as socially and physically.

The older a child gets, the more he or she needs more people and places and experiences than anyone can expect to get at home. During the teen years, children urgently need the company of age-mates. Finally, there comes a time when the main thing a parent can provide is money and information for getting started on an independent existence.

If you look at the daily lives of children at each stage, a surprising fact emerges. Whether the child is an infant, a preschooler, or a grade school pupil, the *economic* level of the family and the *feelings* of the parents make a much bigger difference in shaping a child's daily life than the employment of the mother.

What happens to the 20 million children under 18 whose mothers and fathers both work?

Babies

Few of them are babies. Babies take so much labor that very few mothers can afford to replace themselves in the nursery. Since authorities like Jerome Kagan say that one woman can care for no more than three infants—and she needs a relief shift—group care doesn't bring down the cost much. Nursery schools can't cope with diapers, and few will accept children under the age of two. Some licensing laws actually forbid group care of infants.

Most of the babies of working mothers are cared for at home by a relative, and in a surprising number of cases, the relative is the baby's own father. If the mother can't find a job during hours when the father or a relative can "sit" in the baby's home, she may drop off the baby at her mother's or a friend's house, just as she would to go shopping. If the hours don't jibe, she just doesn't work. Working mothers of infants are most likely to work part time, and more would work if there were more part-time jobs available to them.

Professional baby care is so expensive that a working wife has to hit the top fast to be able to afford it when she is young enough to start a family. Cindy Vaughn was thirty years old when she was promoted to first vice-president of a New York investment banking firm, eight weeks after the birth of her first child. She and her husband, an advertising vice-president, figure child care alone will cost them $16,000 a year. The very rich lure the last of the British nannies from England with middle-management pay and perquisites, while the slightly less rich feel lucky to find a live-in housekeeper, usually foreign born, who will take care of the baby for $125 to $150 a week, but they have to compete for these rare treasures with single-earner families who can afford them, too.

Toddlers

Toddlers—the three- to six-year-old set—are more apt to have mothers who work, but two-thirds of those who do are also cared for during the day by a relative in their own homes or in the relative's home, and half of them have mothers who are able to juggle their working hours so that they are at home during the daytime to care for them personally. A University of Michigan study found that a quarter of white couples and 14 percent of black couples were able to split their working hours so that they didn't have to rely on an outsider at all—and this arrangement was at least as common among the affluent as among wage workers.

Most homes don't have the space or facilities for the exploration toddlers need, so the three-to-six set is increasingly apt to go to nursery school, whether their mothers work or not. In 1976, 21 percent of the children whose mothers were available to take care of them around the clock went to nursery school compared to 26 percent of the children of working mothers. It looks as if "preprimary" schooling has come to be one of the cultural advantages mothers want for their children, whether they are working or not.

Working mothers, then, do not seem to be parking their little children in cold institutions. On the contrary, they are going to great lengths to see that their children are cared for in a family setting while they work. Most parents make a sharp distinction between a nursery school offering an educational experience to a young child for a few hours a day, and a day-care center organized to care for a child while the mother works.

Only 6 percent of American children are in institutions that call themselves day-care centers, and parents have grave doubts about them. Over half the parents responding to a family survey thought that you could never be sure how children were going to be treated in a day-care center. Companies that had been induced to experiment with day care for the children of employees have been folding them for lack of patronage. A study made by the Stanford Research Institute found that many parents who needed child care wouldn't use day-care centers even when they were provided free.

Neither nursery schools nor day-care centers are convenient for working parents. Some keep bankers' hours and few match the schedules of parents who work full time and have to do errands before and after their nine-to-five day. A good one rejects a child at the first sniffle, whether there is someone at home to nurse the child or not. Transportation is a hassle and expense. In New York City, for instance, publicly funded day-care centers were located in real estate owned by friends of politicians rather than near the families who used them. But the real objection is more basic.

Day-care centers meeting Federal standards are just too expensive to provide care for the hours a mother must be away if she intends to work full time. In New York City during the late 1970s, those ill-placed publicly funded centers cost $85 per week per child and were restricted to poverty-level families, while the few commercially run preschools that offered a full day educational program under the direction of trained professionals had to charge $3,000 to $5,000 a year, almost as much as the tuition at an Ivy League college. The numbers were lower elsewhere, but costs were so high that a mother had to be rich or on welfare to afford a full day of acceptable group care for a three- or four-year-old, and in licensed centers there were only places for one out of the six preschoolers whose mothers needed to use them.

Even when they were subsidized they failed to attract working mothers. "Look at it from the mother's point of view," a union steward in an Illinois factory town reasoned. "In our plant she can bring home $100, maybe $130 a week with overtime. Say she has two kids.

That's $60 a week from her pay, so she's working for $40 or killing herself for $70. Because she's young and doesn't have seniority, she may have to take the second or third shift, but the day care center closes at six, so what's she to do? Can you blame her for going on welfare instead?"

There's not much room for improvement in costs. Child care can't be mass produced. On the contrary, a larger child-care group is apt to cost *more* per head rather than less because it requires more administration. Family care—in the child's home or another home like it—makes the most economic sense and it is the arrangement of choice for mothers who can't find a relative or afford a true nanny. In the mid-1970s it was being provided at $25 to $30 a week per child, enough to compensate a woman with a big house who enjoys running a place where, as one day-care mother put it, "little kids can spend the day with other kids, making noise, eating new foods, squishing orange play dough, and being the biggest one in the sandbox." But there are not and can never be enough situations of this kind to go around at the ratio of one supervising adult for every six kids, the maximum most licensing laws allow. If she takes in more, in some cities she may be legally classified as a "school" and required to produce a master's degree in early childhood education.

The most recent vindication of group care for preschoolers is especially persuasive because it comes from an impressive child-development researcher who has bitterly opposed it. Jerome Kagan, Harvard Professor of Human Development, still questions group care on the ground that we "don't know enough about its impact," although the study he conducted in 1976 is by far the most careful to date. To make the test more rigorous, he measured the change in development of pairs of day-care and home-reared children 20 to 29 months old who had been matched for sex, ethnicity, and parent education.

The day-care children had been spending eight hours a day—longer than most centers keep preschoolers—in a research laboratory school since they were three and a half months old. Kagan confirmed that social class and ethnicity made more difference than home or day-care rearing. Caucasian children understood words like "large" and "open" better than the Chinese children for instance.

Children of less well-educated parents scored generally lower than middle-class children on language and on such tasks as remembering where a toy was hidden, or finding a car in a picture, and they learned faster than their lower-class match mates who were being reared wholly at home. Across the board, however, day-care children did better than the home-reared at tasks requiring them to imitate adults, such as building a tower with blocks.

On balance, then, the case against group care for small children is no more persuasive than the case that is sometimes made for it. At present, we just don't know how much difference it makes to the child. Home-reared children differ from children reared in groups in the speed with which they develop some skills, but there is no clear-cut superiority of one over the other. It might turn out, for instance, that group-reared children are more sociable while home-reared children have a better chance to become creative individuals. If reliable differences are ever established, it will be easier to see that the real issue is deciding what kinds of people we want to create.

School Children

The problem of child care is acute while it lasts, but it solves itself in a very few years. When a child enters school, the taxpayers foot the babysitting bill, and both mothers and employers benefit. Mothers are able to go to work with little or no expense, and employers can tap a labor supply of mothers who can afford to work for wages that do not equal the cost of the extensive services to families that mothers of preschoolers are expected to bear.

Once a child is in school, the main part of his or her day does not depend on the physical presence of the mother. Child care narrows down to arrangements for the few hours a child may be home from school before a parent arrives from work. After-school programs, many of obvious educational merit, are available in most communities.

Children do much the same thing when they get home from school whether their mothers work or not. Two out of three working mothers of school-age children manage to arrange their work so that one or the other parent can care for the children without involving any outsiders at all. A special census survey of 1976 discovered that school-age children from poorer families are more apt to be cared for by a relative while their mothers work, while families with income of $15,000 or more are more apt to have the children take care of themselves. Many of the 1.8 million children who come home to an empty house are old enough to take responsibility for themselves for a few hours. And as we mentioned, Eda LeShan says the real issue is whether or not a child knows he or she is safe.

How Mother Feels

Home, nursery school, day-care center, neighbor. Teacher, grand-mother, father, big sister, friend. Where a child spends time and even with whom makes less difference than the message the child gets from Mother that tells the child how Mother feels about him or her and herself—messages she usually doesn't realize she is sending. Mothers who work send as many different kinds of messages as mothers who stay at home.

Working mothers who really want to nurse their babies find all sorts of ways of keeping their milk even when they can't get home to nurse during the day. Some of them duck out to the ladies' room to express their milk manually, store it in a refrigerated water cooler and bring it home for the babysitter to give to the baby the next day. La Leche League, the organization for nursing mothers, has helped many mothers keep their milk while working eight hours a day. Some working mothers arrange their schedules so that they can get home for a midday feeding.

Occasionally, mothers determined to nurse are lucky enough to be able to take their babies to work with them. Faye Wattleton, presi-dent of Planned Parenthood, had to visit many of the branch offices of the organization the year her child was born. She simply packed him up and took him with her—healthy small babies travel a lot more easily than healthy, exploring two-year-olds. Susan Catania, the Illinois Assemblywoman, nursed the youngest of her seven daughters through the noisy Plenary Sessions of the National Women's Conference at Houston.

A lawyer was so excited over the birth of her son that she couldn't bear the idea of being away from him during the day, so she fell into a heroic schedule. She got up early every morning, bathed and fed the baby, then herself, and packed him into the car with food and gear for the day. In the parking garage she set up the collapsible pram and trundled him into the office, where he was installed for the day in a temporarily vacant room beside her own.

Efficient professional women may be able to arrange the logistics of child care, but not all of them automatically can shed their efficient, businesslike selves for the responsive, mothering role they think they should switch into as soon as they get home from work. Instead of relaxing with slippers, drink, and paper, as fathers are expected to do, they work at being a mother as if it were a competitive task on which raises or marks were going to be handed out.

Children, of course, are not deceived by the performance. They perceive that Mother is talking too fast. They may wriggle out of a proffered lap to avoid physical contact with an over-tense nervous system. And they learn that a battery of questions don't have to be answered. A pause, and such a mother will turn her attention to somebody or something else.

"Running after my son for a weekend leaves me limp," the president of a fashion-based company confesses. "I'm just delighted when it's Monday morning and time to get back to an adult world. I know I'm supposed to find business travel a hardship, but I don't mind admitting that when things get tense around the house it's a relief to know I've got to leave it all and fly to Paris for a week." Fathers have long felt this way but they seldom say so—at least to their wives.

FATHERHOOD IS NOT MOTHERHOOD

Fathers do help. On surveys, child care is the household task husbands most frequently share, and the more education a father has, the more likely he is to spend time with his children. Three out of four fathers of our Matching Couples said they helped care for their children. This sounds hopeful until you look a little closer at just what mothers and fathers do for their children. According to one time-use study, women spend their time on "custodial" tasks, such as washing and feeding, while men's time is "interactional," or play.

Fathers do what they like doing with children, mothers what has to be done for them. Observers who visited homes for a study of work and family life were able to document how automatically mothers and fathers fell into sex-stereotyped parenting roles.

A nurse who has to get to work at 7 A.M. gets up at 5:30 A.M., gets out clothes for her 4-year-old son, and puts him back to sleep with his father before she leaves by public transportation at 6:30. The father likes to make the time he spends with the boy pleasant, so he dresses his son, although the boy can dress himself. His mother leaves work at 3:30, picks her son up at day care, drives with him to do the necessary grocery shopping, and then comes home. At home, she does kitchen chores and prepares supper. At the same time she tries to play with the child. Sometimes she has trouble doing both. Her husband gets home at 5:30 P.M. The family has supper. The father then spends time playing with his son and keeping him out of his mother's way while she does the kitchen and other necessary household chores.

Fathers are willing to help—providing it does not interfere with something else they want to do.

ASK THE CHILDREN

"If you think mothers who work aren't hurting their children," one conservative woman wrote, "ask the children!" But the grade school children queried on one study of 1976 favored working mothers more than working mothers favored themselves. Three out of four of the working mothers thought mothers of young children should work only when money was needed, but three out of four of the children said it was all right for mothers to work if they wished to do it.

This doesn't mean that children were more socially liberal than their parents. Most of them were remarkably conservative, especially on sex roles. Two out of three thought it was Mother's job, not Father's, to cook and clean. Children of working mothers were more apt to see Father and Mother as individuals. They were less likely than the children of nonemployed mothers to think their parents' ideas were old-fashioned, and more willing to see parents separate if they were unhappy.

You get a different story from adults whose mothers worked while they were growing up—particularly young adults who were children when the postwar social scientists were looking for signs of "maternal deprivation." Most of them think they learned to be more self-reliant. Many are still proud of the achievements of their mothers. Few think they've been seriously damaged. But there are interesting divergences between the recollections of adult males and females.

Male reactions are simpler. One man remembered his mother hurrying in the morning for fear she would be fired. He imagined flames coming out of the office building that would prevent her from getting into it on time. Like daughters, men whose mothers worked are generally proud of the achievements of their mothers, but they are more apt to see her job through the spectacles of social philosophy. A male college student cited his mother's help in founding the family's business as evidence that the Equal Rights Amendment would be good for the country. A Texas oilfield welder who wrote that he "accepts the Bible principle for wives" complained that he always felt less valuable than his mother's job, when he was growing up. "I cared less that she was supposedly working to give us nice things. I would have preferred a nicer family." The philosophy of these men colors their memories.

Women seem to remember their childhood feelings better, and they are more likely to have specific complaints. Although daughters have more respect for a mother who works, and are more apt to become working mothers themselves, they don't always feel that their own working mothers are models to follow. Ambivalent is the word for the feelings that women faculty and students expressed when invited to talk about their working mothers.

"My own mother's work made it possible for me to attend college and secure a job potential that allows me to set my own hours around my family needs," a teacher said. "But I feel to this day the sense of loss as I watched her waiting for the bus to work in front of our home."

One North Dakota woman recalled being socially disadvantaged in grade school because she couldn't invite friends to her home after school but had to go to theirs. To a woman in Montana, however, the empty house was a social advantage. "We were free to do what we wanted. We could jump on tables and chairs, and all the neighborhood kids could come in and feel free, too." Still another reported that she acquired "teenage habits" from the babysitters, "lying on the sofa and looking at television, snacking instead of dining."

Some are still jealous of the mothering they fantasize their working mothers gave to outsiders. This is particularly true of daughters of teachers. A young New York mother, herself a teacher, remembered feeling left out of the fun when her mother worked long hours coaching school plays. Another thought that her mother worried more about the young women she supervised on her job than she did about her own children. "They were her real family," she observes. "She's still working for that firm, and so dependent on her role in it that when it moved she commuted three hours a day just to stay with them."

More common is resentment at having to help with housework or younger brothers and sisters more than they imagined girls with stay-at-home mothers were required to do. "Every night I had to leave my friends to make dinner," a young working wife complains.

However, very few felt their mothers were not around in personal crises, or failed them because of their job responsibilities. Much more common is the memory of a mother who was always tired, though trying to hide it, a martyr or saint who worked all day and did the housework at night and was undervalued both at work and at home.

"She was a superwoman," a young working wife said of her mother, an editor who worked at home. "She cooked all the meals, and she picked up after everybody except me, because I was the only girl. She did all this juggling to fit into our schedules, so that when we came home from school she would be there to talk to us and read to us. Nothing was ever left out. And in some ways I feel that I couldn't do that, and in other ways I feel that I don't *want* to do all that."

Daughters of working mothers resent the discrimination against their mothers at work, and they flatly refuse to work twice as hard at a job and come home and do the housework, too. They remember the little time-saving devices that kept their mothers always tense. "Over-organized," was how one woman in Montana used to describe her mother. Others remember them as bristling with nervous energy. "She's a crazy worker," one complained. "She'll watch TV, carry on a conversation, and knit at the same time. She's a real Puritan work ethic person. Even sleeping is work for her. She does it so that she can wake up the next working day and have her energy level up. Everything she does is work."

Daughters of working mothers would like to be more relaxed. "I'm not going to have children until I'm so well established in my job that they can't put me down," vowed the daughter of a woman who suffered from antinepotism rules. "I would have more help, and I certainly wouldn't let my husband sit around and do nothing while I was trying to take care of the kids."

Others intend to solve the problem by remaining childless indefinitely. "What's the point of having kids if you can't stay home with them?" Others think of solving the problem by giving up careers.

Whatever complaints grown daughters make against their working mothers, very few say that they've been psychologically damaged by anything like the "maternal deprivation" that the child-development specialists were talking about in the 1950s when they were growing up. Instead, they are responding to the *feelings* of their mothers when they were small. According to Dr. Ruth Moulton, a psychiatrist specializing in the problems of career women, the pressured professional mother may drive her daughter back into total domesticity, while the masochistic, submissive mother may drive her daughter out of the house to avoid a similar fate.

MATERNAL GUILT

In the late 1970s, political reactionaries were still blaming working mothers for neglecting their children. The charge is old and largely disproved, but it was so widely believed among working mothers themselves that it is worth looking back to see where the idea came from, and what behavioral scientists found out when they attempted to test it.

During World War II the government was so eager to lure mothers to work in the aircraft plants that it financed day-care centers for them. Millions of women learned what it felt like to bring home a paycheck of their own, and many of them didn't want to give up working after the war was over and the day-care centers were closed.

Policymakers worried. They were sure that "maternal separation" was bad for children, but they could not say for sure just how and why. Delinquent children often came from poor, ghetto families where mothers had to work, but was it the mother's job that made the child go wrong, or the father's absence, or could it be just lack of money?

In order to find out—and send the mothers home—more than a score of social science teams launched studies designed to identify the impact of the mother's employment. For every child whose mother worked they found a mate of the same age, sex, and family background whose mother didn't work. As far as possible, parents of these mates were matched for schooling, income, occupation, and marital status.

Answers took a long time. Some of the studies followed the children for years. But when the results were in, they weren't any good for scaring mothers out of jobs. The tangle of data garnered by the worried specialists added up to a single verdict: inconclusive. School marks, social adjustment, mental health, and behavior simply didn't depend on whether the mother had a job. A fatherless child whose mother worked had problems that showed up on mental tests and in reports from teachers, but so did the fatherless child whose mother stayed at home. It became clear that troubled mothers with problem children couldn't help their children just by quitting work and staying home, and good mothers couldn't hurt their children just by taking a job.

The matching pairs reminded investigators that what they knew about "maternal separation" had come from the kinds of children they had studied first. These were orphans, easy to observe because they were in institutions or under the care of adoption agencies charged with checking how they did in foster homes. When Mother left these children, she left for good. They cried, kicked, sulked, mourned, and some of them never bounced back. They were slower in walking and talking, didn't do as well in school, didn't make friends as easily, got into trouble more frequently and were more violent or withdrawn than children reared by their own parents. The children of working parents who rejoined their parents every day handled their tears and sulks as easily as the children whose nonemployed mothers left them for a few hours shopping. It began to look as if the early orphans had reacted not so much to separation from their mothers as to the problems that had separated them from their mothers in the first place.

When the child-development specialists who remained interested in working mothers began to look at what mothers and children actually did when they were together, they had to face a reality most of us have forgotten from our youth—the embarrassing fact that whatever else a mother does, she spends surprisingly little time interacting with a small child. Professional child-care-givers say that six hours a day is the most that an interested adult can invest interacting with a child, but according to a review of the literature made by Mary Howell, of the Children's Service at Massachusetts General Hospital, "attentive time" is less, not only here but in other countries as well. In one Boston study, mothers and children "interacted" only one-third of the time that their mothers said they were watching them, even though their mothers knew that they themselves were being watched by Harvard psychologists. Most of the time the youngsters were playing by themselves or watching what went on around them.

Time studies on interacting with children show that working mothers spend almost as much time with their children as mothers who stay at home, and sometimes more. An early study made at the Iowa Child Welfare Research Station, for instance, showed that mothers of nursery school children spent more time with them than mothers of matched children who were kept at home. Lois Hoffman's studies found working mothers were spending *more* time reading to their children, and were more apt to plan activities with their children around their *children's* interests than mothers who stayed at home.

There is evidence, too, that working mothers take special pains with their children. They got high marks on a test devised by Dr. Marion Yarrow and given to 50 pair of working and nonworking mothers of varying incomes in cities and suburbs. Mothers were rated "good" if they enjoyed their children, recognized their children's needs, got along with them without hassling, and applied consistent rules. She found that mothers who enjoyed their jobs were more sympathetic and permissive than the nonworking mothers matched with them, and what their children said bore them out. When given a list of verbs and asked who came to mind, they were more apt to say that mother "smiled," "praised," "listened," "explained," and so on, and were less likely to associate her with "hit" or "punish" than the children of matching mothers who stayed home.

One of the difficulties of comparing working and nonworking mothers is that it is seldom the job that makes a difference to children. Almost always it is something that goes with the kind of mother who seeks a job in the first place, and as we saw in Chapter 2, many working women have personal assets that cannot help but benefit a child. One of these characteristics is a more companionable style of marriage, so that children of working parents are more likely to see parents sharing housework and interests. Another is that many working women are more confident and assertive than homemakers.

There is one way in which a mother's job can hurt a middle-class child, and it turned up on a study of grade school children analyzed by Lois Wladis Hoffman, herself a working mother. Hoffman compared the children of working mothers who liked their work with matching children whose mothers were similar in social class, size of family, and other ways, but differed in not liking the jobs they did away from home. Although predominantly middle class and well educated, the mothers who liked their work felt so guilty about leaving their children that they tended to overcompensate for their absence.

"There was much in her relationship to her children that was very positive," Hoffman wrote of this kind of mother. "She expressed more positive affect, used less coercive discipline. She felt less hostility toward her children and more empathy—but in many cases she was somewhat overindulgent, and the children reflected this in their peer interactions and school performance. They played more with younger children than with their age mates; they were less likely to initiate interaction with their classmates; their academic performance was not up to par." These children actually did less to help around the house than the matching children whose mothers stayed at home.

Hoffman's conclusion will make many a middle-class mother wince: "It may not be employment one has to worry about, but guilt about employment." If guilt does the damage, then we have more children to worry about than ever were affected by the physical neglect suffered by "latchkey" children in the early part of this century. That image dates back to the days when the mothers most likely to work were the desperately poor and deserted. Since no one was home, their children wore keys around their necks so they could let themselves into their dwellings after school. Hoffman has ably marshalled the evidence that the poverty of these mothers hurt their children more than their employment, but the horror of the child with the key around his neck continues to haunt those whose contemporary contact with children is limited.

And there is plenty of evidence that the tide of maternal guilt is rising, not subsiding.

"I have many guilt feelings about working while my child is small," a mathematics instructor in a West Virginia community college wrote. "I feel guilty about doing what I want to do instead of shouldering the responsibilities I don't enjoy."

"As I'm working with a youngster, the thought of my own little one creeps into my mind," a learning disabilities specialist confessed on paper. "I wonder, what is she doing?"

Others wrote at length about how they tried to make up for their absence. In many homes, the children's hour is sacred, no matter how tired mother feels. According to a study made in 1977, two-thirds of working mothers try to make up for their time away from home by attending activities at their children's schools, and more than half try to make up by cooking special food and by taking the kids on outings. And they juggle.

They make extraordinary efforts to be with their children. A surgeon who could never rely on her babysitter to arrive in time found she could take the baby with her, order the hospital nursery to make up extra formula, and leave the baby in his basket outside of the operating room, where she could take care of him between cases.

Women's magazines address the worries of this new working mother. "It's four o'clock and where are your children?" Install a phone monitor so they can leave word where they'll be. Brace for the assault on Mom when she comes home by having a babysitter feed young children just before you arrive. Or cool them down by putting them into a warm bath first thing. Get off the bus a few blocks away and walk slowly to unwind before opening your own front door and confronting their demands. Ads suggest taking Geritol to brace for these rigors.

Do your school-age children reject after-school programs because they would rather bring their friends to their own home? Hire a teen-ager to supervise a party for them. Do pediatricians keep you waiting so long you are docked at the office? Ask for evening office hours and if you are refused shop for a doctor who has them. Do neighbors complain that your children "run wild" when you are away? Keep calm and get the story from your child before replying.

What if you can't make the school play? Get the child's father or perhaps even a grandmother or other relative or close friend to represent you at the school. What if a child wants more time with you? Take her or him out to dinner. In the summer, when there's no school, shift their bed hours around so that children can spend time with Mother and Father in the evening and sleep later in the morning.

But children are not dopes. They know a good thing when they have it going, and they can be merciless. "Who do you love better, Mommy, me or your work?"

"I know it should be getting easier now," a mother of a five-year-old writes columnist Niki Scott. "They've had time to adjust to my working. But I feel so guilty all the time—when my youngest says, 'Do you HAVE to work today?' and when my little girl practically tells me I'm a terrible mother . . . I just shrivel up inside. I spend a great deal of time with them, during the evening and on weekends, but it never seems to be enough." And she wonders why it takes them so long to adjust!

"When I pick up my child at her day-care center, she is exhausted, cranky and hardly able to walk," a worried mother wrote to Jean Curtis, author of *Working Mothers*. "She falls apart, wants me to carry her, fusses at me."

Professor Barbara Harris, of Pace University in New York, explains how her own mother helped her to step cheerfully over the prone body of her two-year-old barring the door when she had to go to class. According to her mother, Barbara herself had pulled the same kind of tantrum, distressing her mother until, at the suggestion of the babysitter, she slammed the door as if to leave and stepped back inside. As soon as the door slammed, the wailing stopped. "Mommy's gone now, Mame," the little girl announced to her babysitter. "It's time to play."

This is separation anxiety. It comes and it goes. According to child-development specialists, it's a normal stage in a child's separation from his mother's apron strings. Jerome Kagan has observed it in lower-class mestizo children in Guatemala, Israeli kibbutzim, nomads of the !Kung San tribe in the Kalahari Desert, and American children, both home-reared and day-care.

Guilt over "maternal deprivation" is only half of the story. For the passionate mothers, there is "child deprivation," too. Eda LeShan, the unflappable working mother, now regrets that she didn't quit work to stay with her child for a year or two. "I might have waited until she was three, or even two, and lost nothing and gained something I can't have now," she thinks. Care-givers often can't understand what drives a mother to employ them. "I am taking good care of Eric," a babysitter writes. "But I would not pay some other person $200 a week to take care of my children."

We come, then, to a rather surprising conclusion to the query with which we started: What does the employment of a mother do to her children?

The question itself is disingenuous and invites a counter question: *Who* thinks mothers hurt their children by going out to work, and *why* do they think so? And as we have seen, the answer to that is: social conservatives who are thinking less about the welfare of children than they are of preserving a society of families as opposed to a society of individuals.

As to the welfare of individual children, the impact of a mother's working turns out to be inconclusive and indirect. We have seen that a mother's job does not radically change the daily experience of children at any age. Studies have failed to establish any reliable correlation between the employment of a mother and the development of her children, and the testimony of children themselves is for the most part neutral.

It turns out that children are less affected by whether their mothers work than they are by how their mothers feel about what they are doing. According to Lois Wladis Hoffman, satisfied women make good mothers. This means that a mother who likes her job is not going to do her child any favor by quitting to stay at home. Because she is home all day, she runs the risk of taking her dissatisfaction out on her child. Hoffman found that the children of Reluctant Homemakers who would rather work are worse off than the children of Reluctant Working Wives who would rather be at home.

So what *does* make a difference? In its report of 1977, *All Our Children,* the Carnegie Council on Children concluded that improvement in the welfare of children could not come from "educating" parents or changing their behavior. It would have to come from improving the incomes of parents and providing families with the services of the many outsiders now intimately involved in the development of children. Their vision of an ideal world for children would be a "society where parents could choose to be effective mothers and fathers and productive workers, even when their children were young."

Good mothers are going to work because they've known all along what the social scientists retained by the Carnegie Council were surprised to discover: "Other things being equal, the best way to ensure that a child has a fair chance at the satisfactions and fulfillments of adult life is to ensure that the child is born into a family with a decent income."

CHAPTER 7

The Truth
About the Money She Earns

Wives contribute 40 percent of the earnings of working couples, but every trick known to accountants is used to ensure that her money doesn't count as much as his. Neither private nor public bookkeeping gives her money the power that the marriage contract accords him.

Couples adopt money management methods that discount her earnings, and so do the banks, employers, suppliers, and Government agencies with whom they must deal as a family.

HER PAYCHECK

The problem begins with her paycheck. Since she isn't supposed to have one, tradition doesn't say what to do with it. "For what it's worth, I don't think there is any generally accepted 'wisdom' as to how couples should handle two incomes," Richard Pratt of the American Bankers Association says. "It's an operation based on about 98 percent emotion, and 2 percent practicality. Money gets translated into emotional intangibles like love, respect and caring, and mechanical methods just can't cope with these aspects." Rather vague for a banker—and not much help.

Family finance advisers are strangely silent, too. Insurance companies and savings banks are quite explicit about how much insurance a husband should carry or how much money he should keep in a savings account at all times, but they mention her money only in passing, and then usually to warn against the hazards it carries.

There seem to be two schools of thought. The old school advises young couples to live on the husband's income and never depend on the wife for anything really essential. "Sometimes a two-salary income deludes young people into taking on far too heavy a financial commitment," a publication of the J. K. Lasser Tax Institute warns. "Then when they are suddenly reduced to one salary, they are in trouble." This obsolete bit of advice dates from the days when wives had to be prepared at all times for unexpected pregnancy that would take them out of the work place.

The liberal school is for accepting her money into the family pot. "Mutual confidence is established," a manual prepared by J. K. Lasser Tax Institute advises. "There is none of the 'holding out' of 'my earnings'—a fruitful source of marital discord." Sidney Margolius, money management columnist, illustrates with a cautionary tale about a witchy working wife who wouldn't dip into "her" savings account when her husband was short of money, so that he was in and out of bank loans all the time.

The holding out that is dangerous is that done by the wife, not the husband. Margolius tells about a husband who couldn't resist impulsive spending that wrecked the family budget. Family counselors probing the man's psyche concluded that his extravagance was "an expression of resentment at his loneliness" because his wife worked from 5 P.M. to midnight. They fixed up the couple with a budget that made it possible for her to quit her job and "re-establish a satisfying relationship." Case closed, with no word about whether the new budget worked or the spending sprees stopped.

Citibank of New York tries to be nonsexist. "A working wife may have a strong need for 'my' money or even 'my' telephone, as is the case for one woman who wants to be able to call her mother long distance often, without arousing her husband's ire," a bank booklet advises. "This plan may be best when a wife has long been accustomed to independence and likes to remain 'free.' " Their careful use of quotations dissociates the bank from any such sentiments and prepares for their conclusion: Family finance authorities generally favor the pooling of earnings and outgo for efficiency and for family teamwork and harmony.

Working couples who don't level with each other about money can get into big trouble even if their combined income is high. This can happen when either runs up credit card charges on the assumption that the other one will take care of mundane expenses like the monthly utility bills. Some of them get so deep in debt that they have to be referred to consumer credit counseling agencies set up by creditors in major cities. Some agencies won't take on a family in trouble unless the husband and wife make decisions on spending together. "Managing money is a form of communication in itself," says Gerard Lareau, President of the Consumer Credit Counsellors of Greater New York. "It's the only way for the lesser-earning spouse to have a fair share in where the money goes."

In spite of this advice, very few husbands and wives really have equal say about how family money is spent. According to a family study on budgeting, three out of five families say they are partners, but a third of these partners admit that the husband has the final decision. Only one wife in five, even though she may "handle" the bill paying and the money, has the last word. Working wives do no better than wives who stay at home: two out of five don't even pretend to be partners but say their husbands decide. These "macho" families have more quarrels about money than those who say they are partners, and half of those who quarrel say they can't talk frankly to each other about money.

Games for avoiding communication are ingenious and widespread.

There are wives who expect their husbands to turn over their paychecks and take back lunch money.

There are husbands who expect their wives to turn over *their* paychecks and take back lunch money, and there are wives who actually like to do so.

There are wives who don't even know what their husbands earn, but only what their husbands are willing to contribute to the household.

There are wives who pay all the household bills out of their own pay and get little or no help from their husbands. "You might say that my paycheck *is* the family budget," one of these principal breadwinners explained. "Whatever he earns he spends on himself."

There are husbands who pay all the household bills themselves and neither know nor care what their wives earn. "It's hers to spend as she pleases," one of these husbands boasted. *"We* don't need it."

Many couples confuse—in an almost deliberate way—the handling of money with power to commit it. When the actual disbursement of money is honorific—as in paying a large restaurant check or buying the car—husbands usually handle it. Whenever it becomes a chore, wives usually do it. Now that there are so many bills to pay and so much female-bookkeeping-type paperwork to do, the actual disbursement of money has become a part of housework.

Responsibility for the annual income tax return can be a delicate issue of couple politics: it can be relegated to the spouse least able to avoid the chore, or preempted by a spouse who regards it as a control center for family finance. In many families the income tax is divided along strictly sexist lines: she keeps and records the hundreds of scraps of paper required to validate deductions; he makes the accounting decisions on which deductions to take, or deals with the family accountant.

Whoever actually handles the money, how many bank accounts of what kind are kept and in whose name, are important not for the "practical" or even financial advantages, but because they are symbols of the way the couple feels about whether it's my money, your money, our money.

Wherever husbands and wives think her pay should go, it actually winds up in the family pot more often than either husbands or wives think it should. As a matter of fact, that's what three out of four of those in the Matching Couple Study actually did with it, and only a little more often when the family pot was under $15,000 as when it was more than $25,000. A third of the couples disagreed about what to do with her pay, but the real quarrels were about what *actually* happened to it. "He says it's mine to spend as I wish," one disenchanted working wife explained, "but somehow it always turns out that I 'wish' to spend it at the grocery store or for clothes for the kids." The question about what became of her money apparently was so traumatic for the Reluctant Working Wives that a third of them skipped answering this particular question.

Four ways of thinking about her money emerged. Each copes with the threat of her money to the marriage contract in a different way.

One way is to segregate it from the "real" support of the family and treat it as pin money she can spend on herself, or earmark for something nice but unnecessary.

Pin Money couples deal with the threat of her money by keeping it out of sight. It's hers to spend as she pleases or to sock away in her own bank account if she chooses. The object is not to give her independence to flout his wishes—but to save him the pain of seeing it.

Traditional husbands who think that a wife should keep her money are apt to think that she *did* keep it, even against the evidence. "Money was a problem until I went to work, but he refused my financial help," one Defiant Working Wife wrote us. "He told me to keep my earnings. He wouldn't let me buy a boat or an air conditioner, but then he did suggest that I buy two tires for the car."

Pin money hoarding wasn't popular with our Matching Couples, but housewives were more attracted to the concept than working wives. Seven percent of the homemakers thought that if a wife did earn money, she should be allowed to keep it, in particular the Submissive Homemakers (12 percent) who had special private reasons for wanting to earn some money.

"How can you feel liberated if you let your husband pay for your rent and your food?" a feminist challenged one of these "Pin Money" conservatives during a public discussion of the issue.

"After twenty years of getting his meals and taking his clothes to the cleaners and asking for every ten dollars, I think I'm entitled to a little money I can call my own," the other woman retorted. "Money of my own" is the special project most likely to attract a traditional homemaker to work.

But only 5 percent of all working wives and 7 percent of Submissive Working Wives surveyed want to earn pin money. Husbands of every persuasion, from Traditional to Contemporary, are a little more likely than their wives to think that she should keep her earnings for herself. Husbands who are not happy about their wives working are twice as apt to "let" them keep any money they do earn as husbands who approve, but this permissive attitude does not seem to have much to do with how badly a husband needs financial help with the household bills. The paradoxical facts are that blue-collar husbands with limited and precarious earnings are more apt to renounce any claim to the earnings of their wives than highly paid professional men. Listen to them talk, and you hear that ability to support a family is a more important as well as more precarious source of satisfaction for them than the breadwinning role can be for professional men who get more satisfaction and prestige as well as more money out of the work they do.

The message the "pin money" husbands are beaming at their wives sounds something like this: "Whatever you want to do with yourself is okay by me, honey, so long as it doesn't delay dinner. And if you run into something that makes you a little money, why shucks, it's yours to blow as you please."

The source of this extraordinary nobility is rooted in forgotten history. "Pin money" (on farms it was "egg money") used to be a concession to wives. Generous husbands "let" them keep, for personal frivolity, small sums they earned from such tasks as sewing. American wives now generally have the legal right to control their earnings, but the presumption that he has the right to "give" her such control lingers on.

Not all husbands are willing to let her keep those earnings even in the enlightened twentieth century. A bookkeeper gives her husband money against her will. "Working buys a woman a certain amount of independence," she says. "After giving my spouse $100 a week out of my check for bills, I pocket $20 for my own needs. I work for $80 a month."

Her husband is a restaurant manager. "My wife and I are from different backgrounds," he says. "She wants material things now, and I want to sacrifice now for better things in the future."

The notion that money belongs to men dies hard. An accountant convinced his wife to endorse her paycheck over to him because "it would cost the *bank* too much money" for her to have a checking account of her own. In less sophisticated circles, wives turn over their paychecks in order to avoid physical battery.

Husbands who do "give" their wives their own earnings expect something back in return. That something is recognition of the power that breadwinning gives them in the family. There are strings to this "gift." She can keep it providing she does nothing to interfere with his comfort, and refrains from spending it on something of which he disapproves, such as a separate vacation, a piece of furniture he regards as a luxury, or help for a child or relative held undeserving. "Pin money," in other words, has to be spent on pins, a commodity men must have thought dispensable.

Earmarker Couples are neo-traditionalists. They deal with the threat of her money by building a Chinese wall around it to show that the family is "really" living on his pay alone. They recognize that a husband can't win all the bread these days, so she "helps" him, just as he might "help" her with the shopping or the mopping.

Like many a young working couple, the Taylors in Milwaukee try to bank her paycheck against the down payment on a house. She's a registered nurse and her young husband is earning at what is probably the peak of his career ladder. He makes $22,000 as a unionized skilled blue-collar worker in a brewery. Both of them come from large farm families and they want first a house and after the house, a child. They try to put away most of her paychecks but a lot of times it doesn't work out and that worries Carol. "Sometimes there's car insurance, life insurance, and everything due at once," she says. "It's just too easy to put some of my check into the checking account."

Earmarkers don't like to see "their" money lost in the family bills, but that's what often happens to it. The piano money has a way of being spent on car insurance or braces. One woman who craves an expensive dining room set estimates she has saved up enough over the years to buy three of them, but the money always went someplace else. Almost two-fifths of the wives surveyed thought their pay should be kept for a special family purpose, but less than a fifth *were able* to keep it separate. Fifty-four percent of the Submissive Working Wives wanted to earmark, but only 10 percent managed to do it. Those who succeeded recommended keeping the money in a separate account and spending it on the intended item as soon as there was enough money in the account to get it.

Wives like earmarking better than husbands do, especially if they earn much less than he does and/or work only part-time (and if the total income of their families is a little lower than the average).

Sometimes a wife will take a part-time or temporary job to buy something she fears her husband wouldn't approve. A wife in the process of raising her consciousness worked as an office temporary to earn the money to go to the 1977 National Women's Conference at Houston. She says her husband was proud that she went, but she didn't want to ask him for the money. Another woman celebrated her liberation by "earmarking" her money for something that everyone in the household would have to concede was essential. When she succeeded in landing a job after years of being a full-time housewife and rearing four children, she reported that her salary was exactly equal to the monthly payment on their house and announced that henceforth she would take care of it. "That's what I'm working for," she told the family. "A roof over all of our heads."

This, of course, is exactly what earmarking is intended to avoid. The idea is to maintain the role of the husband and father breadwinner—with appropriate credit for the nonthreatening auxiliary earner, whom sociologist Alice Rossi has called "the cakewinner."

Pooler Couples deal with the threat of her money by insisting that it doesn't matter where it comes from. Her check goes into the bank with his check and both become "our money" to be budgeted together. A majority of couples believe that this is the way working couples should handle their money. It is especially favored by Contemporary Wives and their husbands, by the young and the college-educated, and by the marriage and money management counselors. Poolers favor a joint checking account because it is a symbol of mutuality. In the notably volatile acting business, Dick Van Patten, star of the ABC television series, "Eight Is Enough," has kept all the money in a joint account with his wife for twenty-four years because, "It helps emphasize that we are one unit." In fact three out of four of *all* couples actually do end up pooling.

Poolers aren't necessarily planners. Many young Contemporary

Couples with an underdeveloped sense of private property are quite comfortable channeling whatever cash floats in to whatever the most immediate demand for it is, regardless of who earned it or who needs it. A young pediatrician says she puts her check into the account of her husband, a surgeon, if his account happens to be low. He pays most of the bills out of his account, she thinks, but it doesn't matter because "we both think of the money each of us earns as belonging to both of us."

Couples who put their money together may think they are sharing and sharing alike, but they are often more traditional than they realize. A young banker and his teacher wife pool their money in a joint account. "I would never say this paycheck is mine," his wife says. "I'm working not for me, but for us." Yet they do not have equal say about what's best for "us." Although she earns more than he, she still thinks that a man should be "head of the household." When she wanted to buy a sewing machine and he thought she didn't need one, "we went into a long session of why we shouldn't, what our plans were, the whole bit." The upshot was no sewing machine, but "I feel fine about it," she says. "We reassessed our goals and reinforced where our direction was."

Pooling does not imply joint decision, let alone equal say. It may only mean that husband and wife have learned what to expect of each other.

"We are so used to sharing, we've become like one person," a wife says.

"When we were newly married she sometimes said she would use her own money for something I didn't want her to buy," her husband adds. "But it isn't a problem any more. She's a good shopper and a bargainer, so I can let loose a little and she won't abuse it."

The money management experts don't recommend total pooling. Financial columnist Sylvia Porter believes that a husband and wife should each have some money that doesn't have to go through the family accounts. "If you want to do something absurd with your personal allowance, that's your business," she advises in her *Money Book*. Rather, she recommends partnership rules: no major decisions without prior consultation; part of each paycheck to go into a common fund from which essential household bills are paid. She suggests that the wife pay for optional household help and entertainment in the home, while the husband pay for entertainment out. She also believes, rather traditionally, that young couples planning a baby should live within the husband's means and earmark part of the wife's paycheck for the initial expenses of the baby. "And if you get into a squeeze—which you will—call it 'our' squeeze, not 'yours.'"

Bargainer Couples are radicals. They look the threat of her money full in the face and accept it at full value. Husband and wife both assume that a paycheck belongs to the person who earns it. They scrupulously divide the household expenses. They may agree that the husband take care of the rent and the cars while the wife pays for food, tuitions, and household incidentals. They may agree to split every bill that comes in down the middle, or in proportion to their salaries.

Bargainers believe in separate accounts. Lynnie Green, co-star of the CBS series "On Our Own," thinks they give each partner a sense of financial independence. If her husband insisted on a joint account, she would suggest that each of them contribute a fixed percentage of their earnings to a joint account for communal needs, and she would increase *her* percentage when they start having children.

"I would really be upset if he tried to get at the money in my checking account," a teacher says of her husband, an electrician. When she was on maternity leave without pay, they joked that she would have to get a loan from him to meet her end of the household expenses.

Most of the bargainers are Contemporary Couples both of whom expect to support themselves. They tend to be feminists, couples who have lived together before getting married, or with obligations left over from previous marriages. Whatever the reason, they openly admit that they cannot or will not commit all their income to the marriage.

Some of the bargainers have elaborate arrangements. "When we moved in together neither of us felt that he had any obligation to support me," a secretary says of the engineer who only recently has become her husband. Now they each put the same amount of cash into an antique developing tank which they call "The Box." Out of it they pay for housing, food, utilities, and joint entertainment. What each has left over goes for personal expenses, clothing, insurance, medical expenses, and transportation.

But counting every penny does not eliminate disputes. "Once he asked me whether the Box could use a calculator," she recalls. "I said the Box could use a $20 machine to balance the bank statement and compare prices at the grocery store, but it did not need the $200 scientific model that he could also use at work. The Box made an offer of $20 toward the expensive model, but he thought that was inconsequential and bought it out of his money."

Transportation is carefully figured. She doesn't drive, so he owns and maintains the car, but when she rides with him the Box buys the gas.

One of the problems of the Box is that she puts in as much as he, although her salary is much lower, so she has much less to spend on herself. "That means," says she, "that when he cooks up an obviously expensive and unnecessary scheme, such as flying all the way across the country to spend Christmas week with relatives, he usually offers to buy my ticket."

Bargainers sometimes sound as if they were planning for divorce. One wife alarmed her husband by insisting that the car she had helped buy be put in her name rather than his, but she says she has no intention of departing. "It's just that the divorces of some of my friends have made me realize that I should be keeping my hands on some of my money."

PHONY BOOKKEEPING

However husbands and wives think about her earnings, the law minimizes them. A husband residing with his wife is automatically labeled "head of household" even if both tell the Census taker that they regard her as head of household, and even if she actually earns more money than he does.

Courts look right through her money. Without bothering about the facts, they assume that anything bought with money was bought with *his* money. This makes joint ownership of *anything* a "love trap" unless she takes certain precautions.

Unless she keeps deposit slips proving how much money she herself put into their joint account, tax collectors will assume that it was all put there by him, and so is subject to a gift tax from him to her if she attempts to draw out too much before his death, or an inheritance tax if she tries to draw on it after his death.

Unless she specifically asks, her bank doesn't have to issue a separate credit report for a wife who opened a joint checking account with her husband before November 1, 1976; unnotified, credit bureaus will go on attributing credit worthiness attained by the use of her money to him alone.

Family accounting can minimize her pay, while making full use of it, by the same devices that corporate accountants use to minimize profits that otherwise would go to stockholders in dividends, the government in taxes, or utility customers in lower gas and electric bills. The trick is to charge every conceivable overhead cost against her pay (as corporations do against profits they would prefer not to part with). Taxes are a favorite cost to magnify.

"Based on tax structures, it almost is not practical to have my wife work," a husband who works in a bank complains. But since he earns less than $15,000 a year, it is very practical indeed for her to work as an administrative assistant for $8,000, taxes or not.

Conventional thinking assumes her income is secondary, and since it kicks the family into a higher tax bracket, the additional taxes the family has to pay should be charged against *her* portion of the income. This makes her contribution seem small compared to the amount the family received from his salary when it was taxed at the lower rate applicable to his salary alone, as many husbands are apt to point out.

On the other hand, a wife who earns more than her husband seldom complains that she cannot afford *his* job. Complaining husbands would, as a matter of fact, be startled at the way the figures would sound if "husband" and "wife" were exchanged on tables set up to show wives how little their earnings add to the family income. In 1977, for instance, a wife who earned $40,000 could gain for the family only $5,137 by "allowing" her husband to take a $10,000 job (see Chapter Notes).

The assumptions that the husband's income is "primary" is one of the premises the Equal Rights Amendment will remove from the law. And who is to say that the spouse who supplies the money for the children's clothes and music lessons is the secondary earner, while the one who buys the liquor and fishing tackle is somehow "primary"?

Taxes, of course, are just the beginning. Smart cost accountants see expense everywhere. "I can't see us saving anything much out of what she could make," the husband of a woman who had gone back to college at his expense complained. "She'll need more clothes—a type of clothes she doesn't need now. She says her clothes will cost less when she's working because she'll be able to make them. She claims that the Levi's she likes to wear in college are more expensive because she has to buy them. As you can see, she isn't very realistic about costs."

Speculation about When-Does-It-Pay-A-Wife-to-Work? has been a staple of journalism for thirty years. They all start out by warning the ambitious wife that the expenses of working will greatly reduce her real pay, and these expenses will vary with her situation, the ages of her children, the commuting costs she will incur, the extra clothes she will need, and even the money she won't save because she won't always be able to bake, preserve, can, get things fixed, and shop around for bargains.

Leonard Sloane of *The New York Times* has compiled one of the most complete formulas for wives to use in figuring out how much a job really "pays" them in money. After subtracting child care, plus taxes, union dues, car expenses or commutation, lunches at work and additional clothing, including "extra dry cleaning and shoe repairs," he figured that a mother of school-age children would have retained $3,255 from a $7,000 job in 1976, while a Detroit mother of two preschoolers who used a day-care center would net only $3,610 of an $11,000 salary. This seems to be par for the course.

An earlier study of North Carolina mill towns made by a home economist reported that wives could net three-fifths of their gross earnings if they didn't have children, but if they had preschool children they would net only about half of their pay in cities, and less than half in the country. Time-Life Books researchers figured out that the mother of small children makes about as much from a part-time job that eliminates the need for a babysitter as she does from a full-time job that necessitates one. An economist who reviewed the evidence available in the 1960s concludes that contributions of many women are rather small and "make only a marginal difference to the family's overall economic position," which is, of course, exactly the conclusion the calculations were intended to reach in the first place.

All of the bookkeeping charged against the wife's paycheck were covered in an example presented to the hearings on the Economic Problems of Women, which Congresswoman Martha Griffiths of Michigan initiated when she was a member of the Joint Economic Committee of Congress in 1973. Although the numbers have changed, the situation has remained much the same. "Mrs. X" is the suburban wife of a $15,000-a-year executive. She wants to go back to work after staying home three years with her child. She turns down a $15,000 job as an industrial biologist, the field in which she worked before the baby was born, because she doesn't think she could swing the long hours and the pressure. She's attracted to a job paying $10,-000 in college teaching, where the hours are shorter and flexible, but can she afford to take it?

She discovers that day care is going to cost $2,400 and that she can't even deduct it from her income tax because the joint income they would have would be higher than the law allows for day-care deduction. A suitable wardrobe is going to cost $1,000, modest restaurant lunches another $500, and commuting will be $600. They could move into an apartment in the city and cut the commuting, but as renters they would lose the income tax deduction they get from mortgage interest and local property taxes. Finally, she adds in $500 for the higher dry cleaning bills and food costs they'll have. Some nights, she figures, they'll just have to eat out.

"Mrs. X totals her estimates and finds that family expenses will increase approximately $5,000 if she returns to work. Yet her employment will not provide the family with any new deductions or exemptions. Her very first dollar of income will effectively be taxed at her husband's highest rate. His taxable income is $8,000 so her first dollar will be taxed at 22 percent. Her employment will therefore increase the family's federal income tax bill from $1,380 to

$3,820 (1972 rates); her share of the bill is thus $2,440. Assuming state and local income taxes averaging 5 percent, her cost is $500. Social security tax amounts to another $468 (1972). Mr. and Mrs. X calculate that Mrs. X's gross income will yield a net of $1,592.

"Mrs. X still feels she would like to return to work. The college believes she is the best qualified applicant and persistently pressures her to accept the job. Mr. X, on the other hand, does not think it worthwhile. He points out that it might possibly be better for their child if she stays home and that he is enjoying her housewifely activities. For roughly $1,600, he says, he would rather have her gourmet cooking, careful housekeeping and constant availability. Mr. X, generally a nice fellow, has lately embarrassed Mrs. X by explaining to their friends how Mrs. X, a highly trained biologist with ostensible good earning potentials, really cannot make any meaningful contribution to their family income. Mr. X does not understand why his wife was offended; he assures her that it was not a personal criticism."

Mrs. X is offended by a double standard of family cost accounting. Mr. X doesn't mentally deduct from the money he brings home to the family the cost of the good suits he buys for business wear, restaurant lunches, and the car he drives to the office. On the contrary, he openly enjoys these signs of success. But if her job requires amenities, they are mentally deducted from the salary she brings home to the family and regarded only as the painful costs of earning it, like taxes. Most enraging of all, they can be regarded as negatives even when they benefit the whole family.

"It costs us more to live when she works," a middle-management professional complained of his wife's rising career. "The boys go to private schools and a private camp. We take more trips. This summer we ended up taking separate means of transportation." When all of these amenities are deducted from her salary, what's left *does* become too small to make a difference in the family's spending.

Economists have another gimmick for belittling the impact of her money. Since it's supposed to be "transitory"—here today and gone tomorrow—they assume that the couple lives on his pay and puts hers in the bank. Economists are, of course, mostly male and husbands. Since it is tedious to track down what couples actually do with their money, economists fall back on the curious habit they have of assuming that people do what they are supposed to do.

The myth that two-paycheck couples save more and spend less than couples supported by his paycheck alone has been perpetuated, for various reasons, by John Kenneth Galbraith, the liberal maverick, and Jacob Mincer, the labor economist who has pioneered in studies of female employment. Galbraith's idea is that working wives don't have the time to spend money on elaborate consumption, while Mincer holds to the old-fashioned notion that the earnings of wives are too "transitory" to be budgeted for daily necessities. Both theories, of course, were evolved before the inflation of the mid-1970s wrecked fiscal theories of every political coloration.

In 1976, Myra Strober, an economist at Stanford University, went to the trouble of proving what every working wife could have told her: the money wives earn goes to buy the things families want here and now. She analyzed data collected by the University of Michigan in 1968 and found that two-earner families spend more of their income than traditional families supported by a single breadwinner alone. We can get clues to where her money went by comparing the spending of one- and two-earner families in a mammoth Bureau of Labor Statistics survey of family expenditures. It suggests that her paycheck went to buy some very nice things indeed, most of them things that could be enjoyed by everyone in the family.

Chief among them is an extra car. According to the Bureau of Labor Statistics, in the fiscal year 1974, two-paycheck families averaged $2,042 a year on transportation compared with $1,520 for families living on one paycheck alone, many of whom must have been stranded when the breadwinner drove off to work every morning. The next biggest place her money went was, as noted, for housing, especially furniture, appliances, housewares: working husbands run up a bar tab, but working wives splurge on the house. And though two-earner families were no bigger than one-earner families —both averaged 3.3 persons—they spent $140 more a year on food, an item hardly consumed by women alone.

BLS didn't confirm significantly higher costs for clothing a wife when she works. Wives always spend more on clothes than their husbands, but when they work, everyone in the family gets to spend more on clothes. In 1973, two-earner families averaged $381 on clothes for females, $62 more than one-earner families spent, and $276 on clothes for males, $54 more than one-earner families. Working wives put more clothes on the backs of their husbands, too.

It was the same with other budget items about which BLS asked. Although the average spending on one- and two-earner families conceals a wide range of lifestyles, two-earner families spent more across the board. They averaged $62 a year more on education, reflecting the many wives who were putting husbands and children through college.

In the real world in which marketers operate, working wives are as apt to splurge on extras for themselves or the family as they are to sock their pay into the bank against the day of their "retirement." If they're young and childless they may actually sock *less* money away against a rainy day on the theory that two paychecks hedge against unemployment.

NONSEXIST BOOKKEEPING

Nobody really has succeeded in figuring in a nonsexist way the cost of both people in a marriage working. The Bank of America suggests singling out from the total family budget any expenses that relate directly to the fact that both work and subtract these expenses from the combined take-home pay. Offset these, the bank adds, against "any present or expected financial benefits of your both working. These might include the greater insurance coverage and fringe benefits, and the additional income you will receive in retirement from two pension plans. Keep in mind, too, that such expenses as full-time child care will drop once your children are in school."

This cleans up the sexist language, but not the assumption, already discussed, that the single-earner family budget is the norm against which the extra costs of a second job must be charged. And it does not address the crucial issue. If it costs too much for both to work, which is the job that costs too much? To determine that, you have to value each job in terms of its benefits and costs, not only in money, but in unpaid services and leisure foregone and in the psychic costs and psychic pay that most people simply call "feelings."

Money, services foregone, leisure foregone, psychic cost-benefit— wives weigh all four when they consider a job. Would it always pay a husband to work if he figured his job the same way? A nonsexist appraisal of the worth of each job would consider all four on an equal basis.

Money is the easiest of the four to figure. On the plus side, count gross pay, pension rights, social security rights, and the value of insurance protection against loss of pay through accident, sickness, or unemployment provided in part by employers. Companies that provide other fringe benefits, such as low-cost meals, recreation, schooling, insurance, stock-purchase and savings plans among other goodies, figure these fringes can add as much as 25 percent to base pay. Generally speaking, husbands get more fringes at work than wives.

From the total dollar compensation of each job it is necessary to deduct the total dollar cost of holding it, and his costs must be figured on the same basis as her costs. Instead of charging the highest tax rate against her pay on the theory that it is "additional," the total family tax bill must be prorated between the two incomes: if she earns one-fourth of his pay, she pays one-fourth of the tax bill. Each charges as costs the job-related expense of extra clothes, transportation, meals, and business-related outlays such as union dues or professional associations, job-training, entertaining, and the like.

Sauce for the goose is sauce for the gander. Couples who charge against her pay the extra cost of the clothes she likes to wear to work must charge against *his* take-home pay the extra cost of the kind of car he likes to drive to work—and if she would prefer an apartment in town, perhaps even the extra expense of maintaining the wife-killing suburban spread that he thinks his position in life "requires."

Services foregone. The biggest cost of any job is the value of the time you give up in order to do it. Under the usual sexist bookkeeping, wives figure the value of the home services the job keeps them from doing. She may count the higher price of groceries that she can quickly cook into a dinner after she gets home from work; the extra cost of the children's clothes she pays because she can't get to the bargain store on her lunch hour; even the business her husband could

have won if she had been on hand to entertain his clients. Traditionally, babysitting is her cost and her cost alone because she's the one
expected to do it.

Under conventional, sexist cost-accounting, a wife has to charge
against her job all the costs of replacing her traditional work in the
home. This means that the value of her job will vary with the number
and ages of her children, the size of her house, or even the help her
husband needs to earn *his* pay. The teacher who resigns after her second child is born because "the cost of working is prohibitive" has no
idea that she has just made a cost-benefit calculation so intricate that
business managers would leave it to a computer. Yet economic studies of what large numbers of working wives actually do show that
most of them juggle these factors rather accurately.

Though accurate, some of the resulting decisions look bizarre. If
that young teacher, for instance, were a systems analyst she might
command a high enough salary to make it worth working even if she
has *three* preschool children. If she had no children, and couldn't
find professional work, she might go to work at wages little more
than she had to pay her cleaning person. On the other hand, a wife
with minimal job skills and a high-earning husband might be able to
save more dollars by careful administration of an elaborate household than she possibly could earn in the job market. A homemaker
may feel that her home work is "priceless" but it is hard to imagine
any home service, no matter how personal and special, worth the million dollars a year Barbara Walters commands.

The traditional calculation of the "cost" of a wife's job charges all
of the services foregone against her pay on the assumption that she
and she alone would be doing all of them if she weren't earning. But
a working couple who have agreed to continue working and to divide
the household chores equally between them have to charge half of
the services they do without, because both work, against *his* job.

They must agree as to how each partner is to discharge his/her
obligation to do half of each task. The task may be split between
them ("It's your turn to change the baby"). It may be swapped for a
task taking equal time that is more congenial. ("I'll do the windows
if you take care of all the diaper work.") Someone else may be hired
to do it. ("I'll pay for the babysitter.") Or the money equivalent of

the time required may be deposited in a fund from which household help or even household goods may be purchased.

The system can be flexible. The spouse who earns the biggest paycheck may commute all of his obligations to money. If he is pressed for time, he may even hire someone to pick up his clothes. All that is required is to time the task and assign a wage scale to it.

Leisure Foregone. Under sexist cost-accounting, leisure foregone is the biggest cost wives bear for working outside of the home. According to the Cornell study made by Kathryn Walker, working wives average twenty hours of housework a week in addition to the hours they put in on their jobs. All over the world, working women have less really free time for leisure than their working husbands. There is evidence, too, that employed men value their leisure more than employed women: a husband required to wash his own socks will sometimes wear them dirty rather than take the time to wash them.

We are just beginning to see that one of the costs of working is the activities you can't do because you are cooped up on the job all day long. All of us unconsciously set some value on our time. What an affluent homemaker means when she says that a job isn't "worth the trouble" is that the time she would give up is more valuable to her than the money she could make.

Her time is more valuable in two ways. The money she could make means less than it would in a poorer family, and her time is worth more because she has the money to make her leisure time more interesting. "What's the use of having the day to myself," a Reluctant Homemaker complained, "if I don't have enough money in my purse to get out of the house?"

Then, too, it takes time to spend money. "If I work all the time, I never get a chance to spend the money I earn," a freelance writer laments. "Once I'm finished with a project, it's the other way around. I travel, I go shopping, I eat out. I spend money like crazy. Pretty soon I'm broke and have to go to work again."

Generally speaking, however, time and money are equivalents. Employers trade their money for time and employees trade their time for money. What we are just beginning to see is that this conventional trade-off is a highly personal bargain that differs from one individual to another. It depends on what you would do if you weren't working.

Most people work in part because they can't imagine what they would do with themselves if they were free to do as they pleased all day long. That's what they mean when they say that they would go on working even if they had money enough to live without a paycheck. (Traditional women are better off in this respect than traditional men. The women can think of things to do around the house—things that sound like housework but turn out to be amusements, such as knitting, caring for plants or pets, or entertaining.)

Some men and women, however, have personal agendas so urgent that they are willing to limit themselves to poverty incomes in order to have time to themselves, and they are as likely to be men as women. A high proportion of breadwinning wives who outearn their husbands are married to artists, mystics, or men engaged in political, scientific, artistic, or religious activities.

An increasing proportion of young college graduates value their personal relationships and "head time" so highly that they are willing to trade only minimal time for earning the material essentials of life. "Nothing we could buy is worth giving up eight whole hours a day, every day," a woman who has become a permanent Office Temporary declares. Many others simply refuse to consider a nine-to-five job. "There are too many other things I want to do," one chronic part-timer explained. "Reading, writing, sewing, making love when it's convenient."

Some occupations, of course, incorporate more leisure during the working day than others. An air traffic controller has to be on his or her alert every second of the shift, while firemen really only work when there's a fire. And contrary to myth, the better paid the work, the longer the coffee breaks, and the easier it is to goof off on the job. There is evidence, too, that men manage to incorporate more leisure on the job than women, in part, perhaps, because women are more apt to do clerical and service work that is closely supervised.

Psychic Cost-Benefit. Finally, the most important aspect of a job is how well you like it—whether it's more fun than grief. Traditional cost-accounting allows women, but not men, to quit a job that is more grief than fun. The result is that working seems to be doing women more good than it does men.

"I just love my job," a rather affluent working wife, who teaches, likes to tell everybody. "We don't need the money. As a matter of fact, I'm having such a ball that I'd be willing to pay for the privilege of working with those kids if that's the only way they would let me do it."

Equally typical, on the other hand, is the advertising account executive who woke up every weekday morning with a headache that became worse when he got to his desk. His wife, a former nurse, noticed that he never had a headache weekend mornings. "She was the one who discovered that the job literally was making me sick," he says. "Now I'm working part time as a commercial artist and she's back working full time at nursing. We don't have as much in dollars, but we're both better off."

This couple appraised the psychic cost and the psychic pay of the work each was doing and made a switch.

It's not hard to make a psychic balance sheet for your job. First you list the psychic costs—all the things you have to put up with in order to hold the job. An unpleasant commute. A dingy office. Boredom some (with hope, not all) of the time. A mean boss. A disagreeable co-worker. A company policy you don't like. Just write down everything you don't like about your job.

Now make a list of what you like about it—all the things about your job that make you feel good about yourself or you like doing. The work matters. You like the people. You are learning new things. You like the food in the cafeteria.

Next you try to balance the two. The costs and benefits sound imponderable, but apples and eggs can be reduced to money and so can the psychic cost-benefit of a job. If you would look into another job at the same pay, the psychic balance is unfavorable. If you'd stay even if they cut your salary, the psychic balance is a plus.

Considering everything, a wife's job may be well worth its "cost" in the psychic pay it gives her to be achieving objectively on her own. As a matter of fact, in many families, a really nonsexist appraisal of the *full* cost of each job might point to *his* job as the one that costs too much. As two earn, leisure and the psychic balance loom larger in everyone's job decisions.

Nonsexist accounting would mean unexpectedly big gains for husbands. When two earn, leisure and psychic aspects of work become more important. Nonsexist accounting will value his leisure no higher than her leisure and assure him of as favorable a psychic cost-benefit ratio as dependent wives have enjoyed when they went out to work.

It's happening already. Many men are becoming as picky and choosy about the kinds of jobs they will take as women have been, and as likely to quit in a huff if things don't go their way. Men, too, are demanding that work have intrinsic meaning, something more than the money.

Meanwhile, wives are beginning to taste the joys of money. Private and public bookkeeping devices try, but even in concert they do not succeed in purging a wife's pay of all the power that money commands in a money economy. At home, her earnings may be ignored as pin money, earmarked for nonessentials, or commingled in the family pot. They may be minimized by employers, creditors, and tax collectors. But money can never be wholly wished away. Like the nouveau riche, the earning wife enjoys an uneasy, illegitimate, and discounted power denied to those who have no money at all.

One husband recalled the days before his wife worked in terms worthy of a central banker recalling the stability of a world ruled by the British Empire. "We used to have this gold standard in our family. I brought home the gold and I set the standard."

This gold standard won't work for contemporary young couples pursuing two serious careers. By trial and error and a great deal of talk they are evolving a new one.

PART THREE:

LIFESTYLE PIONEERS

CHAPTER 8

The Age Thirty Bind

Men and women who came of age in the 1970s had watched their parents try to live out the marital contract all their lives through, whether their mothers worked or not. They saw that their parents were chained to each other by meshing locksteps: a lifelong sentence of nine-to-five, deskbound earning for him; a lifelong sentence of homebound caring for others for her. Together, these locksteps used the power of sex to get the work of society done. They saw that conventional ways of love and marriage impounded sexuality for social purposes, just as a dam impounds the water of a stream to create a fall that will turn a wheel.

The college graduates of the 1970s had their own ideas of what life should be. They set out, diplomas in hand, to develop their talents and discover themselves as individuals, not as members of the world of men or the world of women, but as members of *one* world. The opportunities at hand were love and work. The trick was to get the good out of them without getting caught in the lockstep.

Seldom has a fundamental change of life plan come for a whole generation so fast. The first thing to go was the traditional marriage contract. Pollsters could see it happening almost faster than they could do their calculations. But the results were always obvious when surveys were based on age. In 1976, two-thirds of the students questioned by the National Women's Survey of the International Women's Year Commission thought that husband and wife should share earning and housework on an equal basis, but approval steadily declined with age to a low of 9 percent for those over 65. Age gaps were almost as wide on other questions probing support for the marital contract. Should the man be the achiever and the woman take care of the family? Is it more important for a wife to help her husband than to have a career of her own? Is a marriage headed for trouble if the wife outearns the husband? No, said the student young. Yes, said the old.

College-age men and women were putting their theory into practice, too, by living together without the housework and budget problems that shaped the marriages of their parents. Student couples got lots of practice scheduling time together around their studies. Work came first: survival in college meant passing your courses. Meals and all the other amenities of domestic life were cast aside. Routine? There was none. Sometimes graduation broke off these living-together relationships, and sometimes they continued. But in either case, the experience left them with a new ideal: marriage was going to be a "positive" experience, something to "work at" for "personal growth," or else there would be no marriage at all.

They aimed at personal fulfillment both in marriage and in career.

When Daniel Yankelovich polled college students in 1973 he found that only 22 percent were looking for an undemanding job without pressure; only 28 percent wanted a job with prestige; but 77 percent were looking for *challenge*. Other researchers—as well as employers—have found that subjective states of mind like "interesting work" or "chance to use one's talents" consistently attracted a bigger constituency than the traditional lures of high pay, status, security, fringe benefits.

The effective satisfactions were increasingly inward. In 1978 participants in the happiness study chose as the best kind of job one that gave you a "chance to do something that made you feel good about yourself." This totally subjective value drew even more votes than "chance to accomplish something worthwhile." Farther down the list the chance to learn new things, develop skills and abilities, do things that you do best seemed important to many more readers than pay or praise, while "chances for getting a promotion" wound up the rear as the *least* important of eighteen sources of job satisfaction. Two-thirds said they would turn down a raise if it meant less interesting work. Underscoring this last, is the fact that in 1976, 44 percent of the graduates of the Cornell School of Business and Public Administration actually refused the highest paid job they were offered, preferring to work where other opportunities—for diversification or place of residence, for example—were available.

Work and love on a timetable of personal choosing is not entirely new, but it was an ideal to be accomplished by only the privileged few. In the 1970s more people than ever were demanding this privilege, and the numbers raised a new question: Could everyone march to a different drummer without ungluing the affluent society that had made it seem possible? Or, what would give first, the social structure or the people trying to alter its shape?

The best hope for fundamental solutions lay with these privileged young people who had been brought up with the idea that they could have everything if they worked at it: an equal, rewarding marriage; rewarding careers that go straight to the top; and children who would grow up having everything, too.

For the first few years out of college, it looked easy. Some outlawed—between them—the traditional marital contract by writing a new one of their own to cover all the problems they saw causing trouble around them: who should pay for what; how much time each owed the other; who should take care of any children they might have; how to settle any disputes that might arise.

What they wanted was a relationship that provided for sharing more of their lives than the traditional marriage contract encouraged. They talked endlessly with each other about their work, their feelings, and all the decisions they had to make, both joint and separate. They aspired to take selfless interest in each other. Home chores were all up for renegotiation. But however they were resolved, each task was to be considered a joint responsibility.

It wasn't so bad at the outset. As a matter of fact, it was fun. Instead of look-alike couples in their ticky-tacky boxes all in a row, they envisaged a world of uniquely different couples, each with a unique lifestyle of their own personal devising.

They thought the future would be easy, too. Their careers, well started, would continue upward. Their children, when they arrived, would have more of their parents than they themselves remembered getting from theirs. Fathers would do more than play ball with their daughters and their sons. Mothers active in the wider world would bring more to their children than services. Both would be models of sex equality to their children.

But an entirely new course of action always introduces unforeseen obstacles, too. And that is what happened to the young people who threw out the marital contract. Around the age of thirty, when it all seemed within grasp, they encountered the Baby Panic and the tradition of the two-person career. Both came to a head when their careers began to take off.

Inevitably the question begins to grow: Aren't we going to have children?

Something raises the question: How much higher can we go in our careers and still share everything? As they advance, they realize that the more successful they become, the less time they will have for each other. More than nine-to-five dedication is required, they discover, for a real career, "leading to higher levels of pay and responsibility." A real career takes undivided attention and release from sharing with anyone on an equal basis.

Most of them don't give up. They may not be able to have everything, but they do succeed in making at least one part of their dream come true: Whatever the discomfort of lifestyle pioneering, the lives that they design seem a better fit to them than the lockstep life of the traditional marital contract.

CHAPTER 9

The Baby Panic

Cindy had been her cool, take-charge self with the doctor, but it was harder to keep her thoughts in order on the way home. She sat in the back seat of the taxi trying to be logical, but she didn't know where to begin. Everything was going to be different. She looked down at her body with new interest, seeing it for the first time, as if it already belonged to someone else.

Then terror welled up. She was trapped. *Cut it out,* she said to herself. *You've got to think.*

Often in taxis—or on trains, buses, planes—she would think about her work; how to reconcile one thing and another, how to make the budget for one thing include something else. Traveling seemed to set her thoughts in motion, and often the answer came easily.

This time it didn't work. Trying only tangled her thoughts. Voices broke in on her logic. The voices of friends, parents, relatives, and worst of all, her own voice, repeating all the things she had ever said on the subject of babies:

I will definitely have at least two.

I will definitely experience the whole process: pregnancy, childbirth, nursing.

I want to watch my child grow up and discover everything for the first time.

I want to go to the park, collect shells on the beach, help my child with his or her homework.

I will have all my children before I'm thirty. . . . But then when she had turned twenty-nine, Cindy remembered she had revised this to: *before thirty-five.* And she had also started thinking perhaps she'd have only one child, and maybe she would have to hire help (if they could afford it by then), and . . . well, whatever happened, she'd manage in her own way, when the time came.

When the time came. Maybe that was the real problem. Babies had always been in the future. She would be a mother someday. Later. Not now. It had to be later because she and David were too busy and their lives were still too unsettled.

David's law firm had done well last year, but he really didn't care for chasing after the fat retainers that could keep it financially steady. Any moment he might go off on a case that would bring in no money at all and take up all his time. That was what he wanted to do, and Cindy wanted him to do it.

It was worse when she thought of her own work as an administrative assistant to a Congressman. The timing was a nightmare. It just couldn't happen. The primary campaign was coming up. There would be no sleep for weeks. No getting away from the telephone, night after night. She would not, could not miss it.

We don't have enough time for a baby, she thought. She meant, 24 hours a day isn't enough for work, marriage, a child. A child required time—continuously. You couldn't tell a baby—go diaper yourself! if you were too busy with something else. As it was, she and David had trouble finding enough time just to keep up with each other's lives. When would it get better? Not for years. Cindy started counting: thirty-one, thirty-two, thirty-three.

What if I wake up when I'm forty and realize I didn't have a baby? Cindy thought of all those generations stretching back into the past —all the way back to the beginning of life in the sea. If she didn't have a baby, she would be the end. Her death would be total. End. End. End.

Then it came flooding over her. The full baby panic.

Back home, she summoned up the pluck David admired in her. He'd be waiting, thinking she had worked late at the office. She would have to tell him. If I am pregnant, she told herself, I should be happy. Yes, I should be very happy. And it was in this posture of happiness that she opened her front door and took the glass of wine David had been waiting to have with her.

This was their evening ritual: wine, conversation, and relaxation before dinner. How would that change if they had a baby? She imagined a clamoring toddler grabbing at her knees . . . or . . . She went into the living room to sit down.

"David, I wasn't working late," she said after he joined her. "I think I'm pregnant. But the doctor won't be able to tell for another two weeks."

David's face lit up at the thought. He sounded excited as he began to conjure up what life would be like with a third member of the family—how they would all go to the park together, gather shells on the beach—but soon his voice trailed off.

Both were thinking of themselves: *It's early. We don't have to have a baby just yet.* In the silence, both were pondering questions they had never seriously considered before: Can we afford a baby now? What will it do to our lifestyle? What will it do to our careers? What will it do to our marriage? How late can we wait to have one? What if we never have one?

For couples like Cindy and David, the decision to have a baby is like a toll bridge or a road block on the border of a strange country toward which they are traveling slowly at first, but then with increasing speed. A sudden turn of the road—an unexpected pregnancy or even a thirtieth birthday—and the decision is suddenly upon them, filling the horizon.

A growing majority of women college students expect to have two children and full-time jobs as well. A study made by Ross M. Stolzenberg and Linda J. Waite, sociologists at the University of Illinois, at Champaign-Urbana, has shown that the plan of 20-year-old women to work doesn't have much effect on the number of children they expect to have. Ask the career-ambitious when they expect to have their children and they say "later."

It is surprising how well women have managed all through history to avoid pregnancy when they have had a compelling reason to do so. In Colonial America, for instance, they locked their husbands out when times were tough, and women managed to avoid becoming pregnant in the Depression of the 1930s in a variety of ways without the benefit of the contraceptive pill. In the 1970s, women seldom forget their pills when they are looking forward to something really exciting such as going to college or running for public office.

The universal pattern has always been for women to allow themselves to get pregnant when there was nothing much else for them to do. This is the way it was for the women who quit their war jobs after World War II and filled the suburbs with babies. And this is the way it is today for women on welfare in big city ghettos and wives whose professional careers are stalled. One military wife, for instance, frankly admits she had two children in rapid succession because her husband was stationed in Guatemala where "there was absolutely nothing for me to do, not even a cruddy job of filling in as secretary on the base." It's the same all over the world. An East Indian visitor to the National Women's Conference at Houston in 1977 said that jobs for women would be the quickest way to bring down India's birth rate.

Women who do get jobs out of college have "many better things to do." Ask a 27-year-old what she's waiting for and you get the kind of answer that shows she hasn't been thinking babies lately: "after graduate school"; "when our marirage is going better"; "we want to travel a little first"; "when my job is set." For older women of 27 to 29, Stolzenberg and Waite found that plans for working *did* cut down the number of children they expected to have. They have learned from working and watching friends with children just how hard it would be to combine a full-time job with children.

"When I was growing up, I never questioned that I would one day have a child," a 28-year-old newspaper reporter explained. "But now I'm not so sure. I've found a job that I really like and I now can see what children mean—a lot of time, a lot of expense, a lot of frustration—and I am sure, too, a lot of satisfaction. But I can't see myself quitting my job and staying home with the kids."

"I enjoy working," an anguished wife wrote. "I like my paycheck and the independence it gives me. I enjoy the people contact I get at my job and the challenges I face daily. As a claims representative in a small insurance company I make decisions on workmen's compensation laws and injuries, talk with lawyers, police, other claims representatives across the country and receive the benefits of company educational programs to aid me in my job, not to mention the benefits I receive, such as health benefits that my husband doesn't have at his job. My paycheck contributes to the budget and to savings, and still leaves me enough to splurge on myself, my husband, and our new home. It also helps support my ceramics course and horseback riding lessons.

"Do I give this up for confinement to the house, raising children, soap operas, and housework? I'm almost thirty and I'm facing, along with a lot of other young wives, the decision of whether to give up my job and start a family or to keep my job and forget about having a family."

This is the Baby Panic. It strikes when careers and marriages are most demanding, and the first few promotions have catapulted a Contemporary Couple into the sudden riches of two family-sized paychecks. It's a new dilemma. Cindy belongs to the first generation of wives who do *not* expect to have children as a matter of course. Cindy's mother expected to control the timing of her children, but she would have had to be very careful to whom she confided a decision never to have any at all. The difference is that Cindy can make this decision openly. During the 1970s most people continued to say that they wanted to have children themselves, but a rapidly rising majority said they did not disapprove of those who elected to remain childless. One of the most important social trends of the 1970s was the rise of a socially liberal "New Breed" of affluent young educated couples whom Daniel Yankelovich found were "less child-oriented and more self-oriented" than previous generations. This New Breed think of having children "not as a social obligation, but as one available option freely chosen."

It is the burden of this choice that creates the Baby Panic. First off, it imposes a crushing, Godlike responsibility. When babies were regarded as bundles from heaven, all you had to do was the best you could for them. A comforting folklore assured you that mothering was anatomical. Nature would show you what to do, and if Nature goofed, it wasn't your fault.

Now it is. In 1978, the readers of a young woman's magazine were asked what they thought a couple should attain before starting a family. "A happy, stable marriage" was checked by 54 percent, and "financial security" was second with 43 percent, but these reasonable conditions were followed by subjective factors such as "my emotional maturity," "my husband's emotional maturity," and "my own readiness to take time out from work." Bringing up the rear of the list were "the chance to have traveled or experimented with different lifestyles," "a certain degree of progress in my work," "work that is flexible enough to make my being a working mother easier," and last—checked by only 9 percent—"enough money to afford good child care while I work."

Wives like Cindy brood about whether they are good enough to be mothers. Do we want to create another in our own image? Are we ready? Particularly, "Are we ready?" "I'm not ready to organize family life around children," one potential mother insisted. "I'm too selfish and impatient," said another. Still another confessed that she could never live for her children the way her own mother had done.

Couples in the grip of the Baby Panic devise their own parental aptitude tests. One wondered whether she could rent a child—to see whether she would like to "own" one! Another tried to borrow a baby from a friend for a few afternoons, but the friend told her it wouldn't help her decide because other people's children didn't feel like your own. One couple devised progressively more rigorous tests of their capacity to nurture. "We started with plants," the wife said, "and then when they did all right we tried a goldfish, and then a turtle. Right now we've gotten a kitten, and if that works out all right, we'll try a dog. If we can take care of a dog in a city—walking it twice a day and providing diversion for it on the weekends and some sort of care for it when we go away, then *maybe* we'll do all right with a child. A child is such a big responsibility. How else can we be sure we want it?"

Another problem is that the choice is so new, there's no help in making it. There is a rich literature of advice and inspirational support for a reluctant or a hard-pressed mother. Motherhood is glorified. Men open doors for women, it is said, out of respect for their services in child-bearing. But there is a verbal blackout of advice on how she should decide whether or even when to have a baby.

The blackout is logical. If the baby is the given around which parents must organize their lives, then parents have to look beyond their own preferences for a reason to have one. The tradition that children are a social or a religious obligation is so strong that there is something mildly obscene about considering what's in it for the parents. "I wanted to have a baby for the experience," a forthright mother of two explained. "For that, of course, one was enough. The second was an accident."

It does not help much to say that the choice is now "personal." Cindy's confusion is that she is trying to reason about what Yankelovich calls "an available option freely chosen" by weighing costs against benefits as she does when she makes a business decision. The exercise is about as helpful as weighing apples against eggs. The reasons for, are romantic, emotional. The reasons against, are all practical.

People have trouble articulating why they want a child. In 1975, researchers in seven countries asked a national sample of married women under 40 and their husbands identical questions about the advantages and disadvantages of having children. The American study, under the direction of Lois Wladis Hoffman, of the University of Michigan, disclosed that the most important reason was "love." "Children bring love" was followed, in order of importance, by "to watch them grow and develop," "because life is more interesting with children," and "because children are fun."

If you go by what parents say, at least, you have to conclude that people have children because of a relationship they want to have with the child.

The leading disadvantages of having children, on the other hand, were all practical, objective barriers: loss of freedom; financial costs, including lost opportunities; worries about everything from the state of the world to the health and safety of the child and specific annoyance and inconvenience of having children.

American couples, it seems, are not so self-oriented, after all, unless valuing children for the way they make you feel can be regarded as selfish. Many are actually attracted to parenting because it is hard, like climbing Mt. Everest. When he was a speech writer for President Carter, James Fallows said he welcomed parenthood because it was "one of the few situations in which unselfish love is required . . . Few of us are so naturally led toward sainthood that we can ignore those rare opportunities to bring out our better sides." A young couple who had announced to friends and family that they would never become parents succumbed, at the last minute, because it appealed to them as the only "adventure" they had not already tested.

Neither men nor women are highly motivated to have babies because of what other people think, or because of "what children can do for you." Few checked as a reason "to please your parents or other relatives," "because of your religion," or the economic reasons which ranked high in Indonesia and the Philippines: "to have someone to depend on when you are old" and "because children can work and help the family." As a matter of fact, three-fourths of the supposedly "self-oriented" New Breed parents Yankelovich interviewed said they expected nothing at all in the future from their children.

Psychiatrists can and do ferret out secret and inadmissible motives. To save a shaky marriage (but child-bearing may well wreck it). To prove something, like his manhood (in Latin circles), or her womanhood (presumably essential for Total Woman), or even how much better a mother you can be than your own mother. One woman frankly admitted that she wanted a child "to make up for the mistakes my mother made with my brother and me." The daughter of a professor accused her own mother of having her to improve her credibility as a child psychologist and serve as a role model for her women students.

Now it doesn't take exceptional wisdom to see that the only good reason for having a child is just that you want to have one. Practical reasons for having a child are as suspect as practical reasons for marrying. Practical reasons *against* having a child, on the other hand, make admirable sense. If they deter you, fine and dandy. You didn't really want a baby that much after all.

There are no universal answers to the questions David and Cindy pondered in silence, but there is some data on each of them that will help couples decide what is right for them.

The most immediate question, of course, is the dollar cost.

CAN WE AFFORD A BABY?

It's not the first cost, it's the upkeep. But the first cost is substantial and growing. By the time this book is in print, inflation will have pushed the first-year cost of bearing and caring for a baby to well over $3,000. This amount covers medical expenses of the birth, the baby's doctor, a maternity wardrobe, diapers, baby clothes, baby food and supplies, nursery furniture and equipment, ten rolls of film, plus developing, for baby pictures, and forty hours of baby-sitting for the year.

The biggest item of these first costs is the medical expense of the birth, now well over $1,500 in most cities (and soaring out ahead of the general rate of inflation), of which medical insurance covers about half. If the mother quits work because of the baby, the bills begin coming in just when her paycheck stops.

Out-of-pocket expenses grow every year. In 1979, for instance, a New York City couple in modest circumstances could expect to spend nearly $100,000 to feed, house, clothe, doctor, and service a baby born that year until he was eighteen. College would be on top of that, and no one believed that in the 1990s it could be had for the $22,356 the College Scholarship Service estimated a B.A. degree would cost a freshman entering in the fall of 1978.

Dollar estimates of the cost of rearing a child aren't very helpful. They depend on inflation, on location, and most importantly, on the standard of living of the family in which the child is being reared. The old Rule of Thumb counted 15 percent of family income for the expenses of each child, but birthday presents at parties, Christmas, teeth straightening, music lessons, summer camps, and, later on, cars and trips to Europe are eating up more of a family's income all the time. An estimate of 1977 found that middle-class families with two children were really spending *40 percent* of their income on the kids.

A more realistic Rule of Thumb for the late 1970s is that *20 percent of the income of typically small, middle-class families goes for the out-of-pocket expenses of each child.*

Big as they are, however, these out-of-pocket expenses are not the half of it. None of them count the time spent caring for children. It has to be counted as an expense because you have to pay someone else to do it or forego income to do it yourself. Childwork is work, whoever does it. The most important Rule of Thumb confronting parents caught in the Baby Panic is that *the biggest cost of a child is the cost of caring for the child.*

It is the inescapable work of child care that prospective parents "cannot afford." According to the Population Reference Bureau, caring for three children until the last has graduated from high school involves more than 18,000 hours of parent-time, or the equivalent of a full-time, steady job for nine years. One way or another, parents pay for this time.

If childwork were considered solely as a task and assigned on a purely economic basis, parents who earned more than the cost of competent care-giving—say $8,000 to $10,000 a year—would hire it done, while a parent who earned less would quit earning to do it. And, to some extent, it does work this way.

The third Rule of Thumb on affording a child is a paradox: *The more money you make, the more a child costs you.* Child care can cost the poor less, for instance, because often they are surrounded by friends and relatives willing to sit for little or nothing because they can find no other work. Moving up the scale, the majority of non-career women workers earn so little more than the cost of competent care-giving that they aren't sacrificing very much in dollars to quit earning and do the job themselves.

The cost escalates for career-bound, college-educated couples. According to one calculation, a college-educated mother could lose, on the average, $34,000 worth of income in 1978 for the years she dropped out taking care of her child, while a high-school dropout would lose only $16,000 in pay. The calculation considered both the years out of work and the wages each could earn, which were updated for inflation from a formula.

Women in the Baby Panic know that they can cut the cost of time out for a baby by coming back sooner. Just how much can be reduced to a formula. If you started earning $6,000 a year at 18, and received a 1 percent raise in real wages every year, you would lose $89,402.74 by stopping out for ten years between the ages of 25 and 35. You would lose $131,027.53 if you stopped out 15 years, but only $46,527.85 if you went back in five. And these losses are modest. The more you earn, of course, the more you lose.

A mathematician earning upward of $30,000 a year took one look at the formula, gasped, and refused to apply it to her own situation. "I'm just not willing to put a price tag on a baby," she objected. "And even if I were, this formula doesn't begin to count what I would really lose. It doesn't count promotions."

"Janie is riding a wave," her husband explained. "A wave that is carrying her straight to the top. If she got off the wave for any length of time, it might not be there when she comes back." Janie took no chances with her career. She took three weeks of sick leave to have the baby so she never went off the payroll at all. It often pays a mother to turn her entire paycheck over to a care-giver during the critical, career-building years just to stay on that wave, and many of them do.

In practice, a baby competes not only with time spent earning a paycheck, but with all the satisfaction a paycheck can buy as well. And if children have become, as the economists maintain, a consumer product, then children are no longer the kind of consumer product whose benefit is display, like a diamond, but the kind that economists call "time-intensive." Music lessons, for instance, are "time-intensive" because they take time. They are not worth the money if you don't have time to practice.

Many of the satisfactions that come from having children spring from one's relationships with them, and relationships take time. No matter how much you enjoy observing a child's growth and development, or teaching a child, or gathering shells with a child—these goodies remain academic if you don't have the time to engage in them.

But some of the benefits do not depend on inputs of time. You don't have to spend time with a child to insure your immortality, satisfy the expectations of friends or family, or prove you are a woman (all you have to do is have the children and get them started on a life track). In the recent past these values were more important than they are now.

Nor did career-bound wives in the past era suffer the Baby Panic. They "got their children over with" by having them in rapid succession, planned their deliveries during the slack season—summer, for college professors—and took work to the hospital. Back home, they cheerfully and proudly paid the going rates for the highest possible quality of child care available and expended their not inconsiderable executive talents on proving that they were women as well as whizzes in the office. For these women, children were achievements, not experiences. One advertising woman admitted she saw her children as extensions and symbols of her husband and herself. "My jewels." Status symbols for display, like a diamond.

Young, college-educated couples no longer expect to gain status from having children. What they want is a relationship that takes more time than absentee parenthood and is harder to "combine" with careers. They aren't really thinking about the high cost of college when they question whether they can afford a baby, or even whether they can find suitable child care, or work out sharing the diapering. What they really are questioning is whether time spent having fun with a child is going to be rewarding enough *to them personally* to be worth giving up the many other things they could do with the time.

HOW FATHERS FEEL

The Baby Panic spotlights a difference of view between men and women that dual-career couples have pushed aside during the early years of "roommate" marriage. Up to this point, they have shared the same feelings. Each wants the other for the same kind of love and companionship. She wants a career the way he wants a career. And when they talk about children, they see the same picture. On the Hoffman study, the first four reasons for having children were ranked in the same order by husbands as well as wives.

The only difference was that the relationship with a child meant more to her than it did to him. "In ten years," one brilliantly successful young television time saleswoman promised, "I will have my own radio station, or three children. *But I will not have both.*"

Her husband's feelings echoed her own. His feelings ran to her and through her to their children. Wife and child were a package deal. The nursery rhyme put it best: The farmer takes a wife, and the wife takes a child. It doesn't matter whether this is a biological tie, as Alice Rossi maintains, or merely reversible culture, as the classic feminists maintain. When children are wanted solely for the relationship, mothers are willing to give up more to have them than fathers.

Occasionally a husband wants the baby more than the wife. There are still some patriarchal, upper-class men who expect an unwilling wife to supply them with immortality, if not a son and heir. There are still some male chauvinists whose solution to an "uppity woman" is to get her pregnant so she will have to "go back home where she belongs." And every once in a while you run across the rare and interesting combination of a sensitive, poetic man who is willing to give up more of his time to a relationship with a child then the achievement-oriented woman he has married.

Usually, however, it's the other way around. When husband and wife disagree, it's the wife who wants the baby enough to give up more of her time to do it. She may wonder why a man cannot be more like a woman. She feels as strongly about a career as he does, so why can't he feel as strongly about having children as she does?

"How do you really feel?" she is always probing. "Are you willing to get up in the middle of the night when the baby cries?" The question is not so much a demand for logistical assistance as it is a test of the intensity of his interest. She is trying to find out whether the baby will really be as important to him as it will be to her. If it isn't, she fears for the equality and companionship she values in their marriage.

Now no decent man can refuse to do his share of whatever dirty work there is to raising a child. (And there is plenty.) But they do not and cannot share how it feels to be a mother. If she doesn't want a child enough to carry the emotional burden and give up more of her time than he does, she probably shouldn't have a child at all.

However he feels, it's her body and her decision, and normal, decent husbands are glad to leave it with her.

WHAT DOES A BABY DO TO CAREERS?

"I'd love to have a baby," a television producer told us. "We have maternity benefits in our contract, but I can't afford to be fat and clumsy for four or five months. Some woman is going to get an anchor spot around here next year, and it won't go to a woman who is pregnant."

Her problem was exceptional. In 1977, *The Wall Street Journal* estimated that 1.5 million pregnant women were working and doctors encouraged them to stay on the job as close to delivery as possible. Liz Richards, hostess of Cleveland's "Morning Exchange" television show, came close to having her baby on company time. Cleveland is a family town, and Liz didn't have to worry at all about looking pregnant on camera. On the contrary, public interest in her progress made the baby such news that the minicam followed her to the hospital.

Pregnancy is no longer a bar to high office. In 1970, Eleanor Holmes Norton happened to be pregnant when Mayor John Lindsay sounded her out on becoming New York City's Commissioner of Human Rights. Her news did not dismay him. What better equal opportunity symbol than a pregnant black woman? In 1977, New York City Mayor-elect Edward Koch chose an obviously pregnant woman for one of his deputy mayors and Governor Edmund G. Brown, Jr., appointed a pregnant woman judge.

Pregnant women sometimes embarrass old-fashioned males. Harriet Rabb, the civil-liberties lawyer, argued a case in court when she was eight months pregnant. When she stood up to give her summation, the judge ordered her to give it sitting down. She refused. "All right," said the judge, "then I'll stand up." He did, but when she went right on talking, he felt foolish and sat down again.

A great many very busy women take little more than a weekend off to have a baby. The president of a leading fashion goods company who spends a lot of time in Europe was so intent on a new promotion that she didn't realize she was pregnant until she was five months along. She hadn't worried about missing periods because she had stopped taking the Pill and figured it would take some time for her periods to become regular again. When she did get around to the doctor it was too late to do anything about the European campaign she had been planning, so she just went through with it, seven months pregnant, "bumpy back roads in France and all."

"Our European customers were charming about my condition," she recalls, "but the airlines won't take you if you are more than seven months pregnant, so I had to lie to get back to New York for the birth. He had the grace to arrive on New Year's Day, when everything was shut down, anyway." Time out: zero working days.

A woman who was paid on commission by a metropolitan bank for developing deposit accounts took only one day out for her baby. She worked the day before, had the baby the next morning by natural childbirth. The next day she returned to work in an office she had set up in her home. Normal childbirth seldom disables a healthy woman for longer than the minor illnesses and personal crises for which absence from work is expected.

The real problem is not the temporary disability of pregnancy and childbirth, but the parenting a child requires during the first few years. Although the most common solution is for the mother to stop working during that period, mothers who rise to the top seldom take it. Nearly half the women company officers studied by the executive search firm of Heidrick & Struggles had families, but only 14 percent had interrupted their careers for them. Skills rust during time out, and momentum is lost. Many women who have been on a career track for a number of years adjust poorly to full-time mothering. They seem especially prone to the baby blues. "I was forced to stay home when pregnant," an administrator wrote. "I was miserable until I made up my mind to go back to work." Finally, there is the wear and tear of making two major work adjustments if career mothers stop out and then return to work. Stopping work and starting it up again takes its toll in human terms, and there is evidence that it triggers fits of depression.

What a baby is going to do to your career, if you are the female half of a two-paycheck marriage, really depends on the stage you are at in your career, the flexibility of your schedule, the kind of help you have on the home front, and whether children drain or recharge your batteries. That, at least, is the experience of successful career mothers who have found ways around the bind of the male career timetable. Their experience is worth a closer look.

By accident or design, their children have come during quiet stages of their careers, before or after the crunch years when the payoff for extra effort is biggest. This is more possible than it sounds.

Early babies were the rule for achieving women in the past, when women didn't get a chance to show what they could do until their children were born and well on their ways. Even today, early babies sometimes fit in smoothly with schooling or training that cannot be speeded. The television producer who couldn't afford to look pregnant and clumsy had had no such problems with her first child, born when she had a beginning job and didn't work on camera. A Foreign Service Officer deliberately planned to have her children early because at that stage the work is more predictable and less demanding than in the higher ranks.

Generally speaking, however, in the 1970s, early babies have been career disasters. They interfere with the investment career-bound parents should be making in themselves.

"I'm not sure I'd have children if we had it to do over again," a discouraged professor of modern languages confessed. "You have to go to Europe every summer to get ahead in this field. Since the children, we haven't been able to afford it, even though my wife is working full time again." Before the children, his wife had worked to put him through graduate school. An economist would say that the children diverted her income from investment in his career.

You can have a baby before or after major career investment, but there are some careers you cannot interrupt once you've started up the ladder . . . and those are the careers that lead fastest and farthest to the top. Elementary schoolteaching and social work are ill-paid, dead-end fields precisely because they have adapted to the presumption that women will take time out from them to have babies.

The more promising a career, the more likely it is to lead straight to the top, the more a woman has to lose by taking time out for a baby. If you step off the ladder in any rewarding, advancing field you not only lose your place, but may never get back on it again. This is true of highly paid executive and technical jobs in fast-moving fields such as health care, research, fashion, communications, and entertainment. And these are the fields in which women take the least time out for their babies. Nursing used to be an interruptible career, but new techniques are being introduced so fast that a woman who has risen in it to the administrative level and drops out to have a baby faces a formidable retraining to get back in.

The bind of conforming to the male career ladder will probably be a bigger problem for women starting their careers in the 1970s than it was when all career women were anomalies who weren't allowed on the ladder to begin with and had to make their ways around the system, rather than rising within it.

Those women who got around the bind of the male career timetable often went into work that lent itself to flexible scheduling: teaching, writing, research, promotion and publicity, and the helping professions such as nursing, counseling, and social work. It was easier, of course, for women who had advanced to the point where they had some control over their schedules.

Professors, writers, researchers, and therapists have always done some of their work at home, and so have salespersons working on commission. In almost every field, the study and planning of career-level work involves hours of solitary concentration that can't be done in an office. Even a toddler is less of an interruption to serious thought than the clatter and chatter of many work places.

The woman banker who stayed in the hospital only twenty-four hours after delivering her baby arranged to work at home for the first four months of the baby's life. "There was a bad two months when she was colicky," she wrote, "but I hired a neighbor to sit six hours a day and that got me through it." She had her best quarter ever while staying at home. Her commissions added up to more than the salary of the bank's chairman, so they had "to cut my commission 40 percent," she explained, "to be palatable to everybody."

A surprising amount of career work can be fitted around the schedules of small children if it doesn't matter when and where it is done. There is nothing sacred about the schedules of small children, either. Dr. T. Berry Brazelton, Harvard professor of pediatrics, sees no reason why children should sit up during the day when they are being cared for by babysitters and go to bed when their parents come home. Why not encourage them to sleep on the babysitter's time and spend more of their waking time during the evening, when their parents are around? It's one of the ways that children can get closer to fathers as well as mothers.

And if work is portable, so are children. A shop owner in New Jersey takes her newborn to work with her and her first child as well. Customers are fascinated, she finds. The TV producer who was worried about being pregnant on camera brought her eight-year-old along to watch a film her company made. He didn't trip over the cables, and he knew when he couldn't make noise.

Mothers who bring up children when their careers are going full blast must have good backstops at home. Sometimes it is a mother, a sister, an aunt, a friend who enjoys the role. Sometimes it's a husband whose hours are more flexible than hers. It can also be a professional care-giver for whom a place has been made in the family. When I needed some home backstopping for my son, I advertised for an "honorary aunt" and tapped a plentiful supply of wonderful older women who never would have answered a "Help Wanted" ad for a housekeeper.

Finally, for some women at least, childbirth and nursing can be an invigorating experience that liberates energy for work and generates a surge of self-confidence. When Olive Ann Beech's second child was born, her husband was in a coma, from which he never fully recovered, in another room of the same hospital. The Beech

Aircraft Company was in danger. Olive Ann started running it by phone from her hospital bed and never relinquished control. It became a major manufacturer of World War II planes.

So far as baby care goes some women report—rather ominously —that they are so absorbed by the care of their child that they can't think of anything else. "My brains turned to mush," a writer told us. "The only words I write are the ones I put on the shopping list." They may have no interest in following the news or even in getting rid of the fat that has built up during pregnancy.

For a woman who has been active in her work—even on the verge of success—this narrowing of focus is suspicious. It suggests that the baby is serving as protection against the next step up in her career. Rather than risk a height that may be dizzying, one can cop out by having a baby. For these women, a baby is a failsafe, a respectable way out of confronting what looms to them as an obstacle.

Matina Horner, President of Radcliffe College, would say that these women "fear success." Horner's study of women college freshmen during the 1960s found that they feared that career success would unwoman them. And sure enough, when Lois Wladis Hoffman, the Michigan psychologist, followed up the freshmen who had feared success, she found that they often quit to have babies just when their careers began to blossom. Meanwhile, however, a replication of Horner's original study at Michigan found that men were as likely to "fear success," too, although they could not, of course, have babies to get out of it.

If a woman fears that having a baby will "turn her brains to mush" she would do well to remind herself that there is no physiological basis for this fear, and ask herself why she feels this way. A baby has been the classical solution for problems women don't want to face, from lagging careers to bad marriages.

On balance, it's important to distinguish between the short-term and long-term impact of children on careers. A baby can be an awkward obstacle if it comes at the wrong time. It can deter a parent from taking the risks or making the investment of time that leads to promotion. For couples who have been concentrating on career success, the decision to have a baby is threatening because it forces them to examine the noncareer side of their lives they've neglected. They have to ask themselves, for the long-term is work enough to fill the rest of our lives?

WHAT WILL IT DO TO OUR MARRIAGE?

Baby has always been the interloper who made the family love affair a triangle. Victorians accepted the competition between father and baby for a mother's love with good humor. For two-career couples, the competition presents a very new problem. After studying the reactions husbands and wives had to anticipating their first baby, sociologist Ralph La Rossa suggested that since marriage as an institution is becoming more and more a companionship arrangement, the first pregnancy will increasingly become a crisis for the marital system.

"We actually have to budget time together," a career wife pursuing her first big promotion complained. "How on earth could we ever find time for a baby? It would have to come out of the time we spend together, and I'd hate to choose between a baby and my husband!"

Young couples living on two family-sized salaries have the means to follow their impulses. If they see a thing they want, they buy it. If they think of something to do, they do it. "Last night we decided on the spur of the moment to pack up right away and fly to Canada for a weekend of skiing—next week it could be California—or Europe," one couple told us. "You can't do that when you have children!"

Even more ominous, for working couples, is the prospect of a shift in the delicate balance of marital power they have negotiated to accommodate both jobs. Generally speaking, studies of marital power conclude that a baby shifts power from her to him. Sometimes, a traditional dependent wife can use the baby to get more of her own way than she had before. She may use her pregnancy to get her husband to mop the kitchen floor or take out the garbage, if he hasn't been doing these chores. She may egg him on to make more money, or stay at home nights instead of going out with the boys.

For a working couple where the wife must quit to care for the child, a baby means that she loses the power her paycheck has brought her. "I don't want a baby," a wife with a master's degree told us. "I'd then be 'just a housewife,' a position that means 'lazy' to my colleagues and me."

A husband La Rossa interviewed looked forward to the baby he and his wife were expecting because "I will then be the sole breadwinner and my authority will go up." His wife, a bookkeeper whose career had been going well, laughingly denied this. "He can think that way," she said lightly, "if he wants. I figured I'd better have one before I got too ambitious in my job. I was getting a lot of promotions."

A baby is particularly threatening, however, for two-career couples who are sincerely trying to build an equal marriage. Tact, and a careful avoidance of issues may have made it easy to live out the rhetoric of equality during the early, baby-free years. They may not realize, until they start talking logistics, that their scenarios of family life diverge. Male college students may expect their wives to quit working while children are young without realizing that the women college students they are dating expect to work straight through.

It is easy to agree to having a baby as an abstract proposition. Men accustomed to the rhetoric of equality find it easy to agree to go 50–50 in caring for a child. Wives suspect, and rightly, that they agree all too easily.

"Are you willing to change half the diapers?" one wife inquired. "Not just the wet ones, but the ones with a 'load'?"

It was obvious from his expression that he had no visual image of what he was promising to do. But then the light dawned. "Oh, a *load*. God!"

"I think what would happen," she said, "is that when you found you had a load, you'd ask me to take care of it, even if I were busy doing something else."

Wives have good reason to worry that the cavalier promises to help may not be honored after the child is born. Some of them have drawn up explicit written agreements—you do the child care on every other day, every other diaper, every other feeding. An airline stewardess divorced her husband because he reneged on their agreement to share care. The breaking point came when he hired a babysitter to take care of the child when it was his turn and expected her to pay half of it.

Even when both want the baby, she is willing to give up more freedom for it than he is. Husbands who want a baby when their wives are reluctant almost always expect all the benefits—love, affection, watching the child grow, fun—without any of the loss of freedom that is the biggest disadvantage of children for both sexes. Quite often, husbands enthusiastic about becoming fathers are fantasizing the restoration of the traditional marital contract. "He would like nothing better than to have me stay home and have babies," one working wife wrote us. "I'm simply going to have to say no."

When it comes to an outright disagreement, few husbands want a baby enough to do all of the work of caring for it. A lawyer whose husband kept pestering her to have a baby says she told him to go out and adopt one, and he did. They split all other household expenses, but he pays the salary of a full-time housekeeper-governess who takes full charge of the child. She's glad they have the little girl, but won't let her husband adopt a companion for her. "We know what it's like to be parents now," she argues.

When husbands and wives disagree about having a child, it's usually the other way around: the wife wants it, but the husband doesn't. Men seem to feel less strongly about the advantages as well as the disadvantages of parenthood.

A common bargain is the one made by the wife who worked to put her husband through college on the understanding that she would have a baby when he was able to take over the breadwinning. When the time came, however, he reneged on the gound that the child would "interfere with our relationship." She had the baby anyway, but had to give up her plan for staying home with it.

Many women give up having children because their husbands don't want them, "wouldn't be good fathers," or because they suspect that the marriage itself could not stand the strain of parental responsibility. Their fears may be justified. Children can make some marriages more stable by providing a common responsibility. But this is not to say that they actually improve the *marital* relationship.

An analysis of the national "Quality of American Life" surveys of 1971 and 1974, made by Mary Jo Banes of the Wellesley Center for Research on Women, found that people were most likely to say that their *marriages* were happy either when they were expecting their first child, or after all their children were grown and gone. They were least likely to rate their marriages happy when their children were at home going to school. And one of the most reliable findings on the happiness of marriage is that marriages last longer and are more satisfying if the husband and wife have a few years alone together before the children arrive.

HOW LONG CAN YOU WAIT?

Women old enough to become household words in the 1970s generally have had their children, if any, before they became famous. Secretary of Commerce Juanita Kreps, Congresswoman Margaret Heckler from Massachusetts, feminist author Betty Friedan, and physicist Rosalynn Yalow, winner of the Nobel prize in medicine, are a few of the eminent women of the 1970s who had their babies before they were thirty, while they were just getting started in their life work.

Women starting out in the 1970s are trying to reverse the sequence and establish themselves in their careers before they start families. The biological deadline is a good fifteen years beyond the crisis age thirty, and some distinguished career women have not hesitated to start late. Margaret Mead and Shana Alexander, the television commentator, postponed motherhood until they were more than 35. Yvonne Burke married while running for Congress from California and at 41 became the first Representative to be granted maternity leave by the Speaker.

One of the most candidly reported late families is that of sociologist Jessie Bernard, whose books, *The Future of Marriage* and *The*

Future of Motherhood are feminist classics. In her fascinating *Self-Portrait of a Family,* she tells how she married her professor in college, established herself as a scholar and thought she would never want children. Her husband felt the same. When she was more than 30, she changed her mind and stayed with her husband only on condition that they would have them. The first of her three was born when she was 38.

In the 1970s young women climbing the career ladder are following their example.

These achieving women are too few yet to show up in the statistics, but they tend to be occupational elites who know and reinforce each other. In 1976, only 5 percent of first babies were born to women over 30. One percent were born to women over 35.

The *physiological* danger of late childbirth to mother and child are not all that impressive. Your chances of bearing a mongoloid, mentally retarded child do rise as you grow older, from one in 3,000 when you are under thirty to one in 40 when you are over forty-four. The sharp rise is frightening, of course. It makes you feel you haven't a moment to lose. But the odds are long against it even at the end, 30 to 40 *against,* if you look at it that way. (I probably feel this way because I have successfully confronted them.)

Today older mothers need not worry about the odds. Mongolism and other chromosomal abnormalities now can be detected early enough in a pregnancy for a safe abortion if the fetus is defective. And by great good fortune, these detectable defects are the *only* ones that are related to the age of the mother. Heart disease, diabetes, and a long list of other ailments are more common in older women, but the chromosomal abnormalities are the only conditions that need worry a healthy older mother.

Your chances of getting pregnant decline with age, it's true. And your chances of a complicated delivery are higher. But as my doctor assured me at the time, age alone does not wear out the reproductive machinery before egg production stops at menopause. (Medicine had made childbirth so much easier and safer that my chances of trouble were actually smaller when I was 46 than they were when I was 19.)

The truth is that we have all been oversold on the *health* advantages of starting our families early. That's the considered judgment of Barbara Seaman, author of *Women and the Crisis in Sex Hormones,* one of the few medical writers who has bothered to sort out what we actually know about late childbirth. She puts the optimum time for starting a family between 25 and 35, but concludes that if a woman is otherwise healthy and enthusiastic about having a baby, age alone should not deter her. She warns that the real danger affecting many more women is having a baby in your teens, before the reproductive machinery has had a chance to mature.

The Baby Panic begins at 30, then, for reasons other than medical. Doctors admit as much. According to the medical journal, *Obstetrics and Gynecology,* "elderly primigravidas" (the medical term for women pregnant for the first time when they are more than 35 years of age) "will be more apt to have dysfunctional labor on an emotional basis either because psychologic problems prevented their marrying earlier or because a long period of infertility had a psychogenic base."

What the doctors are saying is that you are in for emotional problems if you don't have your babies when society expects you to have them. That time is reinforced by public opinion. ("All our friends were having babies.") And the policing need not be subtle.

Just before my son was born, a mother of three children all under five wanted to know whether I wasn't "kind of embarrassed to be pregnant" at my advanced age. It stopped conversation at the cocktail party. "As a matter of fact," I told her, "I'm foolishly proud." Instead, I felt I should have asked her whether she felt embarrassed at having three babies as soon and as fast as she could.

The "right time" to have a baby is socially determined and it varies with times and places. If history is a guide, late babies are more "natural" than the assembly-line feats of fertility that became the suburban pride after World War II. Alice Rossi points out that prolonged breast feeding inhibited pregnancy before the age of birth control. The result was that babies spaced themselves three or more years apart—a more comfortable arrangement, the experts now think, than closely spaced families.

The baby boom following World War II goes far to explain why the panic age is now 30. In the 1970s, women of 30 are suddenly aware that they haven't started to have children at the age when their mothers were beginning to be through with childbearing.

There are some drawbacks to having a baby when you are older. After I got my son to bed I sometimes had to turn in myself, and my husband has been known to fall asleep on his bed after getting him into it. Then, too, you worry about dying before the child grows up.

The child of older parents tends to be less childish. He's not tossed around physically as much, and since he interacts more with his parents, he tends to "talk old."

There is much, however, to recommend starting a family after careers and identities are established. Older parents have more money, so if they can't run after a toddler all day, they are at least better able to hire someone else to do some of it. They are more patient, too. And it's easier to dish out consistent discipline if you are under better control yourself.

HOW DO YOU REALLY FEEL ABOUT CHILDREN?

In the end, it comes down to feelings. A couple with the wit for successful careers can cope with the logistics of caring for a baby if they urgently want one. The question is how much they want one. And though the depth of people's feelings about children haven't been carefully studied, the fact is that individuals differ widely in how much they are willing to give up to have them.

Most women have trouble sorting out their feelings because they haven't been encouraged to be candid about them. Not only does every woman blow hot and cold about the impending experience of childbirth, but women differ unpredictably one from the other. If we had reliable measures, we would probably find that women distribute themselves along a wide spectrum. At one end are the passionate mothers who yearn for a child. At the other, the women who find the thought repellent. The vast majority of women fall somewhere in between.

"You know how it is," one woman tried to explain to another who said she didn't want to have a baby. "When you see a baby, you have to look at it, the way men have to look at a beautiful woman."

"Well, I don't," her friend retorted. "I don't look at babies at all."

There was nothing more to say to her. If she didn't understand it, you couldn't explain it to her. Some women are literally addicted to childbirth. "He became prosperous as doctors are apt to do in this country," a woman told us, "and I kept on having babies. I would reach a certain point with each child in two years, when I began to feel I was not totally involved, so I would just have another. I was 31 when we reached number 6, and if it had been up to me I could have gone on until the reproductive machinery gave out."

A passionate mother may not realize, when she marries, that what she really wants out of marriage is a child. When a brilliant young lawyer discovered that her husband didn't want children, she stopped taking her pills and got pregnant anyway. He was so angry he left her, but she happily managed by taking the baby to the office with her. But two years later the baby urge came over her so strongly that she considered reconciling with him long enough to get pregnant again with the understanding that she would take full responsibility for the baby. Why not find a man who really did want children? "Because I'm thirty-four and too busy to go husband-hunting."

It's easy for these passionate mothers to choose a baby over other investments of their time and energy. Their desire for a baby is physically compelling.

The decision against having a baby is easy, too, for those who are physically repelled by the prospect. Society hasn't treated non-mothers well in the past. In the 1970s, they fare much better. They are merely made to feel that they may be missing something life-enriching if they don't have at least one child "for the experience."

The decision is hard, however, for the majority of women whose bodies send them no signals. These women will do well to consider what attracts them about motherhood. If what they need is to nurture, could they be just as happy nurturing plants, pets, friends, patients, clients, or even a whole organization? If what they really want is a relationship with a child, does the child have to be *their* child? "I'm working with children all day long," a teacher explained. "And I love it. I give them my all. But it's very nice at the end of the day not to have to feed children and put them to bed. It's nice to get home and find my husband the only one waiting for me there."

Others have developed continuing relationships with nieces and nephews that allow them to watch children grow. These nonparental relationships can be uniquely rewarding on both sides. "I don't have to deal with her angry moments," a godmother said of her small ward, "and she doesn't see me as one of those grownups who is always saying 'no.' " More objective relationships with children are often more gratifying than ambivalent relationships with blood off-spring.

Contemporary two-career couples are finding other ways to attain some of the benefits commonly cited as reasons for having children. Contemporary wives are finding that occupational achievement is a less risky and even less demanding way to establish identity and the respect of others than gaining accolades through the traditional route of motherhood.

AND IF NEVER . . .

Very few couples start out to be childless. They just put off think-ing about children until something happens to show them that they don't intend to have them. Thinking about babies is hard because the issue is always being approached from the negative side. As soon as the subject comes up, they have to produce reasons why they *don't* want to have children.

This is a puzzling question for people who have nothing in particular *against* children, but no urgent desire to have them, either. Like many other childless couples, Bob and Gloria didn't realize at first that they didn't want children. Gloria was educated in parochial schools, and it was all she could do when she married to talk about birth control with their Catholic doctor. "He asked me how long I'd be on it," she recalls. "And I remember answering, as clear as a bell, 'Until Bob gets out of school.'

"So when he got out of school, I had to go to another doctor. When this one asked me how long I'd be on it I said, 'Until we get the furniture.' And I can give you five different deadlines. The next was 'until we get some money for a house.' "

After six years of this, they finally sat down and agreed that Gloria had better get a tubal ligation, but they couldn't find a doctor who would do it. "That's a technical decision," one gynecologist told her. "You don't know what you are talking about. You'll grow up some day and then you will want a child." She asked him how long she could stay on the Pill without risk and he told her it didn't matter. Some day she would grow up and then she would want a child.

"But I'm thirty-six years old," she expostulated. "Old enough to know my own mind. If I bring a child into the world and change my mind, I hurt the child. If I tie my tubes and change my mind, I hurt only myself."

Gloria found another doctor and had her tubes tied. Just to keep her company in the decision, Bob had a vasectomy. And neither of them has ever regretted the decision for one minute.

Couples who say "No" to babies seldom miss them. "Oh, sometimes I think it might have been nice to have had a kid or two," a career wife of 40 admitted. "But I'm not ever actually *sad* about it. It's pretty hard to miss something you never really wanted in the first place."

The astonishing fact is that in the late 1970s, couples are as likely to regret *having* children as *not having* them. In 1976, when Ann Landers asked the readers of her syndicated column whether they would have children if they had it to do over again, 70 percent of those who wrote in said "no." "I was an attractive, fulfilled career woman before I had these children," a 40-year-old mother of two wrote from Tampa, Florida. "Now I am an exhausted, nervous wreck who misses her job and sees very little of her husband. He's got a 'friend,' I'm sure, and I don't blame him. Our children took all the romance out of our marriage. I'm too tired for sex, conversation, or anything else. Sign me, Too Late for Tears."

The disgruntled, of course, are the ones who write, but the numbers were dismaying. Nobody expected that 7,000 parents were disappointed enough in their children to write in to a newspaper about it. The complaints came from older parents whose grown children ignored them, young people tied down with little children, and people allegedly worried about overpopulation.

Meanwhile, that same year, several hundred of our Matching Couples volunteered the information that they didn't have children, didn't want any, and were happy because they didn't have any. This was surprising because we hadn't asked them how they felt about children, merely whether they had them. Yet many of the unsolicited comments were explicit and even lyrical. "We are happily child-free," a riding instructor in her thirties wrote from North Carolina. "We have an equality and rapport which is delightful. My husband, a potter-sculptor, is a gentle and sensitive (and sexy!) man."

"Our marriage is very happy and so are most of our friends," a computer programmer writes from California. "The wives work, and there are no children." "We don't want children," a medical assistant from California explained. "Because of this I am able to pursue a career which makes me more interesting and I also share the responsibility of our marriage. It's perfect for us." A secretary writes in from Tulsa, Oklahoma, to tell us that the decision to never have children is "the best decision we have ever made."

"We are extremely happily married," a claims representative working for the government wrote from California. "Married 26 years. No children. I've always worked. I think not having children has helped." Her husband, an electronics engineer earning more than $20,000 in a government job is even more explicit. "How does one know how life would be with a mother mate? Kids kill most marriages."

"Children are the worst things that can happen to a marriage," a sprinkler system designer from Little Rock told us. "It is not one of women's God-given rights to have kids and then sit home raising them. Men gave them the right to quit work to raise kids, and men should take it away." His wife, a receptionist, agrees. "All of our friends who had children are unhappy and/or divorced. We do not want any children because they hinder a marriage." Others wrote in to assure us that a couple could be a family. "It isn't that we don't like children," a secretary from Michigan wrote, "but we don't need them because we have each other."

If couples who say "No" are defensive, they have good reason. They have to be "explained" by society, and the explanation is never that they are strong individuals able to resist social pressure, but that they are immature or selfish. The only acceptable reason for remaining childless advanced by respondents to the Virginia Slims poll of 1974 was the high cost of rearing children and the danger of "overpopulation."

Doubts about the value of children are relatively recent. In 1960, for instance, not one of the Detroit wives interviewed by Blood and Wolfe for their classic study of marital adjustment gave the trouble children cause as a reason for not having them. Wives who didn't have them felt frustrated, and none of those who did could see that their children were interfering with their marriages, although it was obvious to the interviewers. "Companionship with children," they suggested, "may be a substitute for companionship with their husbands."

History explains this oversight. Before widespread birth control, childless couples were presumed to be sterile. This was regarded as a catastrophe, and it was always blamed on the wife. A barren wife was in trouble. In some times and places—and even now among the Middle Eastern royalty—her husband might turn her in for a successor who could bear him a son and heir. At best, there was always a cloud on a childless marriage. The wife was expected to make up to her husband for the child that she couldn't give him.

Better health in general and medical advances in particular have made it possible for most couples to have children if they want them, but social attitudes haven't caught up with the change. In the 1960s, childless couples continued to be pitied as people who had missed something they are bound to regret because there was something wrong with them.

Just exactly *what* they are missing is described vaguely as "fulfillment." But if "fulfillment" is anything more than another name for doing your duty, it is a will-o'-the-wisp no one really ever attains. Gail Sheehy, for instance, thinks that women who postpone babies are going to want to have them in their thirties and forties, but according to the stages she sets up in *Passages,* you are bound, at that age, to regret whatever it was you didn't do. So far, the regrets of women who gave up careers to have babies are far more widespread than the regrets of women who gave up babies for careers.

The expectation of regret keeps the voluntarily childless defensive. Rather than say "No, Never," they prefer to keep the door open for the predicted change of sentiment later on.

"Maybe in ten years," a 29-year-old speech therapist took the trouble to write us.

"If I had a rich husband, I'd probably have a child," a usually clear-headed writer told us, not two minutes after explaining she has married her present husband *because* he had two children by a former marriage and didn't want any more. "I won't have time for a child until I'm forty, and then maybe I'll adopt an older child."

"Adopting instead" was popular among the conscientious in the early 1970s, when it looked as if overpopulation would threaten the environment and inundate Mother Earth with more mouths than could be fed from it. College students wore buttons proclaiming their decision to "Have One, Adopt One." One for the experience— lest they miss out on something precious—and one to nurture from among the millions of starving, unwanted, and unloved.

Adopting proved you weren't selfish and that you liked children. An exploratory study of voluntarily childless wives in the early 1970s convinced sociologist J. E. Veevers that the intention to adopt was an attempt to deny the charges made against the childless "while not seriously threatening the accompanying lifestyle."

As it turned out, most of them didn't do it. "Adopting was a sort of way station," a New York City teacher on maternity leave told us. "We thought that adopting a child already conceived was taking less responsibility than deciding to create a human being of your own from scratch. But before we carried out the plan, it dawned on both of us that we were taking on just as much responsibility in adopting a child as we would have had in having our own. And we decided that we needed a tie that was stronger than our own wishes to tide us over the rough spots of relating to a new human being."

There was much less talk of adopting in 1979. The birth rate had dropped so sharply that it no longer seemed particularly noble to refrain from adding to the American population. There weren't enough adoptable children to go around in the United States, and it wasn't proving practical to import very many from India or Vietnam. For one thing, those teeming countries weren't eager to see their children go.

Those who still talked about adopting were frankly concerned with a possible change of mind about children beyond the biological deadline, but few of them had investigated the possibility seriously enough to encounter the objection of social agencies to placing children with parents beyond childbearing age.

Couples debating the baby decision worry too much about "regretting it later." No one is immune to speculation about what life would have been like with another mate or another occupation, but these retrospective fancies seldom darken an otherwise satisfying life. Couples who decide against children do not lead the melancholy lives of couples who were physiologically incapable of bearing children whom they urgently desired.

The evidence is to the contrary. Studies show that the childless are actually happier than parents. Angus Campbell and his associates at the University of Michigan found that childless wives were much more satisfied with their lives and more apt to say that they were happy than counterpart mothers of preschool children, and another of his studies established that childless husbands were happier than counterparts who were fathers, too.

Couples who know that they want something else much more urgently than they want babies are very apt to find fulfillment in their chosen agendas. Some of the childless lead lives that could never have been as productive if they had taken time out to parent. Joyce Carol Oates married a professor of English as soon as she got out of college and settled down to turning out a stream of brilliant novels instead of babies. It is a fair question what rearing a family would have done to her meteoric literary career. Many others less spectacularly successful have achieved identity and satisfaction creating "brainchildren" or nurturing an organization, students, patients, or causes.

An alternative agenda that attracts a rising proportion of young college graduates is the marriage itself. They are right in assuming that children will dull it. All studies of marriage show that the marriage is most satisfying at the outset, drops when children are born, hits bottom just before adolescent children depart, and recovers modestly when the nest is empty again. Couples who say "No" to babies in order to nurture their marriages may succeed in prolonging the honeymoon and even in retaining some of its attractive features throughout their entire lives.

Bob and Gloria have made their marriage into a work of art. They jog together in the morning. They phone each other at least once during the day to say "Don't mind what I said at breakfast." If either is especially busy, it may be only a quick "I love you." They give each other presents for no reason at all. They cook together at night when they don't go out to gourmet restaurants.

"I prolong the drinks and cooking," Gloria says, "because it's our special time together." Dinner takes several hours of leisurely talk. Sunday morning they stay in bed, making love, until Bob gets hungry enough to get up and make waffles. But they are both into so many different hobbies that they feel every bit as pressed for time as busy parents do.

"We're interest-oriented rather than career-oriented," Bob explains. One of their interests is foreign travel. They've been to every European country west of the Iron Curtain and their five-year plan calls for knocking off all the countries in the Middle East as well. Gloria's hobby is investments. Bob likes to carpenter. Gloria's investment club decided in the early 1970s that real estate was the only chance to make your money grow, so they decided to build a house in the mountains, near the wild country Bob likes. They bought it as a shell and have put all the plumbing, wiring and finishing into it weekends and vacations. They've doubled their money.

Money is more of a hobby than a problem. She is a systems analyst; he is an engineer. They met in a math class at college. "We're not your cool supercouple," Gloria assured me. "Time together is much more important than getting ahead. And when we get job offers in different cities we don't resolve the conflict in favor of the partner who has the most to gain, but in favor of the one who has the most to lose. Bob gave up a wonderful career opportunity because it required him to be away from home more nights a week than we wanted. And he turned down another offer because it meant moving to Tucson the year I had a project here I particularly enjoyed."

Lately, Gloria has been teaching math at the local high school. She likes it because she can shop on her way home and take a leisurely soak in the tub before getting dressed up for the evening. She spends a lot of time on her clothes and has a huge closet full of them. One reason is that she can't bear to throw away a garment associated with some special good time they have had together.

Neither has anything against children. They both have nieces and nephews and tend to spoil them like grandparents. They invite each school-age child for a special, solo visit each summer, during which they plan activities around the child's special interests. The high point for one nephew was a three-hour stay at the Aquarium, a longer time than his busy mother ever had been able to spend.

The problems they have wouldn't worry hard-pressed parental couples. One of them is that Bob likes to ski, and Gloria's ankles can't make it. He's bought her special ski clothes and she's taken lessons, but the sport doesn't take on her. He's stopped skiing and that worries her.

She's a reader and he isn't. She sometimes reads while they are watching television, and that hurts his feelings.

Another problem is relatives. Bob's octogenarian father decided they had plenty of room and he came to stay. There was no way of explaining that they liked having the house alone to themselves. "He just doesn't understand privacy," Gloria wailed. Bob finally asked his father to go—but Gloria thinks he resented her complaints about him.

The biggest compliment Gloria has ever received, she thinks, is the comment of an uncle who confided that he and his wife were planning to separate as soon as their children were grown. "There's no reason on earth why you and Bob should stay together," he observed, "yet you do. You have a perfect marriage."

During the whirlwind years of career foundation after college,

Cindy and David—the couple we met in the opening pages of this chapter—had been able to keep most of their options open. Children were merely one of the options to be taken up later on. Only when the biological deadline loomed on the horizon did they start to realize that they couldn't have everything.

Neither they nor their friends knew how to begin thinking about babies. No one could give them good, clear answers to their simplest questions. Whether they could afford a baby, they found, depended on what else they wanted. Doctors couldn't really tell them how long they could safely postpone the decision, and there was no way of predicting from the human record what life would be like— for them—if they never had children at all. What a baby would do to their marriage and career aspirations depended on what they wanted out of life and how they intended to go about getting it.

Once they had researched their personal answers to these questions, they discovered that the panic was not over having a baby, but over the lifestyle they wanted to choose for themselves.

There were infinite possibilities.

CHAPTER 10

The Two-Career Collision Course

If her Age Thirty Crisis is the Baby Panic, his is the Bind of the Two Person Career. Successful male careers have so often involved the support of an unofficial Second Person—a supportive wife who frees him to give everything to his work—that many careers have come to require this backup. At the beginning, while they are establishing their competence, two-career couples need no more help from each other than college roommates. But as soon as they get into serious career politics and need a Second Person, they find there is a limit to what they can do to back each other up.

This is the bind. She sees it first. She may say she needs a wife, but all she has is a husband, and everyone knows that husbands don't do the work of corporate, political, or academic wives.

He has a wife, so it takes him a little longer to see that the rules of the career game have been made by men married to Second Persons. He may not see the bind until something happens to show him that his own wife isn't doing what those men's wives do.

For a rising marketing manager, it was having to meet his boss at the London airport with a cheap canvas duffel bag for luggage.

He had decided to go on the spur of the moment and couldn't find his suitcase. His wife was in a plans board meeting at her advertising agency, but he made them call her out to the phone. "Oh my God," she said. "I never got around to unpacking it. It's in my station wagon full of my summer clothes. Darling, I can't leave and I can't talk now. Just go out and buy yourself a new one." By that time the only store open was the corner drugstore.

It dawned on him, at that moment, that a vice-president of marketing should have instant access to a suitcase that was not full of somebody else's summer clothes. He was right.

Career Rule One says that the First Person of the career couple doesn't have to worry about the logistics of food, clothing, or shelter, while working. Food, clothing, and shelter are to be as available as water from the kitchen tap. Wherever the careerist labors, at home or at work, meals appear whenever he is hungry. Dirty clothes pick themselves up and hang themselves pressed and cleaned in the closet, and plumbing emergencies are strictly for somebody else. The only maintenance time he is expected to take is for matters requiring his physical presence, such as visits to doctors, lawyers, dentists, barbers, or for civil duties such as voting and serving on juries.

Career couples may start to live by the "roommate test" devised by Sandra and Daryl Bem, psychologists from Stanford University. Home chores are divided on the basis of personal preference, hired out to a paid helper, or simply left undone. But as careers advance they both have to find ways to meet the competition from men who have Second Persons managing the home front. Rather than admit they have any "outside" commitments, they may have to keep their attempts at equality a secret. She may feel, for instance, that she has to bend over backward to disprove the suspicion that she is staying at home for family duties, and he may not wish to have it known he has to leave early to do the marketing or pick up a child from the sitter.

An accountant discovered the bind when he was offered a partnership in a growing firm in Phoenix, Arizona, but realized there would be no job available for his wife there. And it said right in their personally written marriage contract that neither would take a job in a place where an equally good opportunity could not be found for the other. It hadn't worried him at the time, because accountants can always find work anywhere—but not an opportunity like this one!

Career Rule Two says that the First Person of the career must be ready to work whenever and wherever it best serves the career. A growing number of young career couples agree to go where the best opportunity offers, whether for the wife or the husband, but this always means violating this Career Rule for one of them. A computer specialist agreed always to follow his wife, on the ground that it was easier for him to find work than for her. A wife with a Ph.D. in nuclear physics, on the contrary, agreed to go wherever her husband, a chemist specializing in law, could find work in his esoteric specialty.

The career needs of a wife can handicap the career mobility of a man in exactly the same way that women traditionally have been handicapped by the presumption that they will always follow their husbands. The experience of Joseph Juhasz, professor of psychology, suggests that the handicap may be more severe for a husband because it is less expected. When Bucknell University refused to hire his wife, he followed her to the University of Colorado at Boulder. Eventually he landed a job in her new location, but only after being snubbed by her new colleagues and suspected by prospective employers. No one believed that a competent man would quit to follow his wife.

A real career means frequent moves on short notice as opportunities arise. Many organizations groom their promising candidates for promotion by giving them short-term experience all over the country. Those who refuse seldom get another chance. Big companies expect a candidate for promotion to be ready to take on the challenge of a new job in another city with little or no time out for the work of moving there.

This is hard on women officers, who seldom have a "corporate wife" to do the packing and relocating. It is particularly hard on a single mother being groomed for promotion, because she has no one to house-hunt for her in the new location or even to watch her children while she attempts to do it for herself. But a candidate whose wife is not a Second Person may be even worse off than a single mother if his wife has a serious career commitment in the area he is being asked to leave.

There are a number of bases on which the couple can make the decision. They can maximize immediate money earnings: if there's no good job for her, they won't go. They can maximize career opportunity: if his prospects are much greater than hers, she'll go. They can refuse any change unless both stand to profit equally.

As the proportion of two-career families increases, bureaucracies may find it harder to groom promising candidates this way. But in spite of public criticism they are not changing very fast. A man with a career wife continues to be at a disadvantage. In the economic recession of the late 1970s, bureaucracies were not hurting for talent. For every middle manager who refused a move, five others were eager to go.

Career Rule Three says that the First Person of the career has a cheering section at home, and there's a reason why. If a dedicated professional is to be coolly objective, he is going to need to get his own emotional support off the job, preferably from someone who won't set up a second set of waves. A career wife may want to give this support, but finds the timing awkward. She may not be available just when her husband badly needs relaxation, recreation, or simply a friendly ear.

Career couples can buck each other up, but they can also buck each other down. This is what happened to an accountant on the day he was promoted to head of his department. The news thrilled him, but it scared him, too. On the way back to his office he avoided the curious inquiries of the colleagues he would soon have to supervise and thought only of what his wife would say when he told her the good news that night. But when he got home he found she had been so badly humiliated during her day at the office that he felt his good news would make her feel even worse. He hid the split of champagne he had brought home to celebrate and settled down to listen. After hours of assuring her that a job didn't matter all that much, he found himself believing his own words and losing enthusiasm for his own recent triumph.

Employers count on continuing enthusiasm in candidates for

promotion, and they recognize the importance of dependent wives in maintaining it. "I'd gone up in the corporation as far as I could go as a single man," an executive vice-president confessed to John Cuber, author of *The Significant Americans.* "Why they are so prejudiced in favor of married men, I'll never know. Maybe it's those psychological adjustment guys in Personnel."

Salesmen need so much emotional support from home that companies woo their wives with presents and trips. At conventions, they may offer wives tips on how to help their husbands get ahead. Much of the advice draws heavily on the crude flattery advocated by the "true womanhood" cults: "Don't nag," one lecturer advised, and, "watch your figure." Since affirmative action, convention programs for "wives" have been renamed programs for "spouses," but no counterpart books or programs school company husbands in fulfilling the supportive role.

This does not mean, however, that emotional support is not going to be demanded of *him.* According to psychiatrist Ruth Moulton, successful women need unusual emotional support from men, and the Hennig and Jardim study of managerial women bears her out. A wife with a rising career may have been launched by a supportive father or mentor and expect the same continual encouragement from a husband. Moulton found successful women patients often used their husbands as sounding boards and support systems for advice about how to handle difficult men, approval of their papers, help with framing letters and coaching about every move ahead. Husbands may have encouraged them in the beginning, but eventually they felt used, bored, and resentful. Moulton goes on to say that a wife denied emotional support at home is tempted to look for it on the job from a boss, colleague, or even a subordinate on the job.

"Somehow, I never got down to finishing the book," a professor explained when he lost out on tenure. "When Joan wasn't working she could run down references in the library for me. She was always available for typing and reading. But when she went to work she lost interest in my project—and so did I. When the time came for tenure review, I just didn't have the publications for the promotion."

Career Rule Four says that the First Person of a successful career gets direct assistance in his work from an unpaid Second Person at home. For those now at the top, it began innocently enough. An ambitious young husband brought work home. His young wife was not only eager to share his work, but she was also the only other person with a financial interest in it. She typed, filed, kept books, checked facts, answered phones, made appointments. Later on she listened, learned, entertained, made friends who could help. Her unpaid work may have been the most profitable use of her time. According to an analysis made by Lee Benham, an economist at Washington University in St. Louis, a woman's college education does more to raise the income of her husband than it does to increase the income she can earn herself.

As the career advanced, so did the staff work for which there was as yet no money. Ministers' wives kept church books. Doctors' wives relayed critical messages. Political wives distributed leaflets, organized meetings, knocked on doors, stuffed envelopes. The wives of authors typed, checked facts, edited, listened.

"I was at the typewriter from 9 P.M. to 1 A.M. every night for a year, while he slowly dictated to me," Jane Cheney Spock told a reporter of her life while her husband was writing his famous manual, *Baby and Child Care*. "Sometimes I'd say, 'That's not clear,' and I did quite a lot of changing of expressions and other things that weren't clear. I consulted all kinds of doctors and nurses, and I wrote down the opinions of experts about what should be in the book on the various diseases. Some of the doctors didn't approve of Ben, so I had to woo them. In those days, there were eight different formulas, and I tested them again and again to make sure they worked, and I found that one, given out by New York Hospital, didn't work. The nipples clogged up."

At first, her help merely saved money. But a wife who has typed, filed, listened, coached, advised, remembered, and answered the phone for decades develops uniquely relevant skills and knowledge that the First Person can't buy in the open market. This is what happens to women like Madeline Steingut, wife of the veteran Speaker of the New York State Assembly who sat in on so many political huddles in Albany during the twenty-six years her husband was in the New York State Assembly that she became a force in New York State politics.

At the very top, the work of a wife can become a full-time executive responsibility. Elizabeth Lyman, wife of the President of Stanford University, traveled with her husband, raised funds, made speeches, spoke out on public issues, and assisted him by entertaining nearly fifty groups in the course of an academic year. To do all this, she kept a full-time secretary, a house manager, a custodian, and a caterer busy assisting *her*.

Rosalynn Carter is a textbook example of the increasingly important work done by a career man's Second Person. Like many wives of small businessmen, she started doing the books at the Carter warehouse when her husband left the Navy to run that business. When he went into politics, she became an aide, a campaigner, and a public relations adviser.

In 1978, Rosalynn Carter was supervising research on issues the President assigned her from her own office in the working quarters of the White House. She attended Cabinet meetings because, "If I didn't, there's no way I could discuss things with Jimmy in an intelligent way." These discussions were not conducted casually, but at weekly working lunches reserved for Mrs. Carter on the President's tightly programmed schedule.

The Carters believe in the two person career. They think they can strengthen family life in America by encouraging other couples to follow their example. Like Mrs. Carter, Second Lady Joan Mondale has been given a White House office, a staff, and specific responsibilities for relations with the arts community. In 1977, at least three wives of high-ranking Presidential aides had quit jobs as schoolteachers to do volunteer work from offices in the White House. Even after her separation from political adviser Hamilton Jordan, Nancy Jordan continued to work a full day as an aide in the West Wing, where large groups are received.

Anne Wexler, wife of Joseph Duffey, head of the National Endowment for the Humanities, expressed the Carter philosophy shortly before she was appointed to the White House staff. "It's easy for us because we both work and the children are grown. But there must be great strains and pressures when only one member of the family is involved in something like this—the other one must feel left out."

The Carters had reason to worry about the health of the two

person career. In 1978, Second Persons were growing restive and a few were striking out for careers of their own. Even southern wives grew uppity. In Alabama, the former wife of Governor George Wallace talked of running for Governor. In Georgia, the divorced wife of Senator Herman Talmadge used all she had learned as a Senator's wife to run for Congress herself, but lost. The Spocks were divorced, and in an interview with *The New York Times,* Jane Spock attributed the breakup to his lack of recognition for her work on the baby care manual that had made him a household word.

In spite of the example of the Carters, the two person career was not attracting the sophisticated young college graduates who were seeking fame in Washington. These young couples wanted it all, and "all" meant two *equal* careers.

THE COOL SUPERCOUPLES

Almost everyone applauded their ambition, but people asked how long a husband and wife could keep their separate careers as well as each other. It was a good question.

Ten years out of college, the promising dual-career couples dwindle down to a precious few.

Some are no longer married.

Some are still married but only one has a career. Usually it's the wife who drops out, and when the career that remains is his, there's no public relations problem. She's having a baby or keeping house or into volunteer work. Husbands who drop out have a harder time explaining themselves. They may be described as going to school, starting a business, or "taking time off to think things out."

The couples who wanted everything, who survive with both careers growing into their forties or fifties, are very special people. First off, they have double luck: if it's a first marriage, their careers have paced each other. Next, they are personally cool, because for both of them work comes first: however much they may think of each other, each has to be able to keep going for weeks on end without daily doses of love and affection. Another point is that the kind of work they do has to make it possible for them to help in each other's careers or keep out of each other's working lives altogether. Finally, they are human dynamos, compulsive planners, and time misers. But when they have to choose, work wins out over friends, family, leisure —even children.

They are Cool Supercouples because work defines the terms of their marriages. Work brings them together, keeps them together, or separates them. A working relationship may even last longer than the marriage. It is surprising how many of the stablest two-career marriages are between people in the same occupation or on the same professional network.

Entertainers marry entertainers. "With our crazy hours, you can't marry anyone else," says Eli Wallach, award-winning star of the film *Baby Doll.* He met his wife, Anne Jackson, when both were in a Tennessee Williams play and they now have three children. They like to spar with each other. "I've looked at Anne up on a 40-foot screen in bed with another man and not many husbands have to cope with that," he once boasted.

"I welcome *vive la différence,* all right," she retorted. "But what I don't like is if he's making more money than I am."

There are academic couples like the sociologists Peter Rossi and Alice Rossi. He's an opinion research specialist. She's an innovator in the sociology of women. Or academics Robert Whitman and Marina von Neumann Whitman: both are professors at the University of Pittsburgh. He took a leave from his job as head of the English department to join her in Washington when she went there to serve on the President's Council of Economic Advisers.

There are literary couples operating their separate typewriters together like Eleanor Clark, author of *The Oysters of Locmariaquer,* and her Pulitzer Prize-winning husband, Robert Penn Warren. Joan Didion was writing her fastidious novel, *A Book of Common Prayer* while her husband, John Gregory Dunne, was writing his own novel, *True Confessions,* which became a national best-seller. They edit each other's work, but he admits she's the better pencil editor.

There are media couples, like Jo Moring, news director of NBC Radio Network and Jerry Moring, news manager of WNBC-TV in New York who each have a phone beside their bed so that both can call their newsrooms at the same time.

Marrying a fellow professional is a career stimulant. Learning and teaching sharpens the skills of both. Each has an in-house resource for work problems. Sociologists married to other sociologists actually have been found to publish more papers than sociologists married to people who aren't in the field.

In work that depends on the exchange of information such as fashion, news, entertainment, publicity, research, and publishing, a spouse in the business can double the flow of vital gossip. Married competitors have more to gain by exchanging information than they have to lose by divulging an occasional "secret." As in the nineteenth-century marriages of property, a mutual economic interest stabilizes these unions.

Although a high proportion of women doctors and lawyers are married to fellow professionals, the wives are not apt to be as distinguished or as active as their husbands. In politics, where a Second Person is practically indispensable, it is hard to find couples whose careers have been separate, equal, and successful. There never had been a married couple serving in Congress until 1976, when Congresswoman Martha Keys, of Kansas, and Indiana Congressman Andy Jacobs fell in love and married while both were serving together on the powerful House Ways and Means Committee. Neither constituency was entirely happy about the marriage. In 1978, he was re-elected, but she was defeated.

Work is so important to Cool Supercouples that a direct conflict of interest may end an otherwise satisfactory marriage. This is what happened to a couple who married while getting their graduate credentials in urban planning. After graduation, their best job offers took them to different cities. Both liked their jobs. During two years of commuting it gradually dawned on them that they never would be able to live together because they both couldn't be city manager of the same city and neither would be happy doing anything else. They divorced to leave each other free to make other commitments, but the divorce brought them closer—it took all the strain out of the relationship. They continued to spend weekends together, making love and talking shop.

The opposite is even more common. A couple drawn together by their work marry, only to discover that their working relationship was happier than their marriage relationship. They divorce, but continue collaborating. Television's Sonny and Cher Bono resumed acting together for a time after their divorce when they found they couldn't hold their ratings with separate acts.

"We've kept the best part of our marriage, which was working together," a former wife said of her business partner and former husband. "The divorce got rid of the worst, the emotional problems."

Some Cool Supercouples are in entirely different but equally absorbing careers. They preserve their marriages and both careers by keeping them strictly separate. Former Congresswoman Bella Abzug's husband is a stockbroker famous for his refusal to talk to reporters. "Nah, if you want a statement," he tells them, "ask Bella." The husbands of political women like Gloria Schaffer, Connecticut Secretary of State, or Frances T. Farenthold, once candidate for Governor of Texas, appear in newspaper writeups only as "businessmen."

Few people know that Charlotte Curtis, editor of the powerful Op Ed page of *The New York Times,* is married to a surgeon who practices in Columbus, Ohio. The marriage is so private that she doesn't even list herself as married in *Who's Who in America.* "It works," she says, "because neither of us has ever had to play a role. He is a man who works. I am a woman who works. It never occurred to me to pull him away from the job he loves any more than he wanted me to quit *The New York Times."* They get together weekends in the home they maintain in New York, the home they maintain in Columbus, or in a hotel in Washington, halfway between.

Like many professional couples, both Curtis and her husband work such long hours that it isn't a hardship to live in different cities. He has to be in the operating room at eight in the morning and doesn't get home until after eight at night, so even if she lived in Columbus all the time, she wouldn't see much more of him than she does now.

Cool Supercouples have a limited capacity for anything that is not work-related. They talk shop at home. They talk shop at parties. If they take a vacation, they go where they can go on talking shop: the Hamptons on Long Island for artists, publishers, media people; Cape

Cod for the doctors and psychiatrists. Some never take vacations at all. Charlotte Curtis once left her typewriter at home for a week of sunning with her husband in the Caribbean, but she wound up writing in longhand.

Those who come close to "having everything" become compulsive about time and canny about priorities. They may spend all the money they make on the logistics of making it.

The first year John Sawhill was president of New York University, every member of the family was being maintained in a separate place. Their son was at prep school. Isabel Sawhill was working in Washington at the Urban Institute, and living alone during the week in their Georgetown house, while a male house manager ran the president's residence for John in New York. When Isabel and her husband gave a party in New York, all she had to do with it was to catch the Eastern Airlines shuttle from Washington in time to arrive with the guests.

One rising young corporate manager with a new baby thinks that entertaining for business at home is an idea cooked up by stay-at-home wives who want to feel important. "No one below the president level is set up to impress other people with the quality of their housekeeping and it really isn't necessary," she scoffs. "If I have to impress someone I'll take them to a restaurant or the theater."

Couples who have everything put a lot of energy into planning their lives. They attack every new day as if it were a suitcase that has to be repacked so that you can get one more thing into it. What goes is spontaneity. In a smoothly run dual-career home, the order of the day is posted in a visible place, such as the refrigerator door, and deviations are avoided because they involve multiple phone calls. There is no margin for emergencies and no room for impulsive gestures in a home that does not have a Second Person. Some couples even make appointments for lovemaking.

Social life is the first thing to go from the schedule. "There isn't any way to produce at this pace and have much of a social life," Dr. Virginia Johnson, of the Masters and Johnson sex research team told a reporter.

Career couples may look as if they are socially active. They sound as if they go everywhere, know everybody, make all the parties. But what goes on at these parties sounds very much like work. Doctors, lawyers, politicians, communications executives, and other people in the so-called "contact" industries spend all their time selling themselves, sounding out ideas, and digging for information that can help them. The people they keep seeing shift kaleidoscopically from rivals to allies. Even when they become friends, they talk primarily business. Frequently they get no further into each others' lives than perfunctory bulletins about how well their children are doing at school.

They may be proud to have "real," "old," or "outside" friends, but even when they cherish them, they very seldom have time to keep up with their lives.

Cool Supercouples often say that they are "each other's best friend," but if they are in different fields, often they don't have time to go to each other's parties. Charlotte Curtis has friends her husband never has met, and he has friends that she never has met.

Not only are parties politicized, but even sports and hobbies. Business organizations maintain memberships in athletic clubs so that their executives can play squash and tennis with clients. As part of his 1978 campaign to woo Congress, President Carter invited rebellious young members of the House to play tennis with him.

Cool Supercouples do relax, but their idea of relaxation is to work under relaxing circumstances. They buy a country hideaway, not for the outdoor activities it provides, but in order to have a place to work in peace and quiet on weekends. The fact is that an advancing career is so exciting that nothing else is anywhere near as much fun.

Cheerfully, they cooperate in the popular pastime of putting their lifestyle down. They complain of lack of time for the reading and thinking that would make them more productive—but they manage to do it. They complain of fatigue, but they look good and their health is superb. For some people, uphill is comfortable all the way.

But not for very many. Most people want rewarding work, but this does not mean that they regard their work as their main source of satisfaction.

For most couples, two lifelong careers are as restrictive as the traditional lockstep. But even these couples can have more of what each of them wants *most* if they know what it is they want, and they are willing to make tradeoffs to get it. And two paychecks enable them to choose the tradeoffs most comfortable for them.

ALTERNATIVES

The most common solution for the Age Thirty Bind is for her to trade in her *career* for a *job* that allows her to do the work of the Second Person and have children while she's doing it. This classic solution works well for most couples. His career pulls ahead so fast that she "naturally" falls into the role of support. When he has an important meeting, she cancels commitments that would interfere with it. If they are just a little bit tactful, they may not have to admit that she really has given up the race for the top. *One Career, His* works fine at age thirty, but if she has put aside career aspirations she merely puts the crisis on ice for a decade.

There are other possibilities. A great deal of the strain can be relieved if there is only one career in the family at a time, but it doesn't always have to be *One Career, His. One Career, Hers* gives him some of the options enjoyed formerly only by affluent home-makers. Warm Supercouples who want both career and more time with each other can eliminate the need for a Second Person by working together in *One Career, Theirs*.

None of these arrangements need be permanent. A versatile couple can take turns in career involvement or trade a few years of Cool Supercoupling for a midlife sabbatical of *No Career* life.

ONE CAREER, HERS

Society doesn't always disapprove of *One Career, Hers*. She gets permission for a career if she is married to a man who can't have one. She actually is encouraged to aspire if her husband is disabled, unemployed, a student, or retired. She's not supposed to *enjoy* this good fortune, of course, and she has to be prepared to give it up gracefully. Breadwinning wives of students have to be particularly careful to extinguish any long-term ambitions they may acquire while earning.

The happiest "permission" is the retirement of a husband. Careers start later in life for women, and if the husband is older, her career may bloom just about when his is over. The Perrys shifted His Career to Hers so naturally that they didn't realize they were doing it. Jack was a promotion man who was glad to retire from the job, but he missed daily lunches with his contacts in the media. Hanging around the house, he got interested in his wife's hobby of matching rare china. Phyllis had long had a home-based business helping people fill out incomplete sets of Haviland. Listening to her problems, he could see human-interest feature stories, which he began to peddle to his old press friends. It was fun to lunch with them as he had always done, and a relief to have a story that wasn't about the old company products. Soon Phyllis was flooded with inquiries both from buyers and sellers. To get more stock, they took trips to small towns where antique china still can be bought. They exhibited at antique shows, put ads in trade papers, and Jack kept the feature stories going. The business grew so large that Phyllis had to rent a shop. Within two years, the income from the shop plus Jack's Social Security had exceeded Jack's earnings before retirement.

But the best thing about the business was what it did to their marriage. The promotion work that had taken him away from Phyllis for so many years now brought him closer to her. A booster by temperament and by calling, Jack thoroughly enjoyed his new role as supportive Second Person.

A rare form of arthritis was the "permission" which enabled the Stintons to discover that role reversal fitted their temperaments. It struck, by sheer accident, just when he needed his hands for his first big construction contract.

It had taken Walt a long time to get started in life. After high school, he "goofed around and played tennis" before trying college, then quit for a hitch overseas with the Seabees, then came home to putter around the big old house in which he had grown up with five brothers and sisters. He liked farming, but he had no illusions about it. He knew that his mother and father would never have been able to rear their big family on the apples and milk they produced. As a child, he had watched them take turns commuting 100 miles to graduate work in the city that had qualified his mother to be a librarian and his father to be superintendent of schools.

Everyone thought that Nancy was the making of him. A shy slip of a girl—Walt's mother was afraid, at first, that she wouldn't stand up for herself—Nancy was a math major with a good job in the multinational corporation headquarters near the Stinton farmstead. To catch up with Nancy, he cashed in his G.I. benefits on a B.S. in "electronic engineering." It was a new field, and to Walt it sounded ideal. You had to have a college degree and work for a big company, but you were really a very highly paid electrician with freedom to move around from place to place. But it was a narrow specialty, and big companies didn't need any more when he got out. He drifted back to construction work while waiting.

Meanwhile, Nancy kept on getting raises. She was an ideal First Woman for her company's affirmative-action program. Shy, young, tenacious, quietly assertive, she blossomed under encouragement. Walt worried about the traveling she had to do, but she worried about the growing income gap between them. "You could be a contractor on your own," she suggested.

Easygoing, friendly Walt was a natural-born salesman. With Nancy's sharp eye on the estimates, he more than broke even on the trial year they had set for it. When he landed two sizable contracts they resolved the Baby Panic in favor of a baby. Both mothers were delighted. Now Walt would shape up. Privately, they congratulated each other on the way Nancy had handled what could have been a delicate situation. And both thought how well he coped when arthritis struck.

Walt had surgery on his hands just before Nancy had the baby. The specialists said it was a success. He'd be able to do normal things, like driving a car, but he wouldn't ever be able to handle power tools or do the strenuous work of construction. When the bandages came off, he couldn't grab anything, not even a pot, so for the first time in her married life, Nancy had to do all the cooking when she brought the baby home from the hospital.

Her six weeks of maternity leave expired before Walt's stitches were out, so she had to bathe the baby early in the morning before she went to work, but soon he was able to get the baby's dinner ready so that Nancy could have the fun of feeding her as soon as she walked in the house at night. Walt took the baby everywhere, tossing her lightly and confidently over his massive shoulder, his thick hand spanning her little back.

When Walt was better, they started thinking about what he might find to do. The vocational counselor they enlisted gave Walt aptitude tests. For company, Nancy took them, too.

The results were a surprise. They showed that the temporary situation was actually ideal for them. Nancy looks like a slightly compulsive schoolteacher, but the Strong-Campbell Interest Inventory which has been purged of sex bias disclosed that she was really a manager and planner. She liked to create structures, not work in those already set up by others.

Walt, on the other hand, liked the structured work that is closely related to homemaking—the indoor, clean-hands, routine, housekeeping-type jobs. The occupations toward which his interests pointed, the counselor told them, were military, headed by "policeman"! He had liked the structured life of the Seabees, where people do what they are supposed to do. And he scored much higher than Nancy on liking for office *practices*. It was the nine-to-five *schedule* against which he had rebelled. And though their mothers wouldn't believe it, the tests showed Nancy less interested in the domestic arts than most women, while Walt's interest topped the scale for men.

And that is the way it is going to be for the foreseeable future. Walt's love is old houses, so they've bought one that looks like the farmhouse in which he grew up. He'll have to hire manual labor, but he'll be on hand to direct the work of restoring it.

Walt can't stop talking about the house. "It's a Dutch Colonial authentic with '1734' on the barn. It will take years to get it in shape, but it's a real beauty. We have three acres so I have apple trees and a garden. It's surrounded by cornfields but twenty minutes nearer her work. And the fellow next door raises buffaloes, real buffaloes like you find on old nickels. What a place to raise a family!"

The way inflation and exurban real estate values have been trending, it may be the very best use he could make of his time.

The Stintons are ideally situated for lifestyle pioneering. They are both rather conventional people who didn't set out to prove anything by their so-called "role reversal." They don't know what strains they might be feeling if Walt's arthritis had not excused him from the career commitment he *didn't* want while giving her permission to become the executive she *did* want to be.

Fewer, newer, and much more suspect are the careers of women who have no excuse for overshadowing the careers of their husbands. Most of the married women in *Who's Who in America* have husbands who are not listed in their own right, including anti-feminists Phyllis Schlafly and Marabel Morgan, author of *Total Woman*. Schlafly's husband is a lawyer who inherited money. Charles Morgan is a tax attorney in the Miami firm of Peters, Maxey, Short and Morgan, who looks after the money his wife has made explaining how she saved their marriage by deferring to him.

A man who gives up his own career for his wife's can expect raised eyebrows—and so can his wife. Friends thought Joe was crazy to stay on in the Air Force to send Marcia to law school. People close to them told them right to their faces that she'd divorce him when she became a lawyer and started making money.

Instead, they are closer than before. They've become, as she puts it, "grooved into each other, like puzzle pieces." He helps her do research, gets books for her in the library. She bounces ideas off him. He's listened to so many cases now for so long that he comes up with ideas about them himself. He helped furnish her office, knows the people she works with, goes with her to the evening affairs to which lawyers bring their wives, and whenever he can get off work, he goes to court to watch her in action.

Neither of them liked their jobs when they married, but Joe didn't mind the life of a sergeant in the Air Force as much as some of the other fellows. He'd beef, but he'd go along.

Not Marcia. "I don't want to be a secretary to a lawyer," she would fume. "I want to be a lawyer myself." She talked about it and he talked about it and they finally decided that she should try.

Quitting to go to law school cut their income almost in half, so they both had to do odd jobs to earn the money for her tuition. They did anything they could find. Janitor work. Yard work. Car fixing. When she had to study, he did her odd jobs as well as his—three jobs in all. And he learned to do things around the house he had never done before. When exams came, he did the cooking, paid the bills, cleaned the house, gave her a massage, listened to her tell him all about torts.

It sometimes made her feel edgy. When the money for food went for law books, she'd sometimes pick a quarrel with him over money. She hated feeling guilty about spending thousands of dollars all on herself. "But look, honey," he told her, "it's not my money, it's our money, and we're doing what *we* want." Inside, she wasn't at all sure that she would have done the same thing for him. Toward the end, when she couldn't cram for exams and work, too, he re-enlisted in the Air Force to get the bonus that paid her last year's tuition.

Now that she's through the bar and working, she urges him to think of what would really make him happy. He could get out of the Air Force. Go back to school. Start an electronics shop with the skills he developed in the Air Force. Be his own boss. But he's not letting her rush him. He's building a boat. He takes every day as it comes. He likes living with Marcia because she's where the action is. What he really wants out of life is to make her happy and that's a big load for her to bear.

Marcia feels guilty. What makes it work? "A lot of talking," she says, "a lot of talking." She works at keeping communications open. To pay him back, she's trying to learn enough about electronics so she can understand what *he's* up against. She'd like to lavish luxuries on him. "If he wanted to go to Alaska," she says, "I'd send him." At home, there's no question about who does the housework these days. She does it.

She reads women's magazines to learn about new ways to pamper him. One of the ways is breakfast. She slips out of bed before he's awake in the morning to make herself pretty. Then, when breakfast is halfway made, she wakes him so he can get himself cleaned up, too. And even if she has to be in court at 10 o'clock, they always have a leisurely breakfast and exchange the day's schedule. "It makes me cuddly inside to think of him during the day and know what he's doing," she says. A nice thing about the morning is that he has to leave ahead of her, so she doesn't have to leave him at home with the breakfast dishes.

They've resolved the bind of the Two Person Career. Whatever he chooses to do when he's out of the Air Force, One Career, Hers is comfortable for both of them.

Sensitive, idealistic men have always had vocational problems. When they marry the assertive women who seem to attract them, they often have marital problems as well. The Dees could have looked like characters in this standard situation if Lila's public relations business did not support Jerry in the full-time volunteer work affluent wives often do. Because he's a man and a minister's son, Jerry has been able to mobilize the conservative business community behind urban re-development. Her best clients were men they met through his church and community involvement.

Neither expected this outcome. Like many ministers' sons, Jerry decided he didn't want to be poor, so he went to Harvard Business School. Thoughtful, sober, a top student, he was snapped up by an international company and sent to their branch in Ohio. A Harvard professor's daughter, Lila had worked in public relations in college and was slated for promotion, and was sure she would find something in Ohio for her to do.

Ohio was culture shock. Lila canvassed every sizable employer in the small city. No jobs. Nobody wanted a Vassar graduate, even as a secretary. Some local company presidents she wrote to had never heard of public relations and others said they didn't need it. Respectfully, literately, Lila demurred. A few finally allowed her to do for nothing some of the projects she suggested. By the end of the second year business was so good that she was hiring other similarly stranded college-educated wives to help her. But by this time Jerry was so disenchanted with his job that he thought of going back to New York.

Corporate life, Jerry had discovered, was not as portrayed in Harvard Business School cases. Told to represent the company in the community, he brought back suggestions for pollution controls, a day-care center for children of workers, and increased contributions to local charities. When his suggestions were ignored, he spent more time with the board members of local charities than he did with his colleagues in the company. His shift to community service enabled him to do more of the work he really wanted to do.

One Career, Hers gives a work-committed woman the advantages enjoyed by traditional work-committed men. The difficulty of finding a husband for the arrangement has been greatly exaggerated. Some men are talented and enthusiastic Second Persons and many more are happy to be relieved of the responsibility of First Career Person if the relief can be accomplished with reasonable tact.

Role reversal marriages yield unexpected fringe benefits. The first is that the partners have to think about each other and take special care of their relationship. Second Person Husbands can't be taken for granted like Second Person Wives. Then, too, the hostile curiosity of outsiders draws them closer: they are two against the world. But the most important dividend is the strength any marriage gains from a more equal division of power than is possible when the traditional head of the household provides all the money and sets all the rules.

WORKING TOGETHER

Most couples meet through their work, and almost all of them wonder how it would be to work as well as to live together.

But that's nepotism, and most employers won't let them do it. Rules against nepotism sometimes prevent couples from marrying for fear of losing their jobs. In the past, the wife was almost always the one who lost out, but since the women's movement, conflicts of interest are no longer automatically resolved in favor of the husband. Some civil rights lawyers think that Title VII of the Civil Rights Act of 1964 forbids an employer to reject an applicant because of the job held by the applicant's spouse, and the National Plan of Action, adopted by the National Women's Conference in Houston, endorses this interpretation.

Companies that try to live up to the spirit of nondiscrimination on the basis of marital status have found themselves hiring couples, many of them newly minted MBAs, who have met and married in college and have looked for jobs from the same few prime employers of their specialties. Couples are beginning to appear in management-training programs of corporations as well as in law and accounting firms. According to Eugene Jennings, professor of management at Michigan State University, they have caused so many "problems" that some companies are quietly trying to avoid hiring any more of them.

More subtle, and much more dangerous are the conflicts of interest that arise when husband and wife are employed by competitors. Since it may be illegal to discriminate against applicants on the basis of spouse's occupation, employers are very careful how they question them. According to a business magazine, a personnel man for an oil company asks things like, "Are you familiar at all with the oil business?" in hopes of trapping the applicant into saying, "My husband has worked in it for fifteen years," if that happens to be the case.

Feminist men concerned about equal opportunity for women sometimes lean over backward to reverse the presumption that a husband's interest is overriding. One lawyer refused to represent a client who wanted to sue a foundation, because his own wife sat on the foundation's board. "People might think she could be influenced," he said. The appearance of favoritism caused a husband to turn down a sales job with the supplier of a company for which his wife was purchasing agent.

Some couples try to solve the problem by not talking shop at home. In 1978 Marcia Grace, a creative group head with the advertising agency, Wells Rich Greene, was married to Roy Grace, creative director at a competitive agency, Doyle Dane Bernbach. According to *The New York Times,* they have a "gentleperson's agreement" to hold out trade secrets from each other. "If it's really privy," says Ms. Grace, "I mentally shred it."

In book publishing, so many executives are married to each other that it's virtually impossible to worry about conflicts of interest. Agents marry editors. Editors marry publishers. Sally Richardson, director of subsidiary rights for St. Martin's, is married to Stewart Richardson, editor-in-chief of Doubleday. They both read manuscripts in bed. The time they discovered they were reading separate copies of a manuscript up for auction, they agreed not to talk about it.

Employers are less tolerant in fields where patent rights control millions of dollars. An oil company executive discovered the career price he was paying for his wife's job when his boss wouldn't let him take papers home because his wife, also a geologist, could read the blueprints.

The way around nepotism is to go into business together. This used to be the universal pattern and millions still do it. Most farms are still run by a husband and wife, and "Mom and Pop" stores still require two to make both ends meet. Plumbers and electricians expect their wives to do the books as well as the dishes. Businessmen who marry their secretaries can't always afford to retire them. Sometimes the unpaid supporting spouse is a husband. Opera star Shirley Verrett is only one of the many highly paid women whose husbands take care of their business affairs.

But working *for* a spouse is not what most couples want. Wives who do the books, answer the phone, or otherwise backstop their husbands resent the slave labor. Many of them wrote us to complain that they never had any money of their own and were short-changed on vacations, Social Security, and other benefits that automatically would have gone to a worker who was paid. One told us a tale of literal slavery. She worked for her husband, she wrote, only because he threatened to beat her up if she looked for a paying job elsewhere.

Working with a spouse as an equal partner is something else. It sounds as if it would solve all the other ways in which jobs get in the way of family life. Working together attracts couples frustrated by employers who send them to different cities, put them on schedules that eat up the time they could spend together, discriminate against one or the other on the basis of their marital status, or unwittingly pit them against each other.

The dream is widespread. A couple blocked by antinepotism rules in rising in the management of the staid conglomerate for which both work, plan to continue drawing their salaries until they have enough money saved up to quit, open a bookstore on Cape Cod summers and spend their winters reading in Florida.

An academic couple commuting to their weekend marriage from appointments in different cities have vowed eternal togetherness once their present contracts are fulfilled. They are going to resign from their respective faculties, say good-bye to faculty politics, and set up their own research service on the West Coast.

Stephen and Babs took the plunge when she became pregnant with their first child. They had talked for years about going into a printing business together. He worked in production at the advertising agency where she was a junior copywriter. They knew the costs of getting out leaflets, mailing pieces, catalogues, brochures, and they knew they could cut those costs by doing the designing themselves and contracting the work directly to the shops Stephen knew. If they built up a clientele and made money, they could start up a shopping center newspaper throwaway, or they could become printing consultants, like a couple they knew, or could even publish specialized books.

The baby brought the plan to action because Babs wanted to nurse the baby without quitting work and it would be easier to do if she could make her own hours. So she sketched a new business announcement card with a stork in one corner and sent it out to all the business people they thought might have jobs for them. They had a little money saved up. Stephen's father, a printer, lent them more. To save money, they planned to work out of their apartment until they broke even.

At first, all was chaos. Babs brought the baby home to an apartment piled high with cartons of stock for their first orders. Bills, orders, letters, and scribbled notes of phone messages littered the kitchen and the bathroom. Still holding the baby, Babs found a place to sit down and cry. Stephen was contrite. He moved out the cartons, picked up the papers. And while the baby settled into her eating and sleeping habits, Babs found time to sketch layouts on the drafting board they set up in a corner of the living room.

The first year was a roller coaster ride. Some weeks absolutely nothing happened. The phone didn't even ring. They sat terrified, watching the bank balance melt. Then there'd be a flood. More work than the two of them could handle. Should they hire help? At the end of the year they netted out about what they had earned between them at the agency. They had worked longer hours—they thought they had, at least—and sometimes under pressure, but they had goofed off a lot, too, sometimes when they wanted the time.

They celebrated breaking even by renting a cheap office and hiring a babysitter so Babs could get away from the apartment three afternoons a week. Next year was better.

Printing isn't the only service that Mom and Pop can deliver cheaper and better than large organizations with high overhead. Employment agencies, editorial services, research services, legal work, counseling services, accounting services, advertising, promotion, public relations are possibilities. Also, landscaping, dog grooming, catering, travel agencies, plant shops. All the many different franchise businesses, from McDonald's to the dry cleaners, are good possibilities if you have the money to buy them.

If Babs and Stephen had wished to bring up their baby in a closely knit rural community they could have teamed her writing and his printing to run a small-town weekly newspaper. The income isn't big, but the life is attractive, and many can be bought at affordable prices.

There are as many reasons for husbands and wives who are doctors and lawyers and accountants to go into partnership together as there are for professionals who do not happen to be spouses to do so. Charlotte and Bob Herberg bought *Southwestern Art,* a museum publication, in Austin, Texas, because they wanted to broaden its editorial appeal. Dr. Elizabeth Goessel and Dr. Colter Rule share an office on the ground floor of the Park Avenue building in which they share a marriage several floors above. They also share research in biofeedback as a technique for reducing disease-causing stress.

Those who aren't willing to go into business together have a harder time working together. An advertising agency or a law firm occasionally will assign married professionals on the staff to the same project, but most employers try to keep their work as separate as possible. Couples who want more time off the job individually sometimes have been able to persuade an employer to let them share the same job for one paycheck, on the theory that two minds on a task are worth the bookkeeping costs of carrying an extra name on the payroll. This gets around the problems of nepotism, too.

Shared appointments are attractive to small, liberal arts colleges because they widen the range of talents without adding jobs to the faculty. In the science building of little Hampshire College, in western Massachusetts, one door reads BEV AND FRED HARTLINE, GEOPHYSICS, another AL AND ANN WOODHULL, BIOLOGY, and a third KURTISS AND COURTNEY GORDON, ASTRONOMY.

A faculty wife hit on the idea of a joint appointment when she and her husband decided that neither of them wanted to work full time while their children were small. Under the arrangement they made with a small Midwest college, her husband stayed home in the morning while she taught a course in women's studies. After lunch, she stayed home while he taught two courses in his field, religion.

Everyone gained something slightly different. The college gained a new course and a role model of sex equality for students on their small campus. She solved her problem of babysitting and continued to use her Ph.D. in education without working full time. Her husband enjoyed the letup from the job pressure of a full-time teaching load and the improvement in family life that went with it, but the enduring benefit to him was professional. He felt the arrangement advanced his career because it gave him more time for research.

Her husband thinks it gets a little too close at times. He wonders whether the intimacy of working in the same institution and knowing the same people makes it harder for them to develop new interests and grow. But she doesn't see this as a problem. Individuals vary in their needs and, indeed, their tolerance for constant companionship.

The danger of too much togetherness looms larger for couples who share the same duties. Ann and Michael Coburn, the first married couple to be ordained as Episcopal priests, schedule their work as assistant to the rector of the St. James Episcopal Church in Danbury, Connecticut, so that only one of them works at a time. They also try to schedule one day a week to spend together alone. Parishioners think they have the perfect marriage but they say they have to work at it. "People can have more equal marriages," Ann says, "but whether they can handle the idea of teamwork is another question."

Teamwork, of course, is what's involved when a husband and wife share exactly the same duties. So far, only a few of the job-sharing experiments have involved husbands and wives, and in spite of government and foundation funded projects to promote the idea, job-sharing between unrelated persons who want part-time work has not proved the solution to the demand for flexible hours.

On balance, working together cannot be wholeheartedly recommended for every couple. Those who succeed differ widely in how they manage it. Some couples in business together try to reproduce the arms-length division of labor of traditional organizations: he is boss on new business, for instance, while she rules over the checkbook. Others talk everything through and make all their decisions together. Some couples have rules about talking business at dinner. Others are resigned to talking about nothing else. A freelance writer who works with her husband thinks that the working partnership is better if it preceded the marriage. One thing seems sure. A couple working together has *more* of a marriage. More to talk about. More to share. More to fight about. And more testing of the weak areas of the relationship. If it's good, it can be very good. If it's bad it can end in a divorce that involves all areas of life, or a marriage maintained for the sake of the business.

RESOLUTIONS TO MIDLIFE CRISES

When a couple hits 40, the partners begin moving in opposite directions. With the kids out of the way, sex and career turn up for her, but they level off and start declining for him. The stage is set for marital disaster.

Successful or not, the bloom is off his career. He begins to wonder whether it was worth the blood it has cost him, whether there's something more to life. If he's bored, he thinks of changing jobs. Or women. A younger woman, eager and new, who takes him back to his twenties, when sex was endless and effortless, and he wanted it more than she did. His own wife knows too much, needs too much.

If she took career time out for the children and never made it all the way back, she may look for something radically new. She may experiment sexually with other men or even with women. Or file charges of sex discrimination against her employer. Join a political movement. Get religion. Nag her husband to go to a marriage counselor, or join a sensory-awareness group.

Statistics of the 1970s showed how often the scenario ended badly. Newly divorced women looked for jobs and became unemployment figures. They inundated the community colleges set up to train high school graduates. So many of their students were older women with children that day care became a burning issue on many campuses.

Literate, restless, well enough off, for the most part, to buy a book or magazine, take a course, or even pay a counselor, these "mature women returning to the labor force" were a luscious market for entrepreneurs in publishing, education, social work, and the so-called "helping professions."

Foundations, states, the Federal government and universities spent money to teach the returning women how to look for a job, how to assess their aptitudes, how to train for a skill, how to write a resumé, what to say on a job interview, how to dress for success, how to feel about themselves, how to be assertive but not aggressive, and generally how to radiate the job confidence that most of them did not feel. Profit and nonprofit, it was a growth industry of the decade, an industry based on the fraudulent, cruel, and counterproductive premise that there was something a mature woman could do to put her back on the career ladder she left to rear children.

They took courses and they read the books, but most of them continued to be unemployment statistics or discontented workers in dead-end jobs. I could think of only one honest thing to say to an audience of returning women who expected me to tell them how to get paid what they were worth: If you don't land a job that utilizes your talents, it's *not* your fault.

Returning women can find jobs, but they are the wrong age and sex for the careers they really want. They can't change their age or sex, but they can help change the male career timetable. And some of them were doing it. All over the country, couples were challenging the male career timetable. Some of them were writing cheerful alternatives to the midlife crisis scenario.

Dan and Julie headed off the crisis because they saw it coming and switched roles in time. He knew something was wrong when he urinated blood in the lavatory of a plane. It wasn't really kidney trouble, as the hospital first thought. Dan is a psychologist who was retained by corporations to advise their salesmen, and he now thinks it was his body's rebellion against the traveling that was taking him away from Julie and the children. At the time he thought he was dying. When he recovered, he resolved not to spend one more day of his life traveling. He made one more trip, then quit, cold turkey.

They had started out, after college, to be equal. Dan had done his diapering and getting up in the night with their first baby, but when the second baby came, Julie dropped out of medical school and went domestic. Dan began to make money and spend more and more time away for his company. He'd be off for three weeks and then back again only long enough to quarrel and make up with her. Once he took her along, but it made her feel worse to see the fun he was having some of the time on his trips while she was stuck at home taking care of the children. That made him feel more guilty. When they got home, he was so close to the breaking point that he blew up at her for breaking a glass. A week later he was in the hospital.

The breakdown was the beginning of insight for both of them. At first, he was manic. He talked about being born again. They'd sell everything and go to California. He'd go into private practice and spend all his time at home with the family. "But you can do that right here," Julie reasoned. "If you want more time with the children, you can take them over. Maybe they'll take me back at medical school."

Miraculously, her old medical school *was* willing to take her back. It was being sued by a woman who claimed she had been excluded on the basis of her sex. Julie had made an exceptional record so she made a convenient double token: older than the conventional medical student and the mother of school-age children, too.

When they started their new life of role reversal, staying home seemed at first like a much needed vacation. He spent a lot of time getting acquainted with the kids. He liked the idea that he was the one to do the nitty gritty things, like making them pick up their rooms. And he learned to cook. He'd alternate between the good stuff and just throwing pizzas at the family. Gradually, he began to see a few clients at the house.

Scheduling his new life was a problem. He'd drive the kids to school, go swimming at the Y, and then come home to read the paper and drink coffee for about an hour, like a housewife goofing off. He'd go on cleaning binges. He refinished the piano and coached the soccer team at his children's school.

When the novelty wore off, and before his practice built up, he had time to monitor his feelings about eventually becoming the house-husband of a doctor. "Sometimes I felt threatened, sometimes I didn't," he recalls. "The medical parties were the worst. The women thought that what I was doing was great, but the men, especially the older men, would just look at me funny and say, 'Oh, you're taking care of the house.' When I could feel the fast track she was on I would make more effort to develop my private practice."

It wasn't a steady thing, the way he felt. "Sometimes I would cook a real good dinner and was keeping it warm when she called at 6:30 to say she would be home at 7:30, and then at 7:20 to say she wouldn't be home until nine, and I would continue to keep it warm and be supportive when she came in. And other times I'd just get fed up and furious and put everything in the refrigerator and take the kids and go out and forget her. I had to find some kind of balance with that."

More money made things better. When his practice improved, and she began to draw a paycheck as a resident, they moved into a condominium and hired a cleaning service. Dan was glad to give up the drudgery and isolation of housework, but he has turned it to career advantage in counseling women patients.

There are no models for their reversal of direction, so they have to do a lot of talking about it. They know that there is only one solution to the midlife career crisis, and that is to help each other switch directions. He has to help her find ways to resume the career she shelved while she helps him pick up the family involvement and personal development he shelved during the work-intensive phase of the male career timetable.

Julie is exceptional: she had a well-defined career goal and was able to get back on the track. But when she starts to practice, she will face the temptation to overcommit herself that led to his breakdown and they hope his experience can help her avoid it. She knows the toll of living vicariously through the family and she is helping him avoid it.

They talk a great deal about dividing their time between the personal and professional sides of their lives. One plan is to set aside an evening a week for each other, another for the children, and another that *each* family member can use for her/or himself.

Reversal of direction is easier if both plan and prepare for it during their thirties. The wife of a college professor became interested in speech therapy when one of her children was slow in talking. Tuition at the university was free for wives, so she started taking psychology courses on the subject as they were offered. By the time her children were in school, she was ready to take the graduate course leading to a professional degree in speech therapy. She thinks she has become a better therapist of young children because she is older and has reared children herself. Her practice at the clinic fits in with the academic schedule of her husband, an experimental physicist. Her exposure to his work has interested her in the relatively unexplored "hard science" of phonometrics, the measurement of variations in speech sounds.

Some couples are able to make the shift of career involvement without dramatic outside upheavals. Most of their friends think that Davis still is the First Career Person in the family, and that Melissa is just spending a little more time on the travel agency she started with a friend as a lark when their children were in school. The fact is that the boom in travel has expanded their business so fast that Melissa now puts in long, exhausting hours as she and her partner cope with the problems of growth. Meanwhile only Davis, Melissa, and a few top officers of his company know that he has gone as high as he's going to go on the corporate totem pole. He'll always have a job there, but they'll move him sideways in the future, not up.

It was hard to take in the beginning. Some of the men who lost out on the last round developed psychosomatic symptoms. One separated from his wife. Several others quit. Davis and Melissa saw the blocked career as an opportunity for Davis to develop the sides of his life that had been neglected while he was bucking for promotion.

He's staying on, but he's shifting gears at the office. He's using the support of a familiar job and work schedule to steady his change of direction, and the company is helping him. He is finding new, noncompetitive ways to help younger men on the job. He takes over high-level public relations chores like talking at length with distinguished visitors the president of the company can see for only a moment of greeting. He's been told to represent the company informally in local affairs. With company approval, for instance, he is using his engineering background to work on environmental issues facing the local county council. These varied assignments make it easy to come in late and go home early.

Home is now where the action is for Davis. He has learned to cook gourmet dishes. He is building a greenhouse for the plants Melissa is now too busy to nurture. The environmental issues he has studied for the county council have interested him in the local wildlife. He and his high school son are taking a census of the animals in a threatened stretch of woodland near their home. And for the first time in his life he is taking music lessons.

Other, more radical solutions to the midlife career crisis are being mulled by couples who haven't reached it yet. Some Cool Super-couples are talking about a midlife career shift they could make to-gether. This means piling up money while both are too busy to spend it, then taking a few years off to start slower, less-demanding occupa-tions that allow them to develop new interests and talents.

One very successful couple is saving the wife's entire salary against his fiftieth birthday. On that day, she will give up her $50,000-a-year salary and he will cash in his share of the group medical practice which is bringing them an income many times that much. She plans to teach. He's going to write a novel. Their children will be out of college, so they could travel if they felt like a change of scene to go with the change of pace.

A plan that is getting a great deal of attention, but so far little actual implementation, is a midlife career sabbatical during which one or both take a few years off from one career for a noneconomic pursuit. The problem is not financial, but re-entry. Working couples can take turns supporting each other while one takes time out, but it is hard to get back to a career without falling back a number of steps on the promotional ladder.

Companies such as IBM, Xerox, Wells Fargo, and Lederle Labo-ratories have at times experimented with a corporate version of the academic sabbatical. In order to attract scientists from prestigious universities, they have offered some high-ranking professionals paid leaves of absence during which they are encouraged to explore in-terests totally unrelated to their work. Some have become social workers or fund raisers for their favorite causes. Others have traveled and studied. One scientist spent his year off studying oriental reli-gions in India. The theory is that the time out is an investment in human capital which will yield dividends in higher levels of productivity when the professional goes back to his profit-oriented work.

Couples are just beginning to explore the more obvious of the options two paychecks afford. Some discover them by accident, when she becomes the temporary or permanent breadwinner. Others plan them. Either way, couples discover that her job makes it possible for both to do work they like better than the work they are doing, to alternate work and leisure, to invest their time in causes, hobbies, leisure, their children, or each other.

Ideally, husband and wife gain equally. But there is a curious paradox. Women most often *initiate* a variation in the standard male career timetable, *but men are most often the winners,* because they never before have been able to opt for anything but paid achievement as a life commitment. Men always have had the right to choose how they earn, but they are only beginning to claim the right to choose between paid and unpaid work that the women's movement has won, in principle at least, for women.

The potential for human satisfaction staggers the mind. "Let us suppose," wrote Midge Miller, Wisconsin state legislator and feminist, "that we were to suggest a method for decreasing early deaths from heart attacks and other tension-related illness in middle-aged men.

"Suppose this plan would also make education more relevant and help young people continue their education without an accumulation of debt.

"Suppose it would give young children more time with both parents, help women find more satisfaction in their lives and enable them to support themselves when necessary.

"Suppose that this plan would help elderly and disabled persons enjoy life more, make further contributions to society and provide themselves a better standard of living without damaging their health.

"There is no doubt that liberals and conservatives alike would respond. Well, we can develop such a plan if we find the means for breaking certain rigid work patterns developed during the industrial revolution. We are overworking some, while depriving others of the opportunity to make a living."

What will the world be like when widespread claim of these options really breaks the lockstep of family and career? Nobody really knows. The experiments of a minority are already changing the meanings of work and love. Ahead—and soon—are new ways of working, a new kind of "family," and basic changes in what men and women expect from each other.

PART FOUR:

THE MOST PROBABLE FUTURE

CHAPTER 11

Fewer People

Eli Ginzberg is a canny prophet. He assures us that the economic independence of women is the most important phenomenon of the twentieth century, but all he will say about what it will do is that "the long-term implications are absolutely unchartable" and "the cumulative consequences will only be revealed in the twenty-first and twenty-second centuries."

The immediate consequence is fewer babies. The birth rate plunged during the 1970s. No one denied that its fall paralleled the rise in the employment of women, but no one could be sure whether it would continue to fall. For the first time in history, the size of the next generation began to depend on the increasingly personal and private decisions of the growing proportion of men and women who were stepping out of the lockstep to plan their own lives.

The sum total of these individual decisions holds the key to our future. If the birth rate goes up, we could have another boom like that of the 1950s, which was based on growing families that kept women at home and slowed their progress toward equality with men.

And since growth has been our history, it would mean business as usual for government, industry, and education.

If the birth rate goes down, on the other hand, the ultimate result is slower economic growth for the nation as a whole, which means fewer rewards for career dedication, more equality and similarity between women and men, and a small world of adults enjoying a wide choice of activities. With fewer children to hold down and regiment their lives, adults will be able to change their minds and their life-style—and they will—often with frightening rapidity. Politics, marketing, fashions, and investing will all become riskier as rapid change becomes the norm rather than the exception.

The future of the birth rate is the primary political issue. It is complex and controversial. Five years ahead is as far as anyone can really see. At the rate at which tastes have been changing, no one knows how 12-year-old girls will feel about babies when it's time for them to have them. Demographers freely admit that they have no professional prescience. None of them really foresaw the baby boom following World War II or the precipitous drop of the 1970s, and they differ widely on what's going to happen next.

The political conservatives, led by Professor Richard Easterlin, of the University of Pennsylvania, predict another baby boom. They believe that there are fashions in babies, so that the birth rate goes up and down in accordance with the law of supply and demand. Easterlin argues that because few babies were born in the Depression of the 1930s, they found it easy to get jobs when they grew up, so they married early and reared big families in the 1950s. Now that these big families are glutting the slow job market of the 1970s, they are having fewer babies, which according to Easterlin's theory is bound to produce a baby boom in the 1990s.

The theory fits the past two generations, but it ignores important differences in the kind of jobs now being created. During the 1950s, hard-goods industries such as automobile production, television and appliance manufacturing, construction, road-building, and particularly war, created jobs for men that allowed them to marry and support families. During the 1970s, the new jobs have been largely for typists, waitresses, health-care assistants, airline attendants and other clerical, sales, and service occupations dominated by women which paid just enough to deter wives from having babies.

The demographic mainstream, led by Dr. Charles Westoff, Director of the Office of Population Research at Princeton, thinks the birth rate is going to drop so low that we may eventually have to pay women to have babies. Westoff has been asking women how many babies they expect for more than a generation. In the 1970s, all the indicators were pointing straight down.

The most probable future—and the happiest, too— will be a small world. There are many reasons to believe that the birth rate will continue to drop until the population of the United States begins shrinking some time during the next century.

The drop has already been faster than most people realize. In 1977, for instance, there were 15 million more women than in 1957, but they produced 1.1 million fewer babies. The population continued to grow, although slowly, only because old people continued to live longer. If the low birth rates continue, the proportion of the population of Social Security age would double to one-third of the American population by the year 2000. But when the baby boom babies born during the 1950s start dying, the total population could start dropping. Though less dramatic, population growth is slowing even in the teeming Orient.

In the United States, the drop could come fast. All classes are planning smaller families, and control over reproduction is rising so rapidly that the plans are likely to be carried out.

Most men and women continue to say, on the surveys, that they want to have children, but two instead of three, and later—always later. Even more indicative is the rise in the percentage of wives 18 to 24 who say that they want only one child or none, up from 7 percent in 1967 to 18 percent in 1977. The black and the poor are cutting down the number of children they want even faster than affluent whites.

Raising a family was a declining priority for college freshmen. In 1972, 68 percent of freshmen women and 62 percent of men checked "raise a family" as one of the things they thought it was important to do. In 1977, a college generation later, the vote was an identical 59 percent for *both* men and women. In five short years, young men and women had become more alike. And there was evidence that the taste for rearing children was likely to recede further. Less than 5 percent of the grammar school girls queried by the National Children's Survey of 1978 looked forward to becoming mothers without jobs.

Easterlin and his party think that babies will become popular because they are scarce. Teenage pregnancies were a concern, during the 1970s, but with the exception of *illegitimate* pregnancies among *white* teenagers the birth rate for teenagers, too, continued to fall. There is no reason to assume that an absence of babies will stimulate the interest of women in having them, the way long skirts create a yearning for short ones.

On the contrary, the evidence is that childlessness snowballs. "We don't think of having babies," a wife from California wrote beside the question on children on the Matching Couples Survey. "All our friends are couples who work, and we just don't see any around." Women often reveal to researchers that they decided to have a baby because they saw other babies and wondered what their own would be like.

But the most important reason why the drop could come fast was the dramatic improvement in the control of women over their own reproduction. In 1976, almost a third of white wives of child-bearing age were surgically sterile. Sterilization had become as popular a form of birth control as the Pill, and its use was increasing. Meanwhile, the Pill was rapidly spreading to poorer and less-educated couples who had formerly relied on less secure methods. And only since 1973 has legal abortion been available as a backstop.

There was no question how women would use the new control they were so rapidly gaining. According to their mothers, less than half of the grammar school youngsters in the National Children's Survey of 1976 were planned, and one in seven was frankly unwanted. When the analysts compared these children with those who were planned they found that unchosen children had more accidents and injuries, poorer health, and more learning problems in school. Imagine what kind of world we could have if every child were actively wanted!

What is really going to happen in the future is easier to foresee than to interpret. The most probable future is that people will continue to respond to the economic imperatives that encourage smaller families, and new technologies will insure that they get them.

When families are formed for the satisfaction of their members instead of the production of children, there will be many different kinds of families instead of *"the* family." Instead of one lockstep life plan, there will be many different life plans rather than the one right way for all.

The possibilities for work are equally exciting. Fewer children means more adults working in a slower growing economy. Relieved of the burden of young dependents, individuals can afford to choose jobs that pay in satisfaction in terms of the work itself rather than in the promise of consumption or power. Instead of universal enforcement of the old "work ethic" there will be many motives for working and many different work ethics.

Equality in marriage, choice over work, and fewer, more wanted people are some of the consequences that can flow from the economic independence of women. These consequences amount to a social revolution. According to William J. Goode, the Stanford sociologist, "No society of which we know has yet come even close to equality between the sexes, but modern social forces . . . did not exist before either. At the most cautious, we must concede that the conditions favoring a trend toward more equality are more favorable than at any prior time in history."

Babies born during the 1970s may not see this world of total equality. They will be freer and more equal than their parents because both sexes will have grown up expecting to earn. But *their* children could lead more rewarding lives because they will be fewer, and they will owe their good fortune to the basic changes brought about by their career-oriented grandmothers.

CHAPTER 12

New Kinds of Families

Our grandchildren who become historians will wonder why we worried so much about the falling birth rate and the decline of the traditional, child-oriented family. They will analyze the dialogue between the viewers-with-alarm and the hailers-of-new-hope.

Amitai Etzioni, the Columbia University sociologist, sees the family as the base of all civilization. His anguish, during the 1970s, was eloquent: "Bringing up children—and I have five of them—is not just fun and joy. Children can be a pest. Children can be trouble. Children can be a nuisance. When you ask a parent, him or her, 'Do you really want to do that? Do you really want to get up in the middle of the night and attend to that little thing, to wipe it clean? Would you not rather be on the beach swimming, would you not rather travel? Or be involved with someone romantically or smoke marijuana or whatever?' Against this 1970s kind of pressure to focus on yourself, no human commitment can survive. Motherhood was once considered sacred, and it has now become, like education, a question mark. If we keep this antagonistic critical searchlight on this particular institution it will destruct, and instead of ZPG (Zero Population

Growth), we will have a zero society, a society that will come apart. Cultures without a family have not survived."

This cry from the heart did not disturb Eli Ginzberg, Etzioni's Columbia University colleague in economics.

"I can relax if the country decides not to reproduce itself," he shrugged. "I'm not so much interested in the world. I am interested in individuals, in individual freedom. Sure, there will be economic problems. We'll have an aging population. But we're the richest country in the world. If we need more young people, we can import them. All we have to do is to make it easy for them to come in."

The dialogue about the crisis of the family was a classic confrontation between hard-core conservatives who believe individuals exist for the sake of society, and hard-core liberals who defend the right of the individual.

"Isn't the central issue whether or not marriage continues to be a supportive institution to those who enter it?" a woman wrote *The New York Times*.

"The answer is no," a physician reader retorted. "Marriage is a social institution. It was devised to further the stability of society."

In the 1970s hard-core conservatives literally believed that the stability of society depended on preserving the traditional family. They proposed government programs to "save the family" in the same spirit that government programs have been enacted to "save the family farm" even though fewer than 5 percent of the population were family farmers. Some spoke of withdrawing from the mainstream, emigrating to New Zealand, or holing up in protected communities, like those maintained by the Amish or the Mennonites. For to them, the stability of society required that *all people live in the same kind of family*.

The Equal Rights Amendment, abortion, affirmative action for women, government funding of day-care centers—all were opposed in the name of "The Family." (It was always "the" family to emphasize that there could only be one kind.) The crusade enlisted the support of every party opposed to social change. The Ku Klux Klan, the John Birch Society, and right-wing fundamentalist churches joined the fight.

For a while, during the conservative reaction of the late 1970s, the so-called "pro-family" forces won skirmish after skirmish. Abortion riders were inserted in many bills. Phyllis Schlafly, the sweet-smiling mother of six children was a favorite on the talk shows. And in 1978, plans for an innocuous-sounding White House Conference on The Family were postponed because the planners couldn't agree on what they meant by "family."

President Carter had talked about different kinds of families. He had specifically mentioned that some had grandparents and some no children, but he didn't say anything about unmarried couples, homosexual partners, single-parent households, unrelated adults, and the growing number of reconstituted families of children whose re-wed parents introduced them as his, hers, and ours. In 1979, the language had no word to identify the male roommate of a daughter, or the relationship of a person to the children of a former mate by a second spouse.

AD HOC FAMILIES

Our grandchildren who become historians never will understand why we didn't realize that people don't have to get married or have children in order to belong to a family. They will write doctoral dissertations about the temporary but intimate relationships adults were forming during the 1970s.

Yale sociologist Rosabeth Kanter saw the emergence of what she called a "post-biological" family held together by a "quality of feeling rather than a biological tie." If feeling is the tie, then a family can be assembled for a specific purpose, the way unacquainted musicians can get together to play string quartets.

Some of these "ad hoc" families were formed because of where they lived. Many graduate students with children, for instance, were pooling their resources to share babysitting and living expenses in the big old houses that often can be rented cheaply within walking distance of the campus in college towns.

Some were occasion-oriented. For many years now, my family has been part of a Thanksgiving and Christmas day "family" headed by a retired college professor who loves to cook for crowds but has no family of her own. We go because we love traditional holidays but never have time to plan them. The other members of the "family" are a divorced couple and their now-grown children for whom the professor's home is neutral territory. There are rituals. Our contingent always brings the champagne. And enough usually has happened in all our lives since the previous holiday to make for an eager exchange of experiences and feelings.

Most of us are learning that roles can be changed like clothing, and that temporary relationships are less likely to be exploitative and uncaring than those that have biological or economic consequences. One of the perennial themes of fiction is that an intense sex relationship cannot be sustained over time without hypocrisy. Men have always known that sex doesn't have to be forever, but in the 1970s, women were beginning to learn it, too.

In the 1970s, sexual experimentation was no longer initiated by men alone. Successful, financially independent women were sometimes shocked by their own sexiness and the ease with which they accepted variant sex practices and partners who would have been inappropriate husbands.

UNISEX, MALE

Equality of sexual experience is only one of the ways in which men and women will become more alike. And as similar experiences at school and work draw the sexes closer together, women will become more like men than men will become like women. Unisex clothing is a good example. Women have borrowed pants, utilitarian suits, and hair styles that require only cutting and combing from men, while men have borrowed only bright colors and jewelry from the sartorial repertoire of women.

"Male" character traits of rationality, competition, and concern for achievement are being assumed by women much faster and more widely than "female" traits of responsiveness, intuition, and passivity are being adopted by men. In the few years since women have been given social permission to compete in athletics, the performance of women has come closer to that of men. "Femininity," it appears, is not an inborn female sex characteristic, but an artifact of powerlessness that will never be missed.

The relationship between men and women will become more "male," too. Revolt against the double standard of sexual behavior raises the question as to which standards—male or female—will prevail. In the future, the male pattern will apply to both sexes. Early initiation into full sexual activity, a variety of partners, experimentation with differing practices and active solicitation of male partners will be expected of women.

At the same time, men and women will be freer to be friends and companions for whom sexual expression may be absent or incidental. It is happening already in coeducational college dormitories. Older people who grew up in an age of impacted sexuality have difficulty understanding how a man and woman can share a room without becoming sexual partners, but they do.

Men and women can afford to be friends because they can explore a relationship without getting married. And while about a third of the couples living together without marriage eventually formalize the relationship, there is no evidence that the women are more eager to do so than the men. On the contrary, many women say they prefer an LTA (Living Together Arrangement) precisely because they don't want the traditional status of a wife.

BETTER MARRIAGES

Marriages are going to be better because brides and grooms will be older and more likely to postpone having children until they have had a chance to get to know each other. Marriages will be regarded not as status attained by the act of getting married, but as an achievement requiring continuing effort, or even as a work of art.

When marriages are more perishable and more variable, there will be open recognition that some couples are "more married" than others. Tax adjusters and clergymen who would like to bring the living togethers into the fold may press for legal or formal recognition of degrees of commitment in marriage. A first step already has been taken. Under a law that took effect in January 1979, a divorced wife is entitled to Social Security benefits if the marriage has lasted for ten years.

Marriages won't all be alike. They will be individually negotiated contracts. Formal, prenuptial contracts spelling out a couple's special commitment will be recognized more widely by courts and eventually may become as binding as any other contract. They will spell out such things as the handling of money, housework responsibilities, child-care decisions, support of one spouse while the other goes to school, residence, tolerance of exclusive interests, and many other issues now regarded as beyond the control of courts or even the marriage partners themselves.

The future of marriage is rosy. Both sexes will get more of what each now finds lacking. Women can expect more companionship, more talk, more power, and conceivably even more help around the house. Men will get more sex, a greater variety in sex, and more freedom for separate interests and even for trying new sex partners. There will be fewer of the "empty shell" marriages held together by reluctant partners "for the sake of the kids." The new marriage morality will resemble the standard of sexual conduct permitted traditional husbands rather than the old double standard that freed husbands but restricted wives. And there will be fewer children underfoot to interfere with the relationship between husbands and wives.

THE FUTURE OF CHILDREN

When children are few and urgently wanted, they will get more of what child specialists want for them. More direct care from their parents during the early, preschool years, and more tax-supported services from a government concerned about the falling birth rate.

The children of the future will be luckier, to begin with, in their choice of parents. When children are not expected of everyone, only those passionately interested in relating to children will undertake the formidable task of parenting. Few, if any, children will be born because their parents think childbearing is a duty, or to "complete" a preconceived picture of a "nice family." Growing support for non-mothers will make it easier for them to say, "No, we aren't having any." Better selection of parents should greatly reduce the problems psychiatrists attribute to feelings of being unloved and unwanted, to say nothing of the damage done by mothers ordered to dish out tender, loving care when they don't feel like it.

The children will be lucky, too, in arriving exactly when their parents have planned to have them, whether early or late. And since they will be wanted for themselves, rather than to fill out the picture of a family, there will be no temptation to space them closely and "get them over with." As a matter of fact, there will be no "standard" size family at all. Passionate mothers may choose to have children throughout their childbearing years, spaced four or five years apart, but most parents will be content to stop at one, a pattern already visible among educated Europeans.

Only-children have always enjoyed advantages that were systematically overlooked when large families were being encouraged. They have, for instance, always been overrepresented among intellectual achievers, in part, psychologists think, because they have had closer relations with their parents while they were growing up. The first astronauts, for instance, were only-children. A rise in the proportion of younger siblings taking the Scholastic Aptitude Test during the late 1960s was even suggested as a clue to the mysterious drop in scores that occurred when the big families of the 1950s came of test-taking age.

These precious, wanted children will get better care from their parents. They won't be born unless their parents are able and willing to make career and lifestyle sacrifices to spend time with them during the first few years. "In ten years," as one of our career wives told us earlier, "I'll be head of a radio station or the mother of three children, *but I will not be both.*" Again and again young career wives told us that they liked and wanted children, "but why have them if you can't stay home and enjoy them?"

Fewer of these parents will want to send their children to day-care centers or turn them over to full-time housekeepers to have all the fun with them. What they really want is work that allows them to spend much of their time with their children during the first few years, and flexible scheduling is in the most probable economic future. Those who can't arrange to spend time with their children will regretfully decide against having them at all.

Those who do will have enthusiastic help from the large number of childless adults who like to have some contact with children. Babysitters will be easier to find and better in the adult world of the future. The big families of the 1950s may turn out to be experienced and eager grandparents, real and honorary. Caring for children may be the midlife career shift for those who opted against children because there were so many underfoot when they were growing up themselves, as well as for couples who talked of adopting children "later" only to find that there were no more children left to adopt.

The low birth rate will make it politically popular as well as financially feasible to offer parents financial and logistical support of the kind many other civilized nations now provide. School systems will lobby to extend the school age downward to cover tax-supported nursery school as every child's birthright, and there will be underused school space and underemployed teachers to get new programs started.

At the same time, professionals will sell Congress on funding direct services to children, which, like the public school system, will be available to all, regardless of need. All children, for instance, will get their teeth straightened at public expense. All will get a chance to go to summer camp. Testing, counseling, and medical care will be available to all alike.

These direct services will be opposed by conservatives whose answer to the falling birth rate will be to strengthen "the family" and its traditional control over children. The conservative program will call for mothers' allowances available only to full-time homemakers, pension credits for homemakers under Social Security, and tax schedules that penalize working mothers even more severely than those of 1979. But the liberal program of entitlement to the child will eventually prevail.

Children will be given legal rights independent of their parents, enforceable, if necessary, by state-appointed counsel directly responsible to and for the child. Some of the newly defined children's rights will include the right of choice of parent for custody in the event of divorce, the right to formal trial of delinquency charges, and the right of access to school records that may be used by employers or colleges in making decisions about them.

But the most important right of every child will be financial. Every child will be entitled, at birth, to an inalienable Social Security benefit for care, medical and legal services, education, counseling, and retirement benefits. This broad floor under every child will be sweetened as children become fewer. It will provide a national children's lifestyle that will equalize the experiences of children regardless of the lifestyle and income of their parents. And since the benefit goes to the child, rather than the parent, it will not make having children profitable, but merely possible to people who want them but can't afford them.

A SCENARIO FOR PARENTRY

The biggest cost of children will be the input of parent time, when both parents are employed. When schooling begins at four, the bulk of the time required will be concentrated during the first four years, and most will want to take "time out" for it. For those who want only one child, the interlude need be no longer than college, and many will be tempted to take it before their careers begin. Time out for parentry could develop as a response to the slower growing economy. The scenario could go like this:

Jobs were so hard to find during the 1980s that college graduates continued to live on part-time, pick-up employment near the campus, prolonging the culture of studentry. Most postponed having children until they were settled in careers, but those who wanted them lived together to exchange babysitting and keep down expenses. Most of them had been funded through college by student financial-aid programs, so when the plummeting birth rate created demand for government aid to parents, they saw an opportunity to adapt the familiar machinery to their new situation.

A brilliant young mother employed as a teaching assistant at a university secured funding from a foundation for a pilot Parent Financial Aid program. Parents of children under two could qualify for outright grants provided that both limited their earning activities so that they could devote themselves primarily to the care of the child until the child was ready to enter the public school system, which by that time required all children to enroll at the age of four. The program offered help in finding part-time employment and created special work for parents on the model of the student job programs.

The major purpose of the pilot was to see how well student financial-aid systems could be adapted to select and fund parents. Grants were big enough to maintain young families on the modest standard of living to which they had become accustomed as students—high enough to make it possible to spend time with young children, but not high enough to induce the reluctant to have children in order to qualify for a subsidy.

College administrators eagerly cooperated. Declining enrollments left financial-aid officers with slack work loads, and administrators saw an opportunity to adapt underused college facilities to the needs of the new parenting families. Publicity on the project and media attention to the declining birth rate and the high cost of rearing children moved Congress to instruct the Office of Management and Budget to divert funds already appropriated for student financial aid to parents. The women's movement succeeded in limiting the funds to parents who undertook to parent equally.

The program rapidly expanded. The young parents adapted the sharing, the informality, and much of the special language and clothing of student life to the enterprise of parenting. Dormitories were easily converted into family quarters with communal meal service and child-care swapping. Industries which could use part-time workers such as mail-order houses, senior-citizen developments, and medical-care facilities moved in to take advantage of educated, part-time workers with a ceiling on the earnings they could make without losing their parent financial aid.

Blacks, Hispanics, native American and ethnic groups protested the college setting of the program as elitism, if not outright genocide, so the program was broadened to recruit parents from groups that had been under-represented in the original pilots. A generation later, the grants had created a building boom and explosion of child services comparable to the growth of higher education during the 1960s.

Children's villages were built from scratch with playgrounds, schools, medical facilities, and parent support groups. Some young couples were attracted to parenting because of the lifestyle, as teenagers were attracted to college, but the subsidies did not create the baby boom some had predicted. The few who became "perpetual parents" of four or five or six became administrators and counselors, a permanent resource for the changing population. Most of the parents were willing to "graduate" to an adult-oriented life and full-time employment after their child was ready for school at four.

ADULT LIFESTYLES

Fewer children—and withdrawal from the mainstream when children are young—will mean that more of life will be led away from home. Without young children, it will be easier to move, and to follow unconventional daily schedules. Living arrangements will be simpler, less permanent, more various, and organized around the needs of individuals rather than a corporate "family."

In the 1970s the ticky-tacky suburban boxes derided by the counter-culture of the 1960s were becoming slums. Couples who had used them as a breeding ground were following their grown children out of them into apartments and trailers, or taking to the road in vans. Younger, two-income couples weren't interested in buying them. If they needed room for their hobbies, they wanted something more individual, and if they had children they couldn't afford the money or time required for both parents to commute.

Housework will fade away as women give up the dream of home. Our historian grandchildren will be puzzled to read about how their grandmothers struggled to get their grandfathers to help with the housework. What housework? Why dress up the bed with traditional spreads and dust ruffles when there will be nobody home to see it all day? For the two-career couples who are leading the parade, there is already just too much else to do.

Homes won't project the social status of the family. Outsiders won't be able to tell anything about a family or any particular member by finding out where they live, or inspecting their living room furniture. The contents of a home will reflect the interests and tastes of the individuals using them rather than a prevailing style. Individuals won't bother to keep up with the Joneses on aspects of life that don't interest them. A woman who buys designer clothes may drive up in her ten-year-old car to play tennis with a man who steps out of his imported sports car in a ten-year-old suit.

Eating, too, will be individual. There will still be "family" meals on occasional holidays, but varying schedules will make it hard to get the whole family together for a roast beef dinner or a soufflé that can't wait for laggards.

Cooking will survive as a hobby. The business lunch will survive as a ritual. But fewer people will spend their time at kitchen stoves. In 1979, many families were already following the rule of the woman in Chapter 6 who wrote us, "If it takes more than thirty minutes, we just don't eat it."

People will eat whenever or wherever they get hungry. They'll raid home refrigerators stocked with prepared food or go to one of the twenty-four hour cafeterias serving schools, offices, hospitals, and entertainment areas. These will offer a menu that can serve as breakfast, lunch, or dinner, depending on the schedule of the patron—and home kitchens will be stocked that way, too.

Recreation will revolve around interest groups rather than families. Husbands, wives, and children each will have individual school friends, job friends, hobby friends, tennis friends, political friends, church friends. Instead of elaborate parties with carefully thought-out guest lists, people will get together on the spur of the moment without advance food preparation or apologies for the absence of a mate.

The success or failure of individuals won't reflect on the reputation of their families or its other members. Individuals will be freer to marry out of their occupational rank, as they already do in Russia and China. Husbands and wives will support each other in private. Parents will help their children. But they will all have to stand on their own when they confront the outside world.

Family members won't tackle each others' emotional problems. They'll be handled by professionals or support groups of others who are coping with them. We've learned that heavy drinkers can get more help from a pickup "family" of fellow alcoholics than almost anyone else, and similar Problems Anonymous groups proliferated in the late 1970s to provide knowledgeable fellowship for drug addicts, single parents, widows, battered wives, nursing mothers, and victims of everything from compulsive eating to stage fright. Some of these special groups had, in addition, auxiliaries providing support for the *spouses* of those beset.

Families will get along better with each other because they will depend on each other primarily as friends. There will be less chance to quarrel over money, behavior, possessions, manners, or each other because neither parents nor children nor husbands nor wives will be each others' only source of emotional support. Families will spend less time with each other, but the quality of time will be higher, and deliberately scheduled, as friends' meetings so often are.

Home will still be important, but instead of the picture-perfect dream we have already seen disappearing in the future, it will be the badly needed relaxing side of life. People will find it in different places. In the 1970s, for instance, the pioneer-commuting couples weren't sure which of the residences maintained in separate cities was "really" home, and overcommitted career couples were saying that they felt more "at home" in their weekend cabins than they did in their city pads. Others would give the title to their boat or cross-country touring van.

This doesn't mean that there *won't* be traditional homes and families. Some will cling to the dream of home and make it a real career. Homemakers replying to the Matching Couples survey reached for titles that would professionalize their home work. One described herself as "in the wifehood business." Another put her occupation as "Nurturer." They had no trouble keeping busy. Crafts and home-improvement projects took up the time their modern appliances saved.

A woman who quit her job to become a "craftsperson" describes the professionalization of homemaking we can expect from those who choose it over equally available alternatives.

"There's pride in my home," she wrote us. "I'm never embarrassed if someone drops in. I enjoy the end results of cleaning, cooking (we entertain two or three times a month), lawn mowing, washing the car, etc. I have my herb garden (twenty-six herbs if they make it through the winter) and we have a vegetable garden." She also quilts, embroiders, makes clothes for herself and her husband as well as all gifts and greeting cards. Her home recreates the Home, Sweet Home of tradition about as closely as the Williamsburg Restoration resembles the realities of colonial Virginia.

For most people, however, home won't be a permanent place. It will change over the course of a lifetime even more than it did in the 1970s, when it could mean the suburban ranch house where you grew up, the apartment you had in college, the van in which you toured the country with your first love, the hospital where you interned, the house you had when your children were born, and so on down to the retirement condominium you bought in Florida.

NEW LIFE PLANS

School. Work. Marriage. Kids. The Empty Nest. The gold watch and chain. The stages of life used to go by age. A girl worried if she was the last in her class to marry, and so did the last boy to find a job.

Every generation assumes that these stages are rooted in biology, but history shows that they are social devices for getting the next generation born and reared. In 1979, people are "too old" to work at 65 primarily because younger people need their jobs to support families.

The "right age" for working depends on the kind of work that the economy of the time provides for supporting a family. At 16, for instance, the author's grandfather wasn't "too young" to start clearing a farm and raising a family, but 16 was judged "too young" for her son to stack luggage at the local airport during the summer.

The appropriate age varies even for childbearing. Sixteen wasn't "too young"—nor 40 "too old"—when children were needed to help work the farm.

School. Work. Marriage. Kids. . . . We used to think everybody had to go through these stages, but the historical record shows that in the past most people weren't all that lucky. Wars, hard times, and untimely death prevented them from doing what was expected of them at their age. The very idea that age-stages could be a lockstep arose only when affluence made it possible for almost everyone to marry, earn, bear children, and eventually retire with some sort of security. Only when everyone was able to get on the lockstep did people actively aspire to get off it.

But the idea of stages dies hard. People want to look ahead, and when they can, plan for what's coming next. One of the new life pathways attracting traffic in the 1970s differed from the lockstep in a way that has usually led to significant advance in the past: it delayed maturity to permit a longer period of growth and development.

The new life track postponed binding commitments to squeeze in a new stage between college and career-building, then collapsed career and family building into ten or fifteen breathless, overcommitted years, followed by a second, post-childbearing lifestyle that invited a change of career and/or mate. But the really novel feature of the new track was that it was almost identical for men and women.

College, 18–22

Since the student rebellions of the 1960s, going *away* to college has become the liberation from parents that was traditionally achieved only by a self-supporting job or marriage.

College is now the place where you are allowed to make mistakes that won't hurt you because all your commitments are reversible. This is a time when both men and women enjoy unprecedented equality in sexual expression, status, and daily activities. Both sexes learn how to make and break relationships, handle and sometimes make money, cope with bureaucracy, and organize their own schedules as single, independent individuals. This four-year exercise in equality and autonomy is very poor preparation for the sex-stereotyped lockstep of the "real" world of the 1970s.

Identity-Seeking, 22–25

Graduates of the 1970s found reasons to delay settling down in the lockstep entry jobs. Increasingly, they embarked on an informal post-graduate search for the right job, the right person, even the right part of the country for them. This was a time for discovering who you were by trying and discarding all the things that you were not, for the tentative commitments of a Living Together Arrangement that might or might not lead to marriage; for a lifestyle experiment in group living; even for graduate study that might or might not lead to vocation. At an age when all previous generations had been most heavily engaged in work and family, the most alert were still window-shopping on life.

Making It, 25–40

Some time between 25 and 30, the identity seekers found a person or a career and made up for lost time. All the long background suddenly became foreground. Now was the time to pour energy and commitment into career, marriage, children, furniture, cars, boats, second houses, connections. Promotions came fast, and with two working there was money.

Couples who had shared similar activities were unprepared for child-rearing. Some fell afoul of the Baby Panic, or stumbled over the sex-role stereotyping they encountered in their rising careers. And even with the best of luck, intense career commitment generated disenchantment. Gluttons for experience, they had run through it all before the age of 40, and were ready for something new.

Women put a formal end to their child-bearing years and its strains by having themselves sterilized. Men daydream about braving the wilderness with only an ax and a shotgun to hunt for food. Both go back to paths rejected in their youth. A man who refused piano lessons at nine may take up the violin. A woman who couldn't do math becomes an accountant to challenge her company's budget.

This is the midlife crisis, moved back so that it comes early enough in life for viable second chance.

Second Chance, 40–50

Headhunters know the symptoms and exploit them. The job they are trying to sell will provide, they say, "a new challenge," a chance "to explore your underused talents." A professor of sociology takes early retirement to open a gourmet cooking school. A hotel chef, on the contrary, quits his grueling $40,000 executive job to go to art school. An army officer retires after twenty years in the service and becomes an Episcopal priest. An executive turns social worker. An engineer goes back to college for the liberal arts education he spurned as unpractical while he was earning his B.S.

This is the time for born-again religion. For moving to California —or away from it. Childbearing past, a woman becomes sexually assertive, ready for a second marriage entirely different from her first.

Interest Orientation, 50 on

At this stage of life, work is for fun rather than income. Couples or singles move into compact, easy-care quarters in the central city or into communities built around a special interest. Golf communities, crafts communities, music and art communities, religious communities of every conceivable kind. There will be an even wider selection in future.

Those who like to work or need income will work on a part-time or limited basis, which, as we shall see, will be more available in the future. Others will choose phased retirement plans that will use the experience of senior staff of large organizations to train and coach juniors or work on special problems.

This life plan may become common, but it will only be one among many. There are several reasons why individuals will have a wider choice of life plan. First, there will be fewer children to anchor couples in an extended family-and-career stage, and more of them will be born before or after the traditional child-bearing ages. Then, slower economic growth will encourage many people to postpone starting their careers or to retire early from them, and there will be so many different lifestyles going on side by side that variations of timing will be easier to arrange. But the most important condition for lifestyle choice will be the sharing of paid work by men and women.

Traditionally, a lifetime has been divided into three boxes. First comes school. Then work. Then retirement, or leisure. For many decades now there has been a steady shift of life from the box of work to the boxes of schooling and leisure, which offer individuals more control over schedule and location. When earning is shared, the boxes can be more easily rearranged: two working together can contrive, for instance, to spend a minimum of time in the work box; a workaholic can be support to a perpetual student or a nonearning hobbyist. When two earn, school, work, and leisure need not come in that order, nor need one be pursued to the exclusion of the other.

The breakdown of these three boxes of life was well under way in the 1970s. School and work were no longer separate domains. A rising proportion of college students were earning at least part of their expenses. Adult education was a growth industry, and the market potential was staggering. More than 40 percent of adults queried on a Gallup poll of 1978 said they would like to take some special course, or more training, and a third had already done so.

Women were leading the way in midlife career changes. With the springiness of youth, post-menopausal women were going back to college, going back to work, creating new careers on the basis of the skills they had acquired rearing children while learning. Those who had learned to make and break relationships without cracking up found it easier to punctuate their new beginning by divorce and re-marriage, and there will, of course, be more with this skill in the future.

What will really happen? The answer is that *everything* will happen to somebody and a lot of it is going to happen to everybody at some stage of life. The result will be a big, buzzing, well-seasoned stew of diversity, rich and many-flavored like the polyglot cities of New York and Honolulu, rather than monolithic cities like Dallas or Chicago which appear, on the surface, to "work."

It is not a world to every taste, but the bottom line for individuals will be a plus. Sex is going to be richer, more varied, and there is going to be more of it. In addition to being sexier, marriages will be later, fewer, shorter, more various one from the other—and much more rewarding. If they aren't rewarding, they simply won't last. Children will be later, fewer, and much more actively cherished. If they aren't preferred to alternatives, they simply won't be born.

Is there any basis for such optimism? Actually, it is simply a projection of the long-term improvement in the way people feel about their lives. In 1954, Dr. Leo Srole, of the Columbia University College of Physicians and Surgeons, surveyed the well-being of a sample of New Yorkers. His classic study, *Mental Health in the Metropolis,* showed that impairments of mental health increased steadily with age, and were twice as frequent among women as among men.

In the 1950s, when sex differences were being emphasized, these findings occasioned no great surprise. In those days everyone believed that women were just "naturally" less stable emotionally than men. But in 1974, when Srole and his colleague, Anita Kassen Fischer, tracked down and reinterviewed 695 of their original subjects, they discovered that while the mental health of the men in the sample had remained about the same over 20 years of living in New York City and other urban settings, the mental health of the women had improved so dramatically that by 1974 they were just as well off as the men!

At first blush it looked as if the women had actually grown out of their problems as they had grown older, but comparison of successive generations showed that the credit belonged to the times in which they lived. The mental health of women in their forties reinterviewed during 1974 had improved significantly over that of women their age who had been interviewed in 1954, and there was the same improvement for women in their fifties. Not so, with men. In 1974, men in their forties and fifties, on the average, did not differ in mental health levels from men their age twenty years earlier. It was happening in society-at-large, and had an impact on the women in the Midtown sample, as well as on other women living in urban areas.

The lesson of this follow-up study is that well-being depends not on sex, or even wholly on age, but on outside conditions that are changing for the better. According to Srole and Fischer, the best prescription for the mental and physical health of the population is "a liberal infusion of equality." They are happy to add that the updated study lends "weighty empirical support to the compelling ethical case for the currently pending and long overdue Equal Rights Amendment."

Optimism wasn't popular in the late 1970s. When conditions improve, expectations almost always rise faster than the changes themselves can be made, and this is especially true of change in deep-seated family relations. But the Midtown Mental Health follow-up illustrates that we are moving in the right direction.

Real choices for more people will set off chains of consequences for government, education, the economy—even religion. Much of what's ahead will mandate new ways of working and new definitions of the meaning of work in a person's life.

CHAPTER 13

New Ways of Working

The most probable future is a world of individuals rather than families in which men and women will earn and spend in much the same way. The falling birth rate will make women the economic equals of men.

We have no idea what a world like this will be like in America, but we do know what happens when an excluded group comes into the economic mainstream. From our very beginning as a nation, we have prospered by making producers and consumers of people denied full economic citizenship for reasons beyond their control.

Women are the last and the largest minority to win equality. As economic newcomers they share with blacks, immigrants, Hispanics and other ethnic groups the handicaps of limited access to jobs and critical consumer goods such as housing and education.

None of the excluded have entered without political struggle. Always there has been a backlash from people who imagined they were being displaced. The motives and tactics of the reactionaries have been remarkably the same over time. Fear inspired the "Know Nothing" campaigns against Irish immigrants before the Civil War, and

racial segregation of the enfranchised slaves after it. The same kind
of fear is behind the conservative attacks on the demand of women
for a fair shake at work in the 1970s. Reactionary *tactics* always
have been to shame, to ridicule, to threaten, and in extreme situations, to terrorize the candidates for equality. A revival of the Ku
Klux Klan formed to terrify "uppity Nigras" actually boasted of
being on hand to monitor the activities of "uppity women" at the
1977 National Women's Conference in Houston.

The backlash of the 1970s against women is sharp enough to
cause some to lose faith. But in the long historical perspective, it
cannot prevail. Most wives didn't go to work for the power of the
paycheck, but they liked it when they tasted it and they are not going
to give it up. On the contrary, their expectations are rising faster than
the capacity of the economy to fulfill them. Women pouring out of
college will not be content with fancily retitled "women's jobs." They
want more.

Women, too, shall overcome. They may suffer temporary setbacks
in the next ten or fifteen years, but equality is inevitable. There is no
viable alternative. Women are no more apt to quit looking for jobs
to lower unemployment than blacks were willing to go back to Africa
to solve America's race problem. They are in the executive suites to
stay.

The transition to full equality won't be easy. The stalled economy
of the 1970s does not provide the jobs that brought in the immigrants
and blacks. The curious situation of women is that they themselves
are the unwitting cause of the economic slowdown that stands in their
way. In the 1970s, the economy was growing slowly precisely *because*
the new jobs being created, after the Vietnam War, were less productive women's jobs that paid just enough to deter women from
quitting to have babies, but not enough to maintain the old rates of
growth. A Rand study of 1978 made for the National Institute of
Child Health and Human Development decisively linked the decline
in the birth rate during the 1960s and 1970s to the availability of
jobs rather than to the Pill, as generally believed.

The economic double bind facing women raises serious questions.
How will a slow-growing, adult-oriented economy provide enough
jobs for all the men and women who will want to work? Will equality

for women change the way work is done? What will it do to the country?

NEW JOBS

By 1990, two-thirds of all women are expected to work as well as more than four-fifths of the men. What will there be for them to do?

There will be jobs enough to go around because they will make work for each other.

New jobs will be made out of the work that is now done without money changing hands. This creation of jobs out of unpaid tasks has been going on for a long time. Driving schools, nursing homes, and lawn services now are supported by people who a generation ago had time to teach their kids to drive, to take care of their aged parents at home, and had teenagers around the house to do the yard work.

There are many more of these tasks to be converted. When everyone goes out of the house to work, we will need more nurses to take care of people too sick to be left alone, but not sick enough to go to the hospital; more teachers for after-school and preschool babysitting that mothers used to swap when there was always at least one on the block at home; more patrolmen for childless neighborhoods that will be deserted during working hours. And when everyone works, the "consumer maintenance" industries grow bigger. Restaurants, hotels, house cleaning, window washing, babysitting, appliance servicing, telephone answering, poodle grooming and people grooming, too.

The growing end of the economy will continue to be in services: government, health care, education, travel, banking, recreation, advertising. Services are limited not by pollution or the price of energy, but by the man hours available to give and receive them, and the imagination to think them up.

New jobs will be carved out of the volunteer work of proven value because there will be nobody left who is able to do it without at least some income. We may, for instance, eventually have to pay Cub Scout den mothers, presidents of the P.T.A., and members of volunteer fire departments. The professions of teaching, nursing, and social work grew out of what women once did for nothing in their homes, and the process will continue.

Women and men active in community work may find themselves managing public-access television stations which will serve as a live, ongoing letterbox for local issues and organizations. Professionals may be needed in the art of organizing support groups like Alcoholics Anonymous for the many isolated individuals who will be coping with common life situations alone.

Another candidate for professionalism is the ombudsman work legislators do on a casual basis for constituents coping with the bureaucracy of government. Some universities have ombudsmen to deal not only with student, faculty, and staff, but with outsiders affected by the campus, too. Why not ombudsmen for corporations, hospitals, the Army, even the church? A professional representative of the individual in his dealing with organizations could go from organization to organization as accountants now do.

Activities undertaken for fun or as a matter of course will be redefined as work and offered on the market. Some people are now paid for accompanying cellists on the piano or for walking dogs. Ever more specialized coaches, counselors, and therapists enter a market essentially directed toward supporting relationships, which only can grow with the proportion of adults who are unattached to family units. More adults will discover, too, that the structured emotional support you buy at the psychiatrist's can do you more good than the haphazard kind you expect to get from your family or friends for free.

There always have been paid relationships, and they vary from one society to another. One of the most paradoxical things that happened at the 1977 National Women's Conference in Houston was the attempt of some members of the Coyote prostitute's organization to explain to mu-mu–gowned delegates from Samoa what they did for a living. They insisted it was "just a job," but the Samoans marveled that anyone was willing to pay money for that. We will have to remain openminded in the future about the range of services for which someone at some time may be willing to pay.

Human services work will expand in the future, in part at least,

because so many people like to do it. A surprising number of people
will make a living helping other people to have as much fun as they
have learned to have themselves. A new profession that points the
way is that of the hospital "activities therapist" whose job it is to
interest convalescents in craft work, excursions, music, art, plants,
or any activity that will improve their interest in life. "Recreational
schooling" was attracting eager students for every kind of fun from
poetry to belly dancing.

Finally, new jobs will be easier to create because they won't all
have to be full-time positions paying enough to support a family.
Many of them will be service jobs that can be added easily with
little capital investment. The productivity of this work cannot be
greatly improved, so the pay will stay low, but more workers will be
able to afford the luxury of earning less at the job they like such as
"working with people." And it will be easier to make this attractive
work go around to more workers because "people work" lends itself
to the flexible, part-time schedules that mothers, students, and the
retired were trying to find in the 1970s.

NEW WORK STYLES

The economic independence of women will do more than create new
jobs. It will change the terms on which work is contracted and the
way jobs are packaged. These changes will come about because of a
massive shift of power from employers to employees.

Two paychecks will do for white-collar workers what the unions
did for the assembly line. Employers perceived their loss of power,
when unions started to become powerful, as a "decline of the work
ethic." They complained that the old incentives of stick and carrot
didn't hold employees to work standards any more, and they hired
psychologists to tell them what to do about it.

There was, of course, nothing mysterious about the new independence of white-collar workers. With an extra paycheck coming
into the house, a man could afford to talk back to the boss. Husbands
and wives could even afford to express their resentment of the degree

to which they felt "the company" was in control of their private lives.

"It bothered me that someone who didn't even know us could determine where we lived," one wife said of an offer to move her husband to another city. A survey made by Atlas Van Lines showed that more men were turning down company transfers, because they were willing to risk their careers in order to live in a place and with people they liked.

Economic independence of women helped men to more independence at work in another way, too. Equal employment opportunity laws that insured equal treatment for blacks and women established a legal right to ask the embarrassing questions about standards of hiring, firing, and promotion that unions had been asking on behalf of their members.

In the future, employers will not be allowed to fire a professional or clerical worker for speaking her mind, or keep her in ignorance of company policies affecting her. During the 1970s, legal precedents were enlarging the grounds on which injured employees could fight back against arbitrary company discipline. Laws were giving them the right to see their own personnel records, and there was growing support for the idea that employers should not be allowed to disclose these records to outsiders. Courts were beginning to protect employees who violated the rule that "everyone always speaks for the company" in order to protest against illegal or unethical behavior of their bosses or defects in the company's products.

In the future, employees will have something akin to corporate citizenship, with the right to due process in management decisions affecting them. They will, for instance, have a right to *know* why they haven't been promoted.

Corporate citizenship is a consequence of equal employment opportunities for blacks and women that can initiate an upward spiral of benevolent outcomes. Sociologist Rosabeth Kanter, author of *Men and Women of the Corporation,* made an intensive study of the people in a major corporation in order to find out how their work affected their lives. She found that employees with little control over their work tend to be politically reactionary, less creative in their use of leisure, and more severe and hostile to their sons than middle managers with more autonomy. More control over a man's job may give him the kind of confidence that makes family life better in exactly the same way that a wife's job makes her a more confident and better companion to her husband.

But the incentive of the carrot is always more powerful than the incentive of the stick, and it is in the nature of the carrot that the biggest management changes will come. The hope of bigger pay has always sufficed to motivate breadwinners, but a cafeteria offering different kinds of rewards will be needed to get work out of college-educated, white-collar workers with two paychecks coming into their homes.

Advancement will be harder in the slow-growing world of the future. It will take the temperament of a racehorse to get to the top, and the competition will be keener because female racehorses will be admitted to the track. Average, everyday men and women will take a good hard look at the odds against success and turn to satisfactions that don't require striving for it. Like the "decline in the work ethic," the "decline of ambition" is a rational response to the real life situation in which workers find themselves.

There was no doubt, in the 1970s, of a retreat from the single-minded pursuit of business success during the male-oriented, expanding economy of the Vietnam War. Money and prestige were not primary goals for professionals, executives, and college students headed for careers. In 1973, for instance, an American Management Association study found a majority of middle-level executives admitting that they didn't look to their work for their main satisfaction, and a bigger majority said they were changing their definitions of "success."

Even high-powered executives were paying more attention to the satisfactions available from their families, their hobbies, recreations, and religion. They were beginning to prefer shorter hours to higher pay, a phenomenon George Washington University's Sar Levitan ascribed directly to the employment of wives. And they were more apt to take early retirement instead of waiting for age 65 or 70.

Workers almost always say that the work itself, and the satisfactions of doing it are more important than pay. "Helping people" was the leading satisfaction for nurses surveyed by a nursing magazine, followed by "doing worthwhile work." Participants in a 1977 happiness survey went even further. Two-thirds of them said they wouldn't move to a better paying job if it meant less interesting work, and opinion was almost equally divided on whether to take a cut in present pay for a chance at *more* interesting work.

In the future, money alone will not be a big enough carrot to get all of the dull and dirty work done. In the 1970s there seemed to be plenty of people willing to make ceramics at the minimum wage. Yet, in spite of recession, there was always a shortage of waitresses and garbage collectors, even though they could earn as much as schoolteachers.

Even in the fanciest offices, files were growing skimpier and more chaotic because women with the wit to keep them were quietly refusing to do what they regarded as a thankless task. In the future, office housekeeping will go the way of housekeeping at home: it won't be done simply because no one will be willing to do it. Future managers will learn to get along writing fewer letters, and keeping fewer papers. Whatever their sex, they'll pick up after themselves in the office as they do at home.

Employers are trying to make dull jobs more "interesting" by involving workers in more of the decisions, but "enrichment" sometimes works against efficiency and it cannot be applied to a long list of important social tasks. Take health care. The only way to hold down some hospital costs is to put procedures such as taking blood samples on an assembly-line basis. Six minutes to approach a patient, stick in the needle, and get it out again. Some of the human service jobs being created can have as much to do with machines as with "helping people."

Let us consider the options open to a future hospital manager who has to keep those blood tests coming with the kind of people he can hire and train. Because people will move around more freely and have fewer children, there will always be many more candidates for employment, but the stick won't work on them any more because they don't have to take the first job that comes along or stay with one that turns out to be actively unpleasant.

He could hire a psychologist or a promotion specialist to "motivate" the blood samplers he already had and to talk up the job in the community, but he will find it cheaper and more practical to hire an industrial engineer to cut blood sampling work into blocks of time that fit comfortably into the daily lives of people whom he wishes to induce to do it.

The biggest problem will be hours. In many organizations of the 1970s the traditional nine-to-five schedule was convenient only for men who had full-time wives at home to get their meals, take their clothes to the cleaners, mind the kids, and wait all afternoon for the plumber to come. And by no particular coincidence, it often turned out that the only people on the payroll in this happy situation were the bosses who decided what hours the rest of the staff should keep.

Working hours had never been questioned when family life revolved around the starting and stopping time of the breadwinner. But when two earned, they were seen as a threat to home life. In 1973, interference with home life accounted for one-fourth of the complaints about working conditions reported on a survey made by the Michigan Institute for Social Research. This complaint had been so rare on a similar survey of 1969 that researchers had not bothered to code it.

Very slight alterations of schedule were often all an individual needed, and some were able to negotiate with their bosses. One woman traded late arrival in the morning for her vacation. Another arranged to work through her lunch hour in order to take the time off at the end of the day. Time off for parents—including fathers—to visit their children's schools was often exchanged for extra work during rush periods. In many offices, earlier restrictions on personal phone calls during working hours were lifted to help parents keep track of the after-school activities of their children or to attend to personal business that had to be transacted during traditional "working hours."

What has begun as individual concessions will be gradually recognized as "employee rights" when employers discover that they improve productivity and that employees actively appreciate them. "Parental leave" and "paternity leave" will be increasingly written into employment contracts on the same basis as sick or "personal days" have been.

In the future, flexible hours will become mandatory in every kind of work that permits them. "Flexi-time," the arrangement that gives employees a choice of starting and stopping times was gaining rapidly in the late 1970s. It cost employers nothing and often improved morale. Pilot studies had shown that part-time workers were no less efficient or more costly than those working full time. It remains only to apply part-time schedules to the professional work that can be handled this way or shared by two partners—in some cases, even a husband and wife.

The decline of the nine-to-five standard was easy to see even in the recession years of the 1970s. Irregular schedules were becoming more common because they were essential in the service industries that were growing. Restaurants, hotels, airlines, hospitals, entertainment had always employed odd-hour workers, and to these were added the night and weekend openings of retailers, adult-education therapists, dentists, and other services catering to the employed.

Parents and the semi-retired who want to work at home will discover new ways of packaging work now done nine to five in the office. Freelance writers will not be the only ones to taste the comforts and frustrations of working at home when computer terminals and closed-circuit television are generally available in the 1980s. Researchers, scientists, sales persons, and even certain kinds of administrators may go to the office only once or twice a month.

Decentralized locations will prove to have many advantages. In the late 1970s, for instance, public-housing authorities discovered that they could train welfare mothers to administer the housing projects in which they lived and raised their children. In addition to giving them professional jobs, the new practice gave the project residents speedy, neighborly service that had been slow and unavailable when the authority was wielded by a white man sitting in an office on the other side of town.

When more adults are earning, more pay will be taken in the form of leisure. Working hours will come down. Time off will be taken not only in shorter daily hours, but in more three-day weekends, more optional days off, double vacations both summer and winter, and in many different kinds of leave without pay. There will be maternity leave, educational leave, parental leave, and just plain we're-taking-a-year-off-to-go-around-the-world leave. All these and many new devices yet uninvented will be used to package work into jobs of different sizes and shapes to fit the diverse lifestyles and changing stages of the people who do it.

Juanita Kreps, the economist who became Carter's Secretary of Commerce, was the first to point out that work could be easier and more rewarding if it came when you wanted it. "Suppose the government offered to pay benefits equivalent to the current Social Security transfer to those who chose not to work in any given year," she wrote in 1976. "A more conservative plan might allow a worker to take a year off with benefits after every seven or ten years of working credits, while specifying perhaps a maximum of 45 years of work for each individual. . . . Concentration of education, work, and leisure in three phases of life creates adjustment problems both at the beginning and end of worklife, as well as maximizing the disutility of work and minimizing the utility of free time."

Lockstep-bound workers were surprisingly willing to go along. Four out of five of one sample survey of employees thought it would be better for them personally, as well as for society in general, if education, work, and leisure were interspersed rather than following each other in irreversible stages. In 1978, Congress took the first step by outlawing involuntary retirement at age 65.

Employers who in 1979 were complaining about poor work attitudes will discover that they cannot apply the same standard to the more various labor force of two-paycheck families. Instead of talking about the "work ethic" they will learn to think in terms of a whole range of work ethics. Some people are career committed, working for the task itself. Some work the way we all do chores—because the job has to be done. Most work quite simply for money. Others—in the past, it was only women—work for the sociability of the work place, or to help other people. In future, the same work may be packaged in jobs of varying schedules and standards to accommodate the motivations of workers at different stages of their lives.

Robert Holland, president of the Committee on Economic Development, a private business research organization, thinks we will have to "unwrap the job package to provide a greater measure of freedom to the job seeker." Some will want the full package of fringe benefits, with pension. Others will prefer a limited contract for a specific task or a period of time. In some circumstances, a worker will prefer cash to a retirement benefit. And instead of the abrupt transition into work and out of it, apprenticeship and retirement could progress in easy stages.

THE IMPACT OF GENDER

Will women humanize work when they gain power? It would be nice to think so.

They certainly defuse the violence of confrontations, which is why you see them more frequently in places where women aren't supposed to go. The loveliest example is the story told by Carol Jenkins, New York City NBC television reporter.

When Jenkins arrived to film the scene of a gory bank robbery with her three-year-old sleeping on her shoulder, she found the way barred by an official of the bank who happened to be a young woman, too. Both women were so intent on stating their respective positions that neither so much as glanced at the sleeping little girl until they had worked out an acceptable compromise, and Jenkins had managed to shoot her footage. "Cute baby," said the bank vice-president as Jenkins turned to go with camera and child. If both had been men, they might well have come to blows.

Some people hope—and others fear—that women might slow the pace of business. But if anything, the opposite is more likely. Women have, in the past, tended to be more efficient than men on their level simply because they had to be better to get the job. As discrimination declines, their edge will narrow. Their temporary superiority is the result of discrimination, not gender.

Eli Ginzberg looks for a one-time boost to efficiency when women are introduced in jobs formerly done by men (or men into jobs always done by women) because managers will see the job with new eyes and discover improvements they should have made long ago.

He recalls that in World War II, employers thought they had to simplify the work of so-called "white jobs" so that presumably less qualified blacks could do them. In the process, of course, they increased the efficiency of the white workers, too. A boost in productivity can be expected from the novelty of the workers rather than their race or gender.

Equality for women will, of course, improve the quality of management because there will be more candidates to choose from, but this is a matter of numbers, not gender. Doubling the number of men in the talent pool would improve the quality of candidates chosen, too.

Women may understand women better. They may be smarter at personnel policies and know what is going on in the typing pool because they once have been in it themselves. But these advantages are due to special knowledge, not gender. If you want to sell the Chinese, you make a point of hiring a Chinese salesman.

Women may bring to management a less hierarchic and more cooperative style of getting things done. Not always, of course. The scars of past discrimination embitter the pioneer women who have overcome. But if women are less apt to "battle" over sales territories or "score" with a new concept, if they are more apt to conciliate clashing opinions and win subordinates rather than command them, it is not because they are women, but merely *because they are not men.* In contemporary working life, the combativeness of males is a handicap women have been spared.

Equality for women will not necessarily "humanize" work but it can go far toward rescuing men from the crippling obligation to prove that *they are not women.*

Women have always wanted meaningful work helping people instead of money, power, or prestige. In the future, men, too, will enjoy the luxury of choosing work for the intrinsic value of doing it.

Women have always wanted work that allowed for life off the job —part-time work with time out that could be scheduled around changing life situations. In the future, men, too, will have a choice over the investment they wish to make in their work.

The economy of the future will be based on individuals who are growing and changing on timetables that have nothing to do with their sex. There won't be many more people than there were in 1979, but they will be better and happier people. More of them will be adults. More of the adults will be earners. And more of the earners will be working at jobs and schedules of their own choosing.

The most probable future is a world that will be more diverse, faster changing, more human, and much, much more fun than the world we came into.

CHAPTER NOTES

CHAPTER 1

The basic data on women and work come from the rival information gathering systems of the Bureau of the Census in the Department of Commerce and the Bureau of Labor Statistics in the Department of Labor.

BLS (Bureau of Labor Statistics) is authoritative on the characteristics of the labor force and presents statistics on the age, marital status, parental status, education, occupation, and earnings of women workers. The Women's Bureau of the Department of Labor issues a Handbook on Women Workers which interprets all available statistics on women, and reports the interest of all other Federal agencies in the status of women. It is updated every few years; the next one is not expected until 1981. A roundup of private as well as public studies on specific discriminations against women was made by Patricia Sexton for Labor's Employment and Training Administration, "Women and Work," R & D Monograph 46, 1977. For a handy index, "Where to Find BLS Statistics on Women," published in 1978, write Inquiries and Correspondence, Bureau of Labor Statistics, Washington, D.C. 20212.

Census is authoritative on the characteristics of the population, including, of course, occupation and labor force participation. Its 1976 Survey of Income and Education (SIE) has added valuable new data on the relative input of family income contributed by husbands and wives. For the Bicentennial, Census issued *A Statistical Portrait of Women in the U.S.,* Current Population Reports, Special Studies Series P–23, No. 58.

An official statement, with supporting research, on the changes women need to achieve equality is available in the two reports of the National Commission on the Observance of International Women's Year. "To Form A More Perfect Union," delivered to the President of the United States in June 1976, details barriers to full equality. "The Spirit of Houston: An Official Report to the President, the Congress, and the

People of the United States," delivered in March 1978 reports the twenty-six recommendations passed by the delegates to the National Women's Conference at Houston, November 18 to 21, 1977. It is especially revealing about credit, employment, homemakers and insurance. Both reports are available from the U.S. Government Printing Office. The recommendations and account of the meeting are available, along with a personal statement of Gloria Steinem and other representative women participating, in *What Women Want,* by Caroline Bird and the IWY Commission, published in March 1979 by Simon and Schuster.

Another basic source is the testimony heard by the Joint Economic Committee of the 93rd Congress, First Session, chaired by Michigan Congresswoman Martha Griffiths in July 1973: "Economic Problems of Women" and a compendium of papers submitted for the use of the JEC's Subcommittee on Economic Growth and Stabilization in 1977.

Although not intended as a summary of research, Rosabeth Kanter's 115-page paperback, *Work and Family in the United States: A Critical Review and Agenda for Research and Policy,* Russell Sage Foundation, 1977, is a useful as well as readable guide to the research on the impact of work on family life, with an extensive bibliography.

PAGE 4—In 1960, women held 32 percent of the jobs; in 1977, 40 percent.

PAGE 5—The median pay of women has hovered just under 60 percent of the median pay of men for the past twenty years, but the gap widened between 1973 and 1976. See "The Earnings Gap Between Women and Men," U.S. Department of Labor, Employment Standards Administration, Women's Bureau, 1976, and update by Edward J. Kelly.

Samuelson's estimate of the impact of discrimination was made for the Joint Economic Committee hearing of July 10, 1973.

PAGE 7—A study by Ralph E. Smith when he was at the Urban Institute showed that women *already at work* suffered no more, in the aggregate, than men, because the recession struck hardest at industries in which they were underrepresented. Mr. Smith is editor of *The Subtle Revolution,* a forthcoming collection of essays on the economic impact of the employment of women, to be published by the Urban Institute.

PAGE 10—Rena Bartos, Senior Vice-President and Director of Communications Development for J. Walter Thompson Company, the nation's biggest advertising agency, has been a pioneer in assessing the impact of employment on the market for consumer goods. Her presentation on women going to work, "The Moving Target" was influential in alerting the business community to the impact of women at work on American industry.

Media Decisions, an advertising trade paper, estimated that there were only two TV campaigns directed to working women in 1976.

PAGE 11—The Phillips Academy at Andover had 2,600 applicants for 400 places in the fall of 1977. "Preppies" used to be primarily rich. Now they are primarily bright.

PAGE 11—For statistics on working women see Heather L. Ross and Isabel V. Sawhill, *Time of Transition,* Washington, The Urban Institute, 1975.

PAGE 12—The best analysis of family formation trends is a 41-page booklet with charts and graphs, prepared by veteran Census demographers Paul C. Glick and Arthur J. Norton for the Population Reference Bureau of Washington, D.C., "Marrying, Divorcing, and Living Together in the U.S. Today," *Population Bulletin,* vol. 32, No. 5, 1977.

PAGE 13—"The Economics of Marital Status" by Fredericka Pickford Santos is one of the many excellent reports in *Sex, Discrimination and the Division of Labor,* edited by Cynthia B. Lloyd, Columbia University Press, New York and London, 1975.

PAGE 13—Isabel Sawhill's "Economic Perspective on the Family" in the Spring 1977 issue of *Daedalus* is both rigorous and perceptive on the economics of marriage and baby decisions. For analysis of the rise of single women heads of families see Heather Ross and Isabel Sawhill. *Time of Transition.*

PAGE 13—Becker and Michael report their findings in the February 1978 issue of the *National Bureau of Economic Research Reporter.*

PAGE 16—"What Every Woman Should Know About Social Security and Income Tax Laws," an unpublished paper by Isabel Sawhill, clearly explains the marriage penalty in the tax laws.

PAGE 17—The $1,816 "marriage penalty" for man and wife each earning $20,000 in 1978 is from the Tax Report column of *The Wall Street Journal,* September 20, 1978.

PAGE 18—The concept of unemployment insurance is to protect those who are involuntarily dismissed, but in 1978, New York State teachers who became pregnant could be put on inactive status that did not qualify them for unemployment insurance even though they wanted to continue working.

The California law is more liberal and provides benefits for those who quit a job for "good cause." In 1977, the California Unemployment Insurance Board awarded unemployment benefits to a waitress who quit to follow her husband to another state on the ground that "maintenance of the marital relationship" was the kind of "good cause" the law contemplated. The law is intricate and it changes. Consult *Employment Practices Decisions,* a 16-volume reference work published by the Commerce Clearing House of Chicago, Inc.

CHAPTER 2

My interest in the problems of working wives began in 1966 while researching *Born Female* and continued as I realized how family responsibilities impacted on the careers of women. Many of the issues addressed in *The Two-Paycheck Marriage* emerged during research for *Everything a Woman Needs to Know to Get Paid What She's Worth.*

The specific data base for the Study of Matching Couples began with discussion groups I arranged with wives returning to the labor force at colleges in California, Montana, South Dakota, New York, New Jersey, and Michigan during 1975 and 1976. Marjorie Godfrey and I talked with scores of couples, separately and together, to identify the issues and reported some of our findings in "Husbands Talk About Working Wives" which appeared in the April 1976 issue of *Family Circle.*

In order to get a statistical grip on the salience of the issues we had discussed with our couples, *Family Circle* magazine devised a matching questionnaire for wives and husbands to fill out separately. Highlights from that survey, which is entitled "The 1976 *Family Circle* Survey on Working Wives," were printed in the November 1976 issue of *Family Circle.*

The Mark Clements Research Organization analyzed at random 5,000 replies out of the more than 30,000 responses received. The size of the sample and the matching of husbands and wives made it possible to analyze significant but numerically small populations. We were able, for instance, to find the earnings, ages, occupations, education, and opinions of both husband and wife of 402 couples in which she outearned him. And by matching the opinions of husbands and wives we were able to pinpoint areas of disagreement which could be followed up in interviews both with respondents to the printed questionnaire and with additional couples we located to study the specific issue in question.

By this method we were able, for instance, to compare what couples thought they ought to be doing about budgeting and child care with what they actually were doing and even to identify and analyze the population of mothers of preschool children who were working when they thought they ought to be staying at home. We were able to study the impact of a wife's pay on her power in the family by finding out which partner's view was actually followed when the couple disagreed—as well as to analyze the kinds of couples who were most likely to disagree.

Most important, perhaps, we were able to define the demographics of the problem of working wives by comparing the couples who were attracted to the questionnaire with the U.S. population as reported in the Census. *Family Circle* readers are only slightly upscale of the general population, so those attracted to the questionnaire represented the kinds of people who felt that the rise in the proportion of working wives was a problem to them personally. Not all, of course, are working couples: the most vociferous respondents were homemakers who felt they had to explain in personal terms, and often at great length, just why they had chosen to stay *out* of the labor force.

Briefly stated, the couples concerned about the problem were younger, richer, better educated, more likely to be employed in professional or technical occupations, much more apt to have a wife in the labor force and a little more apt to have children under six than the population in general. From our interviews it was apparent that the population most urgently concerned were the college-educated working couples under 30 years of age with reasonably high incomes and preschool children.

Matching couples were younger: 48 percent of the wives were under 30 compared with 25 percent for the whole country; 74 percent of the husbands were under 40, compared with 40 percent for the whole U.S.A.

Richer: Average mean income for responding husbands was $14,670, compared with mean income of $13,231 for all husbands living with wives; and $7,500 for working wives, compared with mean income of $4,721 for other wives.

Better educated: 35 percent of the wives and 45 percent of the husbands were college graduates compared with 14 and 18 percent of the population in the labor force as a whole.

More prestigious: 54 percent of the husbands were in professional, technical, or management occupations, compared with 28 percent of all male workers. Thirty-eight percent of the wives were in professional, technical, or management jobs versus 21 percent of female U.S. workers.

Stratified or true cross-section samples of working couples have been made by both public and private organizations. The two major publicly financed sources are continuing studies following the same group of families over time. One is the continuing survey of income dynamics made by the Institute of Social Research at the University of Michigan under government funding. Its major findings have been reported by James N. Morgan, Katherine Dickinson, Jonathan Dickinson, Jacob Benus, and Greg Duncan in *Five Thousand American Families—Patterns of Economic Progress,* vols. 1 and 2, Ann Arbor, Institute for Social Research, University of Michigan, 1974.

The other, the so-called "Parnes Data," is based on National Longitudinal Surveys of Labor Market Experience and is collected for the U.S. Department of Labor at Ohio State University on the basis of samples drawn by the Census. It has followed four cohorts of 5,000 young men, young women, middle-aged men, and middle-aged women with special reference to their labor force activity, and has been the basis of hundreds of special studies.

Both of these large, government-funded, longitudinal surveys provide information only for the 1960s and occasionally for the early 1970s, and little on attitudes. Since both behavior and attitude have changed radically, they are less helpful in assessing change than private studies made for marketers or magazine advertisers.

Two private studies are of special value. One is the General Mills American Family Reports, "Raising Children in A Changing Society," 1976–1977, and "A Study of the American Family and Money," 1974–1975 both conducted by Yankelovitch, Skelly and White, Inc. Another is "How Women Feel About Housework," a research report based on responses to the Housework Survey in the October 1976 issue of *McCall's*. Opinion polls by Gallup, Yankelovich, Harris, National Opinion Research Corporation, and others contain isolated questions bearing on some of the issues.

A study that addressed itself to attitudes is the National Women's Survey, a national survey of 1,522 women conducted in the fall of 1975 by Market Opinion Research for the National Commission on the Observance of International Women's Year, under the direction of Dr. Barbara Everitt Bryant. Dr. Bryant found that about a third of the women were traditional in their outlook on the role of women, a third were in favor of expanding their role, and a third were trying to balance the two views.

PAGE 21—Social status—"socioeconomic status," or "SES," as the social scientists call it—traditionally has been determined by the income, education, and occupation of the husband-father alone. Dr. Marie J. Haug, of Case Western Reserve, points out that the contacts a wife makes at work can provide information on work opportunities, shopping bargains, insider tips, and upward mobility strategy. She argues that social researchers should count the income, education, and occupation of the wife in determining the SES of families. See her "Social Class Measurement and Women's Occupational Role," *Social Forces,* 52 (1973) 86–98. Our interviews bear her out. According to one wife, her blue-collar husband wanted her to work "so that he could say that his wife worked at _____ company." Another blue-collar husband cited the "people we get to meet through her work" as an advantage of her working.

PAGE 24—Varying proportions—usually a majority—say they would go on working even if they had enough money to live without earning. In the past, women have been a little more apt than men to quit if they had money, but there was no difference between the proportions of men and women who would go on working if they didn't need money among readers of *Psychology Today,* answering that question for a survey on work reported in their May 1978 issue.

Of wives responding to the survey printed in *Family Circle* in 1976, however, 83 percent said they wanted to work for money, but only 76 percent said they would work for money for their own satisfaction, even if the family didn't need money. Husbands, on the contrary, were less likely (13 percent to 23 percent) to object to a wife's working if it was for her own satisfaction only than if money were the object.

PAGE 34—The study of wives who gave up jobs to stay at home was reported by Linda Dannenberg in "Back-to-Home Movement? 'We Gave up Jobs to be Full-time Mothers,' " in the May 1976 issue of *Family Circle.*

PAGE 35—Comparison of the health of housewives and working wives comes from the National Health Survey conducted by National Center for Health Statistics of the U.S. Public Health Service, reported in "Limitation of Activity Due to Chronic Conditions, United States 1974," Series 10, No. 111, published in June 1977.

PAGE 35—The "housewife syndrome" was based on data from the National Health Service reported in "Selected Symptoms of Psychological Distress," National Center for Health Statistics, Series 11, No. 37, August 1970. The sample of adults representing the U.S. population was asked in 1960 and 1962 if they suffered from nervous breakdown, feelings of an impending nervous breakdown, nervousness, psychological inertia, insomnia, hand-trembling, nightmares, perspiring hands, fainting, headaches, dizziness, heart palpitations. "Women had higher rates than men for all 12 symptoms . . . Lower rates were reported by never married individuals, particularly among white women compared with their married, divorced, separated or widowed cohorts; by working men and women compared with retired men and women housekeepers respectively, and by residents of metropolitan areas compared with residents in other urban and rural areas."

During 1971–1975, NCHS resurveyed the psychological well-being of the general population, including the prevalence of self-reported nervous breakdown and impending nervous breakdown, and scored respondents on a scale constructed on the basis of answers to questions about how good they felt rather than the presence of psychological symptoms. They found that the mental health of housewives was as good as that of working wives except for ages 25 to 29 and 45 to 55. Private communication from Dr. Dupuy.

PAGE 36—The psychologist who surveyed the ego strengths of college women was Janice Porter Gump, who reported her findings in "Sex Role Attitudes and Psychological Well-Being," *Journal of Social Issues* 28(2): 79–91, X 1972.

PAGE 36—For mental health of employed women versus housewives, see Myrna M. Weissman and Eugene S. Paykel, *The Depressed Woman: A Study of Social Relationships,* University of Chicago Press, Chicago, 1974. The impact of unemployment on women in Detroit was measured by Rachelle Warren of the Institute of Labor and Industrial Relations in a study of Detroit funded by the National Institute of Mental Health. The regression of intellectual interest among homemakers was reported in James W. Trent and Leland L. Medsker, *Beyond High School: A Psychological Study of 10,000 High School Graduates,* Jossey-Bass, San Francisco, 1968.

PAGE 38—J. Walter Thompson, Simmons Research, Campbell Soup, William Esty Co., the Supermarket Institute, Leo Burnett, and the Bureau of Advertising are among the market researchers who have done comparative studies of housewives and working wives. Almost every woman's magazine has data for advertisers.

PAGE 39—A Gallup poll of December 1970 found the young, the rich, the college-educated more likely to say they were happy than their opposites. In "Does Money Buy Happiness," *The Public Interest,* Winter 1973, Richard Easterlin summarizes data from 30 happiness studies and concludes that money makes you happy only when you have more of it than other people. He calls this the "hedonic treadmill."

Extensive investigations of happiness have been reported by Norman M. Bradburn and David Caplovitz, in *Reports on Happiness: A Pilot Study of Behavior Related to Mental Health,* National Opinion Research Center, Chicago, 1965; Hadley Cantril, in *The Pattern of Human Concerns,* Rutgers University Press, New Brunswick, 1965; and Angus Campbell, Philip E. Converse, and Willard L. Rodgers, in *The Quality of American Life,* Russell Sage Foundation, New York, 1976. In *Here to Stay, American Families in the Twentieth Century,* Basic Books, New York, 1976, Mary Jo Bane analyzed 1973 figures from the National Opinion Research General Social Survey tape on happiness, see her note p. 000.

PAGE 40—The flat charge that marriage makes women sick was made by Jessie Bernard in *The Future of Marriage,* Bantam, New York, 1973.

PAGE 42—"Your Pursuit of Happiness" by Phillip Shaver and Jonathan Freedman, *Psychology Today,* August 1976 reported results of a comprehensive survey of the magazine's readers.

PAGE 44—Ronald Burke and Tamara Weir report their findings in "Some Personality Differences Between Members of One-Career and Two-Career Families," *Journal of Marriage and the Family,* August 1976.

PAGE 46—Jan E. Dizard followed 400 university-educated couples married in the 1930s and found that marital discontent was highest for very successful husbands married to homemakers. His findings are reported in *Social Change in the Family,* Community and Family Study Center, University of Chicago, 1968.

Lotte Bailyn of the Sloan School of Management at Massachusetts Institute of Technology studied M.I.T. alumni and their wives and found that professionally employed wives of husbands whose satisfactions came both from work and family life had the happiest marriages, "Career and Family Orientations of Husbands and Wives in Relation to Marital Happiness," *Human Relations* 23:97–113, 1970.

CHAPTER 3

PAGE 53—The power motivation of men was studied by David G. Winter of the Department of Psychology at Wesleyan University, in a paper entitled "Male Power Motivation and the Status of Women." In 1960, power-oriented college freshmen were identified by thematic apperception tests. Ten years later, they not only were less likely to be married to career women, but were associated with an unusually high incidence of divorce and bachelorhood.

PAGE 54—Dr. Ruth Moulton is a psychoanalyst specializing in the problems of women. For more on the problems of middle-class husbands and working wives, see her paper, "Some Effects of the New Feminism—On Men and Women," presented to the joint meeting of The American Academy of Psychoanalysis and the American Psychiatric Association on May 11, 1976.

CHAPTER 4

PAGE 58—A good introduction to the legal marital contract in the mid-1970s is Riane Eisler's book, *Dissolution: No-Fault Divorce, Mar-*

riage and the Future of Women, McGraw-Hill, New York, 1977. See also, "Toward a True Marriage Partnership," a report of the Wisconsin Governor's Commission on the Status of Women, 30 West Mifflin Street, Madison WI 53703.

PAGE 58—The California Supreme Court decision that challenged the generally accepted consortium rules was made on April 26, 1978, in the case of *Coulter* v. *Coulter.*

PAGE 60—In the 1970s, rich people were still making prenuptial contracts to safeguard property in the event of divorce, but feminist couples of modest means were going to lawyers to ritualize their commitments to each other. Many of these feminist contracts followed the suggestions made by Susan Edmiston in her article, "How to Write Your Own Marriage Contract," appearing in *Ms* Magazine's first issue, December 20, 1971. The article examines marriage contracts of the past—such as that of Mary Wollstonecraft and her husband William Godwin—and suggests general lines for a contemporary contract.

PAGE 62—William J. Goode gives a humane as well as sociological account of the response of men to the new demands of women in his speech, "The Male Sex Role: An Insider's View," made at Northwestern University in May 1978.

PAGE 71—Lee is quoted in *Parade,* February 19, 1978.

PAGE 73—Dr. Virginia Abernethy is a member of the Division of Human Behavior in the Department of Psychiatry, Vanderbilt University, Nashville, Tennessee. See her "Feminists' Heterosexual Relationships," *Archives of General Psychiatry,* April 1978. See also Marilyn Whitley and Susan B. Poulsen, *Journal of Marriage and the Family,* August 1975, "Assertiveness and Sexual Satisfaction in Employed Professional Women."

PAGE 75—The Matching Couples survey indicates that 17 percent of men feel that working wives are more apt to be unfaithful than home-makers, compared with 10 percent of the women. These general percentages may be broken down as follows: blue-collar husbands are more apt to fear unfaithfulness than white-collar (23 percent to 15 percent); though wives are less suspicious, blue-collar wives are more suspicious than white-collar wives (15 percent to 13 percent). Higher education makes both men and women less suspicious: for husbands, 11 percent of college graduates thought working wives more apt to be unfaithful; 17 percent with some college, 23 percent with high school or less; for wives, 7 percent college graduates, 10 percent some college, 15 percent high school or less. The perception of a job as a threat to a wife's fidelity is a stereotypical "hard hat" view, but it is a fear that persists through all levels.

PAGE 76—These suspicious husbands want their wives at home: 62 percent of them, as compared to 27 percent of husbands in general, would take a second job themselves if the family needed money, rather than allow their wives to work.

PAGE 78—Their fears may not be groundless. A study by John N. Edwards and Alan Booth, "Sexual Behavior In and Out of Marriage: An Assessment of Correlates," *Journal of Marriage and the Family,* February 1976, indicates that the most dominant wives are the ones most likely to report extramarital involvements—and these are the women most likely to insist on working in the face of a husband's opposition.

PAGE 79—For an overview of the literature on the impact of the work of wives on marriage, see Rosabeth Kanter, *Work and Family,* see note, Chapter 1. The Matching Couples confirm the importance of a husband's approval: working wives whose husbands don't want them to work rate their marriages less happy than average, while working wives whose husbands approve generally rate their marriages happier than average.

The increased communication of working couples can be bad as well as good. F. Ivan Nye and Felix M. Berardo, in their book *The Family,* Macmillan, New York, 1973, find that conflict and argument is more frequent among couples in which the wife works.

For a feminist perspective of the literature on marital happiness, see Judith Long Laws of Cornell University's article "A Feminist Review of Marital Adjustment Literature," in *Journal of Marriage and the Family,* August 1971.

PAGE 81—The Matching Couples survey included 400 couples in which the wives outearned their husbands. Husbands tended to be students, retired, unemployed, or ill, but some were Contemporary Couples who had gone through college and started working together, but the wife had advanced faster than the husband.

Wives queried on what would happen to their marriage if they were to outearn their husbands were more likely than their husbands (21 percent to 14 percent) to think that the marriage would suffer. The actual data, however, indicates that marriages in which the wife makes more than the husband are no more likely to be rated by the partners as less happy than average. The wives are a little happier and the hus-

278 CHAPTER NOTES

band no less happy than average, but the wife has more power; they are, for instance, less likely to have disagreements on how the wife's earnings are to be used.

CHAPTER 5

PAGE 84—The information on dreams comes from "Dreams and Sex Roles in Two Cultures," a paper read by Deborah I. Offenbacher of Brooklyn College, CUNY, at the 1976 Annual Meeting of the American Sociological Association.

PAGE 85—Time-use diaries are slippery and inexact, as anyone who has ever had to keep one knows, but they are indispensable to understanding the housework bind. "Time Spent in Housework" by Joann Vanek, *Scientific American,* November 1974, is a conscientious review of the evidence to that date. She relies principally on the "United States Time Use Survey" made in 1965 and 1966 by John P. Robinson and Philip E. Converse for the Survey Research Center of the University of Michigan. A more widely quoted study was made by the New York State College of Human Ecology at Cornell University during 1967–1968, of 1,318 households in Syracuse, N.Y., and 60 rural households in Cortland County and later translated into 1971 wage rates to give dollar values. "The Dollar Value of Household Work," by Kathryn E. Walker and William H. Gauger, in Consumer Economics and Public Policy No. 5, Information Bulletin 60, is available from Cornell University for 25 cents. The findings on housework of an ambitious international time-use project sponsored by UNESCO is summarized by Alexander Szalai, Professor of Sociology, Karl Marx University of Economic Sciences, Budapest, Hungary, in "Women's Time," *Futures,* October 1975. Time diaries of adults in twelve countries disclose that it's much the same all over the world: employed men have the most free time, and employed women the least, with housewives in between.

PAGE 86—Detailed data on how much time women spend on a long list of household tasks, and who else in the family helps is presented in "How Women Feel About Housework," see note, Chapter 2.

PAGE 87—For the housekeeping activities of women physicians, see Dr. Marilyn Heins, Sue Smock, Dr. Jennifer Jacobs, and Margaret Stein, "Productivity of Women Physicians," *Journal of the American Medical Association,* October 25, 1976.

PAGE 88—Division of labor on household tasks was observed by the Work and Family Life project sponsored by Wellesley College's Center for Research on Women. Observers visited the homes of dual-working families, and their findings are printed in an unpublished manuscript which may be obtained by writing the Center for Research on Women at Wellesley College, Wellesley, Mass. 02181.

PAGE 90—Data on tasks done by children and tasks skipped came from "A Report on How Working Wives Cope," in *Woman's Day*, September 20, 1977.

PAGE 93—Data on the budgets of one- and two-earner families have been collected and analyzed by the Bureau of Labor Statistics; see page 000 of Chapter 7 and note.

PAGE 93—Richard A. Berk, Professor of Sociology at the University of California, Santa Barbara, reports that the working wives in Evanston, Illinois, he studied got up 30 minutes earlier than nonemployed wives. See *The Organization of the Household Day*, by Richard A. Berk and Sarah Fenstermaker Berk, Sage Publications, Beverly Hills, 1979.

PAGE 96—Sylvia Porter's estimate of the value of a homemaker was made in her book, *Money*, Doubleday, New York, 1975, and Dr. Peter Senn's estimate of the value of a homemaking mother of three was made on the "Today Show," August 31, 1976.

PAGE 98—This was based on a multinational Time-Budget Research project carried out by the UNESCO-sponsored European Coordination Center for Research and Documentation in the Social Sciences. The project involved twelve countries. It is printed as a book, Alexander Szalai, ed., *The Use of Time: Daily Activities of Urban and Suburban Populations in Twelve Countries*, Mouton, The Hague, 1973.

PAGE 99—Compare the lives of two wives keeping house in nonmetropolitan communities who kept time diaries for us. Each has two grade-school daughters, a husband in business for himself, and family income of more than $25,000. The principal difference between the two is that one helps earn part of that income and the other is a full-time homemaker. Both live near parents. Both go to church.

Here's what nonworking Betty did one Thursday, Friday, and Saturday in May:

Thursday
       7:30—Up, breakfast, packed lunches, girls off.
       8:30—Bowling (I'm in a league).
    12:00—Home, load of clothes in washer, lunch, read paper.
      1:30—Ran errands.
           Stopped at a friend's for coffee.
      3:45—Home, helped Marjorie with her last Solar System report. (She is 9 years old and had to write fifteen reports

on the Solar System. It was much too complicated for her to do alone and understand, so I helped her. Don't usually help the girls. Am thinking of asking for a grade on my contributions to her reports!)

6:30—Supper, cleaned up kitchen.

7:30—Folded load of clothes.

8:15—Went to visit a neighbor.

11:15—Bed.

Friday

7:30—Up, breakfast, girls off to school.

8:30—Lay back down, it's cold, raining, and just an "ishy" day.

10:00—Got up and cleaned the house.

Load of clothes in washer.

1:30—Went to Arts and Crafts Fair with a friend.

4:00—Sewed up Karen's ripped coat.

4:45—Showered and got the three of us ready for Mother-Daughter dinner.

6:30—Mother-Daughter dinner at church.

9:15—Home, folded clothes, watched the news.

11:00—Bed.

Saturday

8:30—Up.

10:15—Left for a luncheon and style show.

1:45—Home, wrapped a birthday present.

2:15—Took the girls to Cherry Vale Shopping Mall (they wanted to look around).

3:30—Load of clothes in washer, read paper.

More clothes in washer.

Telephone call.

5:30—Got ready and left to take Larry's Mom out for her birthday.

10:00—Folded load of clothes and put them away.

10:30—Watched "First Saturday" (News program), not sure that's the name.

Folded and put away another load of clothes.

12:00—Bed.

Jane is a medical technologist living in a small town in Montana, within walking distance of her hospital, the school, and a great many relatives. She does all the housework with a little dishwashing help from her daughters. Her husband does not help.

Here is what Jane did during three days in December.

Friday

> 6:30—Got up, fed cat, showered, etc., jumped rope, fixed lunch, at work by 8 A.M.
>
> 4:30—Home from work; went to photographer for my ski pass picture; went to grocery store; stopped by folks to pay father for Great Falls stuff he got for me.
>
> 5:30—Home, started dinner, put groceries away, talked on phone 10 minutes to a friend; took Martha her birthday gift and had a glass of wine.
>
> 7:00—Sat down to dinner; Tami had eaten and gone to Senior Class play.
>
> 7:10–7:20—Picked up dishes and loaded dishwasher; dust-mopped floor; husband helped with dishes!!
>
> 7:20–8:30—Finished addressing and writing Christmas cards; got caught up with budget book and bills.
>
> 8:30–9:15—Read *L.H. Journal* and fell asleep on sofa until 10:30.
>
> 10:30–11:00—Read and went to bed.

Saturday

> 6:30—Got up. Fed cat. Showered and washed hair. Jumped rope 5 min. Made up face. Made coffee. Read paper. Fed dog. Fed husband—bacon & eggs (I eat only bran and applesauce). Fed guinea pig. Went to work by 8 A.M.
>
> 12:00—Home, met friend for lunch at community "Winter Fair." Picked up mother and friend, went to greenhouse open house. Picked up girls and went back to Winter Fair. Had coffee with folks. Went to grocery store and liquor store. Spent hour on phone with friend.
>
> 4:45—Cleaned bathroom and bedroom (the girls had cleaned their bath and bedrooms). Mopped kitchen floor (on hands and knees). Washed load of clothes. Fixed dinner (pork chops, potatoes, veg. and salad). Polished work shoes. Wiped up back entry and basement steps. Changed cat box.
>
> 6:00–6:20—Coffee with neighbor.
>
> 6:20–6:35—Folded clothes.
>
> 6:35–6:50—Sorted through three days' mail.
>
> 6:50–7:20—Wrapped Christmas packages.
>
> 7:20—Put dinner on table.
>
> 7:40—Sat in living room and folded towels.
>
> 8:00–10:00—Watched "Hailey's Money Changers" and addressed Christmas cards.

After 10:00—Wrapped and addressed three Christmas pack-
ages; read for half hour.

Sunday

7:30—Was corrupt and stayed in bed until this hour. First
day off for seven days. Fixed oatmeal, toast, and orange
juice for the family. After everyone was gone, treated
myself to a facial masque with my second cup of coffee
and the paper.

8:15—Counted Christmas cards and put return addresses on.
Sorted three loads of wash, started one load, folded
clothes, pre-soaked next load. Showered and washed hair.
Went to give neighbor girl a shot and had coffee with
her Mom. My Mom and uncle stopped by for coffee.
Cleared up kitchen. Ran dishwasher. Washed knickknacks
on shelves. Hung some clothes on the line. Made bed,
put chicken on to stew for supper.

10:40—Walked uptown to post office to get mail and stamps,
stopped at hospital on the way, picked up couple of things
at the store. Came home to fix lunch for girls. Folded
clothes. Put last load in wash.
Went to work 12 P.M., returned from work 2:45 P.M.
Stamped Christmas cards. Took chicken off bone.

3:30–4:30—Took our three-mile walk. Mailed cards.

4:30—Went to store.

5:50—Put other ingredients in soup. Cleaned up kitchen for
second time. Made bran muffins. My folks and uncle will
eat with us.

Folks left at 9 P.M. Made Christmas charm for front door,
wrapped Aunt's present. Folded clothes. Dust-mopped
kitchen.

10:00 P.M.—Marsha and Charlie came for coffee, sat with
Walt while he watched "Rookies" on T.V.

11:30 to bed, read a while.

CHAPTER 6

PAGE 101—For the time fathers spend interacting with infants, see
"Fathers' Verbal Interaction with Children in the First Three Months
of Life," *Child Development* 42:1971, by Frieda Rebelsky and C. Hanks.

PAGE 101—The biological justification of sex roles is traditional,
but feminists felt betrayed when Alice Rossi seemed to be supporting it
in her paper, "A Biosocial Perspective on Parenting" in the Spring 1977

issue of *Daedalus*. Another Rossi article, "Equality between the Sexes: An Immodest Proposal," opened the academic front of the new women's movement when it appeared in *Daedalus,* Spring 1964, the year the Civil Rights Act launched its legal expression and Betty Friedan's *The Feminine Mystique* opened the eyes of millions of suburban housewives. A sociologist by discipline, Rossi spent several years delving into biochemistry and anthropology.

PAGE 102—The findings of the Matching Couples survey on the acceptance of working mothers by various groups were corroborated by the General Mills American Family Report of 1976–77, *Raising Children in a Changing Society,* see note, Chapter 2.

PAGE 102—See Karen Mason and John L. Czajka, "Change in U.S. Women's Sex-Role Attitudes, 1964–1974," *American Sociological Review,* August 1976.

PAGE 103—Everyone sounds off on working mothers. Margaret Mead was quoted in *The New York Post,* April 18, 1978; Jessie Bernard in her book, *The Future of Motherhood,* Dial Press, New York, 1974; Lee Salk in *The New York Daily News,* April 2, 1978; Eda J. LeShan in her article for *Childhood,* "The Working Mother"; Urie Bronfenbrenner and Joan Huber in *U.S. News and World Report,* June 7, 1976; Bruno Bettelheim in his classic work, *Children of the Dream,* Macmillan, New York, 1969; Alice Rossi in "A Biosocial Perspective on Parenting," *Daedalus,* Spring 1977; Juanita Kreps in *The New York Times,* April 19, 1976; Rosabeth Kanter in *Women and Work,* see note, Chapter 1.

PAGE 105—Jerome Kagan is a professor of human development at Harvard University. Once a staunch opponent of day care, he has revised his position to one of careful neutrality as a result of recent research and experiments. His finding that children turn to their biological mothers whether raised by an unrelated care-giver or not is described in *Infancy: Its Place in Human Development,* by Jerome Kagan, Richard Kearsley, and Philip Zelazo, Harvard University Press, Cambridge, 1978.

PAGE 106—For Lillian Carter's views, see *Ms* Magazine, October 1976. For a psychiatric perspective, see papers given by David R. Beisel of Rockland Community College and Paul Elovitz of Ramapo College presented at the International Psychohistorical Association, June 8, 1978, and "Thrice-Born" by Bruce Mazlish and Edwin Diamond, professors of history and political science, respectively, at MIT, in *New York,* August 30, 1976.

PAGE 109—Shift splitting for child care is covered in *Five Thousand American Families—Patterns of Economic Progress,* see note, Chapter 2.

PAGE 110—The General Mills American Family Report, "Raising Children in a Changing Society," see note, Chapter 2.

PAGE 110—A Carter administration view of day care is ably presented by Suzanne H. Woolsey, associate director of Human and Community Affairs, Office of Management and Budget, in "The Child Care Debate," *Daedalus,* Spring 1977.

PAGE 111—Parental antipathy to day care is documented by Mordecai Kurz, Philip Robins, and Robert Spiegelman, *A Study of the Demand for Childcare by Working Mothers,* Stanford Research Institute, August 1975. John Hess of *The New York Times* unravelled the politics of the location and funding of day-care centers in New York City for *Working Woman,* May 1977. The Bank Street College of Education, 610 West 112th Street, New York, N.Y. 10025, will give you current information on day care in New York City if you enclose a stamped self-addressed envelope.

PAGE 113—A nursing mother who needs instant help can usually get it by phone. Information on the La Leche League nearest her can be obtained by phoning their international office at 312-455-7730.

PAGE 115—Division of child-care functions between fathers and mothers has been established by two especially good sources. The first is the Use-of-Time project conducted at the Survey Research Center at the University of Michigan, reported by John P. Robinson, *How Americans Use Time* (Praeger, 1977). The second study is the examination of work and family life, sponsored by Wellesley's Center for Research on Women.

PAGE 115—The General Mills American Family study queried children of working mothers.

PAGE 117—The author interviewed women faculty and students on campuses in California, Iowa, Montana, New York, North Dakota, Vermont, and Wisconsin in 1976 and 1977.

PAGE 119—In 1952, the author was dispatched to San Diego by *Ladies' Home Journal* to report on the neglect of children by mothers called back to work in the aircraft plants reopening for the Korean War effort. In 1967, *Woman's Day* asked her to report what had become of the studies of the impact of working mothers on children launched after World War II. In 1963, the inconclusive answers had been rounded up in *The Employed Mother in America,* by F. Ivan Nye, a family sociologist, and Lois Wladis Hoffman, a child-development psychologist (Rand McNally, 1963), but "What We Are Finding Out About Working

Mothers," in *Woman's Day,* September 1967, was regarded as news and widely reprinted. An update of the earlier work ten years later didn't change the picture. The current authority on the subject is *Working Mothers: An Evaluative Review of the Consequences for Wife, Husband and Child,* by Lois Wladis Hoffman and F. Ivan Nye, with Stephen J. Bahr, Jossey-Bass Publishers, San Francisco, 1974. Note that since the new women's movement, Hoffman, the woman author is mentioned first.

PAGE 120—The study that found mothers and children interacting only one-third of the time was made in Boston by White and Watts, 1973.

PAGE 123—The problems of working mothers are usefully discussed by Jean Curtis, in *Working Mothers,* Doubleday, New York, 1976. Barbara Harris relates the story of her childhood protest in *Career and Motherhood: Struggle for a New Identity,* by Alan Roland and Barbara Harris, Human Sciences Press, 1978.

PAGE 125—For the contemporary view on the welfare of children see *All Our Children,* by Kenneth Keniston and the Carnegie Council on Children, Harcourt Brace Jovanovitch, New York, 1977.

CHAPTER 7

The proportion of family income supplied by wives is usually given as 27 percent, which includes couples, one partner of whom works part time: it's 40 percent for couples both of whom work full time. Carolyn Shaw Bell, Katharine Coman Professor of Economics at Wellesley College, maintains that federal statistics are collected and presented in a way that systematically undervalues the contribution of wives. She has rearranged the data to give the proportions by income bracket in "Working Women's Contribution to Family Income," *Eastern Economic Journal,* April and July 1974. Both Census and BLS are reviewing their statistical practices to avoid the assumption that the husband is the sole or the principal earner.

PAGE 127—The Lasser advice comes in *Managing Your Family Finances,* a publication of the J. K. Lasser Tax Institute, New York, 1976. Similar advice is given by Sidney Margolius, the financial columnist in *How To Make the Most of Your Money,* Appleton-Century, New York, 1966. Citibank of New York and Bank of America in California deal with the issue briefly in leaflets and brochures on family budgeting.

PAGE 128—Attitudes as well as practices are explored in *The General Mills American Family Report, 1974–75: A Study of the American Family and Money,* see note, Chapter 2.

PAGE 134—Sylvia Porter's *Money Book,* now available in paperback, is a refreshing improvement on the traditional manuals of advice, written by an authority on finance who has lived most of her life in a two-paycheck household, see note, Chapter 5.

PAGE 136—The 1980 Census will drop the term "head of household," and the Bureau of Labor Statistics has already begun to analyze family income on the basis of the contributions of family members.

PAGE 137—Progressive taxation makes additional dollars of family income "worth" less in after-tax net, it's true, but the fiends who designed the system knew better than to wipe out *all* the gain. In its September-October 1977 issue, *New Woman* Magazine demonstrated the sexism of assuming that her income was always "additional" regardless of how much she earned by exchanging the words "husband" and "wife" in a table printed in the July 11, 1977, issue of the male-oriented *U.S. News & World Report,* under the headline, "Does It Pay To Have Your Husband Work?" and the short caption read as follows:

> *"When your husband takes an outside job, how much can you and your family count on in added take-home pay—after allowing for Federal taxes?"*
> It can come as a jolt to find out how much less than your husband's salary is your and his actual gain in dollars and cents. The second income pushes your combined earnings into higher percentage brackets for Federal income tax purposes. So a bigger tax bite comes out of his pay, which in effect, comes on top of his salary. In addition, he must pay Social Security taxes at the rate of 5.85 percent of salary, up to a maximum of $965 a year. The table below will show you what a husband has left in take-home pay after Federal income and Social Security taxes.
>
> Note these points: It's assumed in these calculations that the couple has two children old enough not to require child-care services. Also, the couple files a joint return and takes either the standard deduction or itemized deductions equal to 17 percent of the husband's income, whichever is larger. All income is assumed to be earned. No allowance has been made for State and local income taxes, which would further cut the husband's net income.

PAGE 138—Leonard Sloane's calculation of the cost of a wife's job was reported in "Does it Pay A Wife to Get a Job?", *Woman's Day,* November 1976.

A careful, but sexist account of the extra expenses of working wives was reported by Emma G. Holmes, Consumer and Food Economics

Research Division, Agricultural Research Service, U.S. Department of Agriculture in Home Economics Research Report No. 34, "Job-Related Expenditures and Management Practices of Gainfully Employed Wives in North Carolina" issued in November 1967. It counted taxes, transportation, meals at work, gifts and donations at work, paid service for laundry, general housework, child care and sewing, and extra clothes and personal care.

PAGE 139—In his widely quoted book, *Women in the Labor Force,* Seminar Press, New York, 1973, James A. Sweet admitted that there are "some women who make substantial contributions to family income" though "many" do not.

PAGE 141—For theories about how a wife's earnings are spent, see Myra H. Strober, "Wives' Labor Force Behavior and Family Consumption Patterns," *American Economic Association, Selected Contributed Papers,* February 1977. Practical evidence can be drawn by comparing the expenditures on various items of one- and two-earner families on the Consumer Expenditure Survey Series of the Bureau of Labor Statistics. Diary Survey, July 1973–June 1974, "Selected Weekly Expenditures Cross Classified by Family Characteristics."

CHAPTER 8

PAGE 153—The new, intrinsic work ethic was dramatically illustrated in a survey of readers of *Psychology Today* reported in their May 1978 issue.

CHAPTER 9

PAGE 157—Women don't realize that babies will limit their careers until they have been working: in "Age, Fertility Expectations and Plans for Employment," *American Sociological Review,* October 1977, Ross M. Stolzenberg and Linda J. Waite found that the effect of labor-force participation plans on fertility expectations varies from a mild inhibiting effect for 19–20-year-olds to a strong negative influence for 27–29-year-olds.

PAGE 160—See Claire Safran, "What 80,000 Women Can Tell You About Your Biggest Decision—Having a Baby," *Redbook,* May 1978.

PAGE 161—See "The Value of Children to Parents in the United States," by Lois Wladis Hoffman, Arland Thornton, and Jean Denby Manis, *Population: Behavioral, Social and Environmental Issues,* vol. 1,

2, 1978. The other countries were Korea, Indonesia, the Philippines, Taiwan, Thailand, and Turkey.

PAGE 163—The cost of a baby was calculated originally by Claire Williams, "How Much Does A Baby Cost?" *Redbook,* April 1976, and updated for 1978 prices according to the Consumer Price Index published by the Bureau of Labor Statistics, with allowance for a faster rise in prices for hospital costs. The cost of rearing a baby born in 1978 to age 18 is based on a similar update for inflation of a 1976 estimate made by the Community Council of Greater New York. The College Board is a nonprofit educational association serving students, schools, and colleges. They estimate $5,110 for a private four-year residential college in 1978–79 and a 6 percent yearly increase which brings the total cost of a B.A. degree to $22,356 for a freshman entering in the fall of 1978.

PAGE 164—In *Money,* Sylvia Porter estimated that the yearly cost of raising one child was "approximately 15 to 17 percent of income," see note, Chapter 5. In a July 24, 1977, article in *The New York Daily News,* Robert Zintl reported that middle-class families with two children think they are spending only about 15 percent of their income on their children but they are usually spending 40 percent.

PAGE 165—The assumptions behind the $34,000 worth of time spent on a child are presented in "Family Investments in Human Capital: Earnings of Women" by Jacob Mincer and Solomon Polachek, *Journal of Political Economy,* 82, 1974. The Michigan longitudinal study shows that educated mothers spend more time in child care than those with less schooling, see "Time Inputs to Children" by Russell Hill and Frank Stafford, in James N. Morgan, editor, *Five Thousand American Families —Patterns of Economic Progress,* Survey Research Center, Institute for Social Research, University of Michigan, vol. II, 1974.

Isabel Sawhill was kind enough to construct this formula when she was Director of the Program of Research on Women at the Urban Institute in Washington. She is currently Director of the National Commission for Employment Policy of the Federal Government. Her formula considered age of starting work, original wage, age of dropping out, age of re-entry, rate of increase in real wages per year compounded annually, and retirement age.

PAGE 169—Susan Welch and Alan Booth, of the University of Nebraska at Lincoln, found that housewives who had never been employed had better mental health than those formerly employed, while those who had gone back to work in less than a year were worse off than those who had worked right along for more than a year. In a paper,

"Employment and Health Among Married Women With Children" given at the annual meeting of the Southwest Social Science Association in San Antonio, Texas, in March 1975, they concluded that the transition between work and homemaking was itself stressful for women.

PAGE 172—Dr. Brazelton's unconventional suggestions for changing baby's schedule to fit adult convenience shocked tradition-oriented Beatrice Glickman and Nesha Springer who report it in *Who Cares for the Baby?* Schocken Books, New York, 1978.

PAGE 173—Matina Horner's "fear of success" was presented in her doctoral dissertation for the University of Minnesota in 1968, "Sex Differences in Achievement Motivation and Performance in Competitive and Non-Competitive Situations." The follow-up was reported in 1973 in Lois Wladis Hoffman's "The Professional Woman as Mother," *Annals,* New York Academy of Sciences, vol. 208, p. 211, and verified in a private communication.

PAGE 174—See Ralph LaRossa, *Conflict and Power in Marriage: Expecting the First Child,* Sage Publications, Beverly Hills, 1977. Angus Campbell of the Institute for Social Research has found that childless married men are more satisfied with their lives than childless married women. See Angus Campbell, Philip E. Converse, and Willard L. Rodgers, *The Quality of American Life,* Russell Sage Foundation, New York, 1976.

PAGE 176—A great deal of relevant and hard-to-find research is presented by Mary Jo Bane in *Here to Stay: American Families in the Twentieth Century,* Basic Books, New York, 1976.

PAGE 178—The author's first baby was born when she was 19, her second when she was 45. Improvement in maternal mortality has been so substantial between her two pregnancies that her second childbirth was safer than her first in spite of her great age.

Jessie Bernard's books are *The Future of Marriage,* World Publishing Co., New York, 1972; *The Future of Motherhood,* The Dial Press, New York, 1974; and *Self-Portrait of a Family,* Beacon Press, Boston, 1978.

PAGE 179—Barbara Seaman presents the evidence on the safety (or danger) of late childbearing in "How Late Can You Wait to Have a Baby?" *Ms.,* January 1976.

PAGE 179—For primitives, at least, there seems to be some truth to the belief that nursing protects a mother from pregnancy. There is evidence, cited by Alice Rossi in her "Biosocial Perspective on Parenting" that the rich diet and physical inactivity of modern life lead to a build-up of fat in women that makes it easier for them to become pregnant while nursing. She suggests that the close spacing of American babies during the 1950s is new and stressful.

PAGE 182—Some women are just too squeamish to be comfortable bearing children. One of my childless friends is affronted by jello and raw eggs. She loves plants but can't garden because angle worms set her shrieking, and her husband knows better than to laugh. She invests emotionally in plants and animals, but the death of her dog was so traumatic that she now keeps only her cats. She's opposed to furs because they involve killing animals and not at all sure that it's morally right to eat meat. Most mothers have trouble adjusting, at first, to cleaning up diapers and upchucks, but my friend might never make it, and has had the wisdom to follow her temperament.

PAGE 185—The classic, traditional study of marriage is still Robert O. Blood and Donald M. Wolfe, *Husbands and Wives: The Dynamics of Married Living,* Glencoe, The Free Press, 1960.

PAGE 185—The glamorous Shah Mohammed Riza Pahlevi of Iran divorced two empresses who did not present him with sons. *The New York Times,* November 7, 1978.

PAGE 186—See J. E. Veevers, "Voluntarily Chiildless Wives: An Exploratory Study," in *Sociology and Social Research,* vol. 57, April 1973.

PAGE 188—The evidence of the impact of children in a marriage is presented by Jessie Bernard in *The Future of Marriage.*

CHAPTER 10

Hanna Papanek coined the term "two-person career" in "Men, Women and Work: Reflections on the Two-Person Career," *American Journal of Sociology,* 78:852–872. In *Work and Family in the United States* (see chapter notes for Chapter 1), Rosabeth Kanter discusses the unpaid contribution of wives of executives, Foreign Service Officers, politicians, farmers, small restaurant and store operators, Peace Corps volunteers, teachers, and police in small towns.

PAGE 193—The plight of the Juhasz family was reported by Marlys Harris, "Couples Wedded to the Same Careers," *Money,* January 1978.

PAGE 195—The emotional support career women need is discussed by Ruth Moulton, M.D., in a paper presented to the Joint Meeting of the American Academy of Psychoanalysis and the American Psychiatric Association (see note, Chapter 3) and by Margaret Hennig and Anne

Jardim, in their book, *The Managerial Woman,* Anchor Press/Doubleday, Garden City, 1977.

PAGE 196—In "Nonmarket Returns to Women's Investment in Education," Lee Benham, Associate Professor of Economics and Preventive Medicine at Washington University in St. Louis, applies sophisticated statistical methods to finding out the extent to which college benefits women by improving their chances to marry high-earning men and the extent to which they make the men they marry more productive. The paper is in *Sex, Discrimination, and the Division of Labor,* edited by Cynthia B. Lloyd (see note, Chapter 1).

PAGE 196—Jane Spock's complaint was reported by Judy Klemesrud, "The Spocks: Bittersweet Recognition in a Revised Classic," *The New York Times,* March 19, 1976.

PAGE 197—For Rosalynn Carter's "second person" activities, see Donnie Radcliffe and Judith Martin, *The New York Post,* March 4, 1978, and Martin Tolchin, *The New York Times,* May 30, 1978.

PAGE 208—A spot check of women's names beginning with the letters "D," "E," and "G" in *Who's Who in America,* 1978–1979, found four unmarried women and six married women, only one of whom had a husband who was listed in his own right. It confirmed the pattern of women surveyed for inclusion in *Enterprising Women,* by Caroline Bird, W. W. Norton, New York, 1976.

PAGE 212—See "Husbands, Wives, and Rivals," by Georgia Dullea, *The New York Times,* July 13, 1978.

PAGE 215—The Herbergs appear in "Partners in Business and Marriage" by Claudia Jessup Chipps, *Family Circle,* May 31, 1977.

PAGE 216—For information on job-sharing, see General Information Packet prepared by New Ways to Work, 457 Kingsley Avenue, Palo Alto, CA 94301. In 1977, Gustavus Adolphus College, St. Peter, Minnesota, had four couples sharing academic tenure and full benefits.

PAGE 222—IBM, Texaco, Xerox, and Smith Kline and French are among the companies which have at one time or another offered senior managers paid sabbatical leave for public service or research not related to their company duties.

CHAPTER 11

The Easterlin theory enjoyed popular attention in "The Coming Baby Boom" by Linda Wolfe, *New York,* January 10, 1977. The response to Easterlin was made by Charles Westoff in the December 1978 issue of *Scientific American,* "Marriage and Fertility in the Developed Countries." Westoff expects that within 50 years we will have zero population *growth.* We are, of course, already below the replacement fertility rate. Total births hold up because we have an unusually large number of women of childbearing age.

A Rand study of 1977 made for the National Institute of Child Health and Human Development decisively linked the decline in birth rate during the 1960s and 1970s to the availability of jobs rather than to the Pill, as widely believed. See William P. Butz and Michael P. Ward, "The Emergence of Counter-Cyclical U.S. Fertility," *American Economic Review,* March 1979.

Birth rates are compiled every few months by the National Center for Health Statistics. The Census asks a sample of American women how many children they expect to have every few years and analyzes their expectations in terms of age, education, employment, race, marital status.

PAGE 230—Attitudes of college freshmen come from comparing the same question on the survey administered to entering college freshmen by the American Council on Education.

The National Survey of Children was designed by the Foundation for Child Development, formerly the Association for the Aid of Crippled Children, and administered in 1976 to 2,200 children aged 7 to 11.

Attention to the problem of teenage births has given many newspaper readers the impression that a birth explosion is under way because kids are having sex before they have sense enough to use birth control. The concern is based, however, not on an absolute increase in the teenage birth rate, but the failure of the teenage birth rate to decline as fast as the birth rate for older women. The facts are that there has been a steady decline in the overall birth rate and the proportion of illegitimate babies for women 15 to 19 as for women of other ages. When these rates are broken down by race, however, the rate of illegitimate births to black teenagers has declined from very high levels, while the much lower illegitimacy rate for white teenagers has actually risen a bit. Black kids are improving, but white kids, who are better off, haven't changed very much.

PAGE 230—In 1976 the National Center for Health Statistics reported the increase in sterilization and slight decline in the use of the Pill in "Contraceptive Utilization in the United States: 1973 and 1976."

CHAPTER 12

Most Americans still believe that "the family" is more important than the individuals composing it, but the individualists are increasing. The

General Mills American Family Report of 1976 labeled 57 percent of parents "Traditionalists" who valued marriage as an institution and were willing to sacrifice for their children. The remaining 43 percent were "the New Breed" who were described as "less child-oriented and more self-oriented."

PAGE 233—In 1978, the "Right-to-Life" party polled enough votes to become important to politicians in New York and Minnesota. In 1977 the Supreme Court ruled that states may decide not to fund abortions and many states have elected not to do so. The Pregnancy Disability Act of 1978 passed only with an anti-abortion rider.

PAGE 244—See "The Changing Success Ethic" by Dale Tarnowieski, 1973, distributed by AMACOM, the publishing arm of the American Management Association.

PAGE 245—Before she became Secretary of Commerce, Juanita Kreps suggested that Social Security could be used to fund time out of the work force in midlife, for a more flexible and meaningful allocation of life span between work, education and leisure. She makes the suggestion in *Sex, Age, and Work: The Changing Composition of the Labor Force,* with Robert Clark, The Johns Hopkins University Press, Baltimore, 1975. When questioned, most employees think their lives would be better if education, work, and leisure were interspersed rather than confined to specific life stages.

PAGE 250—The update of the findings of *Mental Health in the Metropolis* was reported by Dr. Leo Srole and Anita K. Fischer in a paper entitled "Generations, Aging, Genders and Well-Being: Current Long-Range Effects of Women's 'Liberation' in the 1920s" presented to IX World Sociological Congress, Uppsala, Sweden, on August 18, 1978.

CHAPTER 13

PAGE 253—The slow-growing economy of the 1970s was analyzed by Eli Ginzberg, Director, Conservation of Human Resources at Columbia University, in his article for *Scientific American* (November 1977), "The Job Problem." See also his interview with the author for the September 1976 issue of *Working Woman.*

PAGE 257—The survey by Atlas Van Lines was made for their 9th Forum on Moving, 1976, and appears in the "Report and Survey" section of the Forum Report.

PAGE 257—Alan Westin examined the landmark legal cases that were clearing the way for employees' fight for rights in a *New York*

Times article, "A New Move Toward Employee Rights," May 23, 1978.

Rosabeth Kanter's findings on employees of a major corporation are printed in her article for the Winter 1978 issue of *Daedalus,* "Work in a New America."

PAGE 258—Sar Levitan is quoted in a *New York Times* article by Ann Crittenden, "Women Work and Men Change," January 9, 1977.

PAGE 259—The survey on work satisfaction was done by *Psychology Today,* and their results are printed and analyzed in the May 1978 issue. The nurses' reports on their job satisfaction come from a survey in *Nursing '77.*

PAGE 260—The 1975 Michigan survey findings that list interference with home life as one-fourth of complaints about working conditions can be found in an article by Robert Quinn, Thomas W. Mangione, and Martha Mandilovito, "Evaluating Working Conditions in America," in *Monthly Labor Review 96,* November 1973.

PAGE 261—A good study on alternative work practices, especially flexitime, can be found in the June 1977 issue of *Atlas* magazine, "Humanizing Work."

PAGE 261—The practice of training welfare mothers to administer their housing projects is being followed by HUD programs.

PAGE 262—So far as poor work attitudes go, on tests, younger sibs generally do less well than the first and second child in the family, but according to George Hanford, senior vice-president of The College Board and Staff coordinator for the Advisory Panel on the Scholastic Aptitude Test Score Decline, this theory accounted for very little of the decline of the 1970s. Younger siblings were so much less apt to aspire to colleges requiring the test that their poorer showing was not an important factor.

INDEX